New England Streams

TEXT & PHOTOGRAPHY BY
Thomas Ames, Jr.

WATERCOLORS BY
David B. Tibbetts

Frank Amato
Frank
PORTLAND

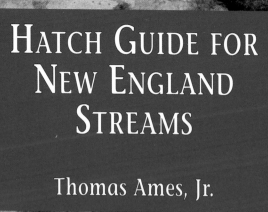

HATCH GUIDE FOR NEW ENGLAND STREAMS

Thomas Ames, Jr.

Frank Amato Publications, Inc.
P.O. Box 82112, Portland, Oregon 97282
503•653•8108 www.amatobooks.com

All photography © Thomas Ames, Jr.
Cover photo © Thomas Ames, Jr.
Watercolors © David B. Tibbetts.
Book and Cover Design: Kathy Johnson

PRINTED BY STAR STANDARD INDUSTRIES IN SINGAPORE
Softbound; ISBN: 1-57188-210-3   UPC: 0-66066-00424-6
Hardbound; ISBN: 1-57188-220-0   UPC: 0-66066-00434-5
3 5 7 9 10 8 6 4 2

Contents

Acknowledgments

If you have even an inkling of how much collaboration is involved in a project like this, you will not begrudge me the small indulgence of thanking a few friends, both old and new, for their invaluable contributions. They are:

A generous handful of entomologists, both professional and amateur, for their invaluable guidance with insect identification: Pat McCafferty of Purdue University, Steven Burian of Southern Connecticut State University, Brad Robinson of Clemson University, Ernest Schwiebert, Jr., Dave Reutz and Carl Richards.

Stephen Fiske and Rich Langdon of the Vermont Agency of Environmental Conservation for data on stream fauna and chemistry.

Nick Wilder of Hunter's Angling Supplies, for providing flies and encouragement.

Randall Kaufmann, of Kaufmann's Streamborn, who provided many western patterns for which there are no eastern equivalents.

Gary Soucie and Tom Rosenbauer, for good advice to a first-time author.

Howard Strathie for his FFF and TU newsletter items about fly patterns.

Dave Tibbetts, for teaching me, among so much else, to laugh at my blunders.

Jim Ehlers of *Vermont Outdoors*, for leading me to some great Vermont fly tiers. Several patterns represented here were first published in that magazine.

Harold McMillan Jr., for giving me, among many things, a home on the Housatonic.

Bob Skowronski, for teaching me the fundamentals of fly fishing and tying, and for sharing his knowledge of the White River and its fauna.

Jim Schollmeyer, for setting the standard with his *Hatch Guide to Lakes* and *Hatch Guide to Western Streams.*

Frank Amato, for taking a chance and encouraging an unknown author to write this book.

And especially to the fly tiers, who carry on the rich tradition of Northeast fly tying: Harold McMillan Jr. (Housatonic River Outfitters), Fran Betters (Ausable Wulff Products), Mary Dette Clark (Dette Trout Flies), Dick Stewart, Nick Yardley, George Schlotter (The Angler's Nook), Dave Goulet (Classic and Custom Fly Shop), Bob Braendle (Great Lakes Fly Fishing Company), John Blunt (Grants Camps), Dan Noyes and

Sumner Stowe (The Fly Rod Shop), Don Sicard (Casco Bay Fly Tying Studio), Bill Thompson, Jack Pangburn and Del Mazza.

This book is dedicated to the memory of Michael Martin, who gave me my very first lesson in fly fishing.

The Madness Behind the Method

Not long ago, on a late September evening, as I labored over my fly-tying desk at my home in Vermont, a large, pumpkin-colored caddis suddenly fluttered about my magnifying light before settling quietly on the desk in front of me. Had any insect behaved with such impertinence a mere two years before, I would have snuffed it in an instant. After all, it was only one player in the large ensemble of moth-like creatures that gathers on our screen doors on warm fall nights with the evident intention of gaining admittance through the slightest opening. But lately my entire attitude toward such nocturnal intruders had changed, from mere annoyance to deep interest and curiosity. So I quickly grabbed one of the slide boxes I use to store my finished flies and captured the intruder, alive and unharmed, a fit subject for a photographic portrait.

The following season, on a June afternoon, I watched a swarm of a different caddis over a fast stretch of Vermont's White River. From the time of year, the hour of the day and the large size and dark wings of the insects, I recognized them as *Psilotreta labida*, the Dark Blue Sedge.

Their flight behavior told me that they were hatching, not egg laying, so I tied a black and gray Deep Sparkle Pupa to my tippet and cast it upstream from a spot that I knew held fish. As my fly reached the spot I halted its drift and allowed it to swing up to the surface. When I saw the line move I drove the hook into the upper lip of a healthy wild rainbow.

These were but two episodes of many along a continuing odyssey, some might say obsession, which began with my first bumbling efforts to tie flies. Like many novice fly fishermen, I had spent a handful of years learning the rudiments of locating a fish and placing a fly more or less in front of it. I had a vague sense of the different sizes and shapes of the hatching insects, all of which appeared to be a sort of creamy white as they lifted skyward. I accumulated boxes and boxes of flies that worked as if by magic some of the time, and had no effect whatsoever at others. I thoroughly enjoyed my time on the stream in the most pleasant hours of the evening. But I was catching few fish, and even fewer big ones. Most of those were on streamers.

It was time, as they say, to fish or cut bait, which for me meant learning to tie my own flies. I placed myself under the tutelage of my friend Bob Skowronski, the acknowledged master of our home river, the White, and an accomplished tier, although he is something of a mystic. Soon I could tie a fair Woolly Bugger, a functional Light Cahill wet and a lumpy Light Hendrickson dry fly. My early masterpieces were far from pretty, but my pleasure was undiminished when a few of them actually fooled fish. I had learned about profile and proportion, shape, taper, and color. There was hope that, with practice, my clumsy hands could bring these qualities to life.

In tying those first flies I also started to learn the relationship between the materials used in the artificials and the anatomy of the naturals—why we use certain kinds of hackle for the tails, specific furs or stripped quills for the abdomen and whether unmarked or grizzly hackle best represents the legs. I wanted to know more about nature's design for each of the insects that hatch on our local rivers, and how to tell one from the other. Bob then placed before me a timeless classic on tying accurate imitations: Ernest Schwiebert's *Matching the Hatch*. Schwiebert's monumental work is packed with information, and his excellent drawings give a good color rendition of most North American mayflies then known to fly fishers. But I am a studio photographer, and I needed a picture of the real thing as a reference. I started carrying a camera to the river and, when that proved impracticable, I brought the insects to my studio. Finally, coming full circle, I constructed small "studios" that I could bring to the river.

Thus began a project that became the basis for this book. As the process unfolded, I learned that the world of New England trout stream insects is very different from the one described by most fishing entomologies. These texts, in describing the fauna of the better-known Pennsylvania and Catskills streams, ignore many insects and life stages which are important to our region while overstating the importance of mayfly dun hatches. It is easy to succumb to their allure. After all, such fabled waters form the cradle of American fly fishing, placing the Garden of Eden at the junction of the Beaverkill and Willowemoc rivers. In those Promised Lands, early twentieth century American anglers adapted the methods of the dogmatic English chalk-stream anglers; a systematic approach based on their understanding of aquatic insects. Some forty years later Preston Jennings added his detailed studies of entomology to the accumulated knowledge of the Catskills "school" in *A Book Of Trout Flies*, in which he formally introduced many of the most popular patterns still in use today.

In the years since Jennings, volumes have been written about aquatic insects and their relationship to trout-fishing west of the Hudson River, in the rich waters of the upper Midwest and the increasingly popular destinations of the American West, overshadowing the unique qualities of our New England streams and the insects and fish that inhabit them. Our flowing waters support an amazing diversity of species from all of the major orders. Maine, alone, has, at last count, 162 species of mayflies, the most of any state. But New England habitats, population densities and emergence dates differ considerably from those of Pennsylvania and the Catskills, and the bugs seldom behave according to the textbooks. Only occasionally do these species emerge in sufficient density to bring large numbers of fish to the surface (except in a few isolated, limestone-rich pockets). If you are looking for clouds of Sulphur duns to appear like clockwork each evening in early June you may end up feeling that everybody else knows the hot spots except you. We have weather patterns that change with maddening frequency and a hatching season that seems to compress geometrically as you travel north. Our rivers are also, on average, more acidic and lacking in calcium and other minerals needed to sustain large populations of many insects.

This is not to imply that the big fish aren't here or that the fishing isn't good. Nothing could be further from the truth. We have our tales to tell, like John Blunt and his wife, on Maine's Kennebago above the lake, encountering a hatch of giant stoneflies so dense that the skies darkened. They wanted to run for their lives, but couldn't pass up all those rising fish. Then there was the time that the dam was shut off on the West Branch (in New England, that invariably means the Penobscot), triggering a massive caddis hatch during which there were fifty fish in the air at any one time. Our supposedly "fished out" rivers contain large trout and landlocked salmon that just aren't very easy to fool. I've managed to hook more than a few of them by adopting different, more regionally appropriate strategies that bring our bigger, better-educated fish to the fly. Primary among these is the realization that many of the most celebrated dun hatches are ignored by our conservative Yankee trout. The evening and morning spinner falls, on the other hand, routinely bring good fish to the surface while many anglers are sipping their evening cocktails or their morning coffee. We also have a few hatches that are less widely known, and more than one genus of mayfly whose multiple species provide overlapping hatches to create, in effect, a season-long emergence.

It was Vincent Marinaro, the famous innovator of the fertile limestone streams of Pennsylvania, who noted that "the character of the stream and its fish always establishes the best pattern of fly and the best manner of fishing it, not the fisherman." Marinaro, and the English chalk-stream anglers who gave birth to the dry fly, fished glassy, smooth-flowing alkaline rivers that not only provided an abundance of predictable surface insect life but a veritable window to the fish below. Our New England rivers are certainly not without their stretches of clear, gentle pools where you can see the trout taking nymphs. But much of our best stream fishing is done in fast-flowing and turbulent riffles, runs and pockets, putting us at a decided disadvantage when it comes to sighting our prey. But as much as the fish are hidden from us, so are we hidden from the fish. We can often make a closer approach, fish with a shorter line, and use heavier leaders and tippets than placid waters would allow. Under such conditions the high-floating Catskill or thorax styles of flies give a satisfactory impression of the naturals.

In some ways the spottiness of our New England hatches can be regarded as an asset. After all, a man who eats but once a day is less likely to complain about the cut of his steak. The fish of our freestone rivers and streams feed more opportunistically than those of food-rich limestone streams or spring creeks. Until they imprint the characteristics of a hatching insect, fish cannot become selective. At the same time, they can ill afford to spend precious energy in charging after particles in the drift that don't distinctly resemble food. Accuracy in both imitation and presentation are of paramount importance, all the more so as fish grow larger, warier and more discriminating.

I've often heard the complaint that the entomological approach to fishing is "too technical." I'll be the first to agree that I don't always have to catch something to enjoy an outing on the stream, but I can think of no occasion when I've had a better time not catching fish than catching them. I cannot promise that by matching the hatch and presenting your fly flawlessly to the fish you will catch them at will. This is, after all, not science but fishing, of which an important component is the possibility of failure. If catching trout could be reduced to a mathematical certainty it would quickly lose its appeal. But in studying both the appearance and behavior of the naturals you can significantly improve your odds while adding yet another fascinating dimension to a multifaceted pursuit. For me, the study of aquatic insects and their transformations is engaging in and of itself. It also increases my understanding of the river, the fish and their prey. Learning where the food is will help you find the fish.

I've had no professional training as an entomologist. That's very good news for you, because it means I won't be asking you to look up words like "benthic," "tergites" or "osmoregulation," which are terribly important to aquatic biologists and amateur enthusiasts (like myself) but won't do much to improve your fishing. But I've studied these insects at the river and under the lens, where I've made a few discoveries that I have been able to corroborate with the help of entomologists and the existing body of literature written in the tradition of Jennings and Schwiebert. Not the least important of these is the incredible variation in color (and size) between individual specimens of the same species, determined usually, but not always, by habitat. *Stenonema vicarium*, the mayfly known as the March Brown, for example, can appear as anything from a rich yellow size 12 to a deep gray-brown size 8 and has led over the years to the development of three distinct patterns to imitate a single species. This underscores the importance of obtaining live samples on the streams where you fish before tying up your patterns or choosing them from the bins of your favorite fly shop. Insect colors reproduced in books are, at best, accurate only for the particular species on a particular stream at a particular time of year. For this reason, I always carry with me a plastic-handled, child's butterfly net, available in any variety store. It has a fine mesh and a deep sock. It's lightweight and easily carried in my wading belt or hip boot, and, at three bucks, it's infinitely replaceable.

Each insect in this book is labeled with its common nickname. Many of these are derived from patterns developed years ago to imitate them. To the appropriate level, you will also see the classifications used by biologists. The insects are first separated by order, then family, then genus (whence the term "generic") and, finally, species (whence the term "specific"). These employ the "Latin" (or, more properly, Greco-Latin) names, the very sounds of which cause most anglers to roll their eyes as if you'd just offered to enliven their afternoon with a soliloquy on the use of leitmotifs in Wagnerian opera. Nicknames, unfortunately, are not standardized. When your friend on the next pool tells you that he's just seen a few "Sulphurs" hatching he is really just suggesting a fly pattern, because the name might mean anything from a size 24 Baetid mayfly to a size 10 *Anthopotamus distinctus*, two insects with very different behavior. It doesn't tell you about nymph activity, or where and how the emergers will appear, or how fish will respond to them. By using scientific names we can accurately describe the insects and predict their behavior. Of course, even these keep changing, for the process of classifying insects is fluid, a work in progress by the best of our entomologists.

Few entomologists claim the ability to look at a photograph of an adult insect and tell you its species, and no fish on record has ever done so. Some insects, like the colorful Golden Drake, are easily recognized, but at least a half dozen eastern *Epeorus* species are more or less identical. Positive species identification requires microscopic examination of details like adult male genitalia. No self-respecting trout will admit to inspecting that particular minutia. As for the angler, such information is of no practical value. For that reason, a number of mayflies are presented here generically where differences in appearance and behavior between species are only slight. Some species are quite distinctive and deserving of individual attention. Fewer angling studies have been done on the other orders, and for the most part we'll limit our examination to the family level.

Observing the trout's food supply hasn't exactly taught me how to think like a fish, but it has vastly increased my enjoyment of the sport. Even on days when I seem to be doing everything right but just can't hook a fish, I feel more connected with the river and the flora and fauna that either depend on it for their existence or just get swept up in its relentless journey toward the sea. It is possible to pay too much attention to the insects and not enough to the fish, and wading can be treacherous if you're looking skyward when you ought to be watching your step. But after a while it gets easy to recognize and even predict the arrival of a swarm of *rotunda* spinners or the unique way that a Golden Stonefly takes off, a colossus next to the diminutive, simultaneously hatching *Leucrocuta* duns and clouds of midges. And there is enormous satisfaction in being ready with the appropriate fly. In the following pages, we'll examine a few ways to induce the fish to take that fly. But first, let's take a look at the contents and character of our New England streams.

CHAPTER 1

The Life of a New England Freestone Stream

In New Hampshire, trout season begins on January 1. New Year's day finds most of the New England landscape covered in snow with air temperatures well below freezing. Ponds and lakes are decked in a thick layer of ice, and spring seems impossibly far away. But beneath the ice and snow new life is beginning. The rains and wet snows of autumn have restored the groundwater from which the springs flow, and tiny rivulets are forming. Eggs that were laid in autumn have hatched, and the larvae are busily devouring the fallen leaves. As the days grow longer and the sun slowly works itself overhead, these springs and rivulets will swell into the headwaters of our streams, even in places that were dry at summer's end.

Fed by rain and melting snow, these infant rivers are composed mainly of sterile water. By the time they've collected with groundwater seepage and perhaps a spring or two to form a steady flow they have absorbed few nutrients and support little in the way of insect life. They are also marginally acidic, except where limestone or marble provide the predominant bedrock, not a common feature of the region. Biologists call these headwaters first order streams, those without tributaries. They are also known as young streams. When two of these join, they form a second-order stream, and so on until you've got Old Man River himself. As the river grows and ages, the amount of nutrients it supports and the kinds of insect life that inhabit it change significantly. Oxygen levels, silt, current and water temperature are all affected by the age of a river. Many larvae that can live quite happily in first-order streams would perish in a fifth-order stream, and vice versa.

In New England, we call these headwaters woodland or upland streams. They trickle or tumble down the hillsides, forming small pockets and pools under the trees where they collect fallen leaves and other bits of organic trash. This detritus is food to a number of caddis, stoneflies and other leafshredders, who not only reduce the leaves to particulate matter but also contribute nutrients in the form of their own wastes. Even large detrivores like the mammoth *Pteronarcys* stoneflies can live in these tiny streams. Molds and fungi hasten the decay of fallen plant material and provide an additional food source for other insects. The canopy that provides this initial food also reduces exposure to sunlight. Combined with the acidity, this relative darkness limits the production of algae. With such a scarcity of food to choose from, fish inhabiting these young streams remain small. They are also extremely non-selective, but spirited, chasing after just about anything that resembles food.

On the first day of a recent spring, my then-6-year-old daughter and I decided to explore the tiny brook that runs along the dirt road on which we live. We found two different genera of clinging mayfly nymphs, two different crawling mayflies, small stoneflies from three different families (including the locally rare "roach-like" Peltoperlodids) and two caddis larvae, a free-living form and a tube-case maker—all leaf and detritus eaters and all within a twenty-yard stretch of the stream. But we only found one or two specimens of each, and most rocks that we inspected were vacant.

As this brook makes its way down our hill it meets the flow of other small tributaries. The gradient begins to soften, reducing the turbulence and the water's ability to aerate itself. It has picked up inorganic solids that alter the chemical balance. The streambed begins to widen, allowing sunlight to penetrate. This not only warms the water, but provides the opportunity for plant life to thrive, especially as the acidity drops. These second-order streams support new life forms, including herbivores that consume living plant tissue such as algae or other aquatic plants, either by foraging or by filtering their food from the drift. Some, like the cased *Brachycentrus* larvae, employ both methods.

Oxygen is also, of course, tremendously important, not only for insects and fish but for the aquatic vegetation on which many of the insects feed. The solubility of oxygen in water is inversely proportional to temperature, decreasing as the water gets warmer. It dissolves as water comes into contact with air, and with the agitation caused by turbulence. In the early spring, when the water is cold, there is plenty of oxygen and fish can be anywhere, but as the water warms fish move to cold spots and to places just below rapids and riffles where the oxygen supply is replenished.

As small streams come together they form what might properly be called large streams or small rivers. Here is where the waters reach the maximum diversity of habitat and, therefor, insect population. Fed by mountain streams and canopied by forest growth, they remain hospitably cool throughout the season. With plenty of rocky structure, there is sufficient tumbling to maintain a comfortable level of oxygen. As the number and variety of larvae multiply there is enough food for carnivorous insects like hellgrammites and the fierce Perlodid stoneflies. Drift-feeders like *Isonychia* mayflies and the netspinning Hydropsychidae family of caddisflies have plenty to sustain them. *Baetis* and damselfly nymphs can forage among the weeds, and silt settles in the slower pools to provide a burrowing habitat for the larvae of the big summer mayflies like the Green Drake and the golden *Anthopotamus*. Small New England rivers have enough diversity of insect types, but also sufficient populations of a given species, that fish become more selective and will key on the minute differences. They also get a better look at your imitations in water that is typically still clear, of moderate current and of adequate depth. Still, there is neither the richness of food supply nor the expanse of a particular type of habitat to support any single species in the huge numbers that provide blanket hatches. So while the fish are more selective, they are still opportunistic. If several similar species of caddis or mayfly are on the river at once, fish often blur the distinction, especially if they key onto a common indicator.

Riffles and Pools, Reaches and Runs

Streams and smaller rivers are where the structures by which we recognize good feeding lies are most apparent—the classic riffles, reaches, runs, pools and tail-outs. Riffles occur when water passes over cobble or small stones, which in turn cause turbulence. The water is rarely more than a few feet deep, nor is the current especially strong under normal conditions, for the stream has spread out and its force is dissipated. Riffles are nurseries for insects with inefficient gills and that require fast-water habitats, where the constant agitation promotes oxygenation. Such larvae include the netspinning and free-living caddisflies, the clinging mayfly nymphs and most of the stoneflies. As emergence approaches, many larvae or pupae drift out of the riffles to hatch in slower currents. At such times fish will temporarily move up into the faster, shallower water and hold in the slower pockets to intercept the vulnerable and plentiful migrating insects.

Below the riffles the river may slope gently into a pool, or it may narrow and gather depth and force to form a run. The fast water of a run

is a poor place for fish to hang out, but the areas immediately adjacent to this high-speed conveyer belt are ideal holding spots from which to snatch passing mouthfuls. As long as there is some structure provided by rocks and large stones, even the fastest sections of a stream will have marginal areas where pockets, eddies and slack waters occur. When casting to such likely spots, it pays to remember that fish feed with their heads up into the current, which is not necessarily synonymous with facing upstream. Sometimes a run will come at a bend in the river where the inside of the curve is shallow and gentle. Such spots offer an efficient food delivery system as well as quick means of escape. Fish also hold on the outer edge, especially where the force of the water undercuts the bank, but only if there is some protection against the current, such as a large boulder or deadfall. These fish can be among the largest, for the bulk of the food is carried to the faster side.

The strength of a run is its own undoing as it carves the bed that forces it to relax into a gentle pool, where once again the river widens. As tranquil as it may appear, a pool is complex in its arrangement of currents as the force of the run meets the static depths. There is usually a main current tongue creating swirls not only on the edges but also on the floor below, and fish holding in the depths may be facing in unexpected directions. The current slows as it enters the pool but speeds up as it exits. Controlling drag can be quite a challenge. Pools are collection sites for silt and debris, and harbor insects like dragonfly larvae, midges, some of the case-building caddis, and swimming and burrowing mayfly nymphs that thrive in slow-water environments where detritus and diatoms collect on the mucky bottom.

The head of the pool is where the food is concentrated as it enters, and here the fish will line up in receiving lines on either side of the current tongue with the biggest brute taking the most advantageous position, and defending it tenaciously. Anglers will also line up there according to the same hierarchy. In warm weather, and especially in low water, the pools are where trout seek protection from heat and from predators. Cool water remains at the bottom, but the otherwise scarce oxygen is found at the head where fast, turbulent water enters along with the food supply. Under cover of darkness the fish venture up into the riffles or the backwaters to feed on emerging or foraging insects. From midsummer on I won't spend much time fishing the riffles unless there is good holding water nearby.

Reaches are much like pools, except that the flow is more uniform. They occur where the gradient flattens out, the surface becomes smooth and the entire stream moves along at an easy pace. Fish choose their holding lies according to the speed of the current, and either pick their meals out of the drift or cruise the slower edges in search of food. Locating fish can be difficult if you don't know the water, for there are few clues to guide you. On the other hand, reaches are particularly rewarding when a hatch is on, because their tranquil surfaces make it easy to spot rises, and because the simple currents allow for long, drag-free drifts.

Reaches and pools can go on for quite a distance, but sooner or later gravity prevails and the current accelerates. Sometimes the water's depth decreases as a new riffle forms, or the river may be funneled into a new run. These tail-outs provide places where fish can hold behind stones or in depressions and pick out the morsels that concentrate in the drift as they speed by overhead, especially those insects, like the Green Drake, that spend their larval stages in the pool and collect in the tail-out as they hatch. Because the current speeds up as it reaches the tail-out, it is a difficult spot to control drag.

Pocketwaters contain elements of riffles, runs and pools all mixed together. They occur where the grade is fairly uniform over a substantial distance and where the stones are large enough to create numerous, widely distributed holding lies in water that is only moderately deep. A pocketwater with a steep gradient is a rapid. The stones break the current into a complex tapestry of smaller currents that quickly rejoin and then separate once again. This constant agitation means a good supply of oxygen all season long. Trout hold behind, in front or just to the sides of the stones and dart into the current when tempted by items in the drift, with little opportunity for prolonged scrutiny. The dead spot in front of a stone allows a better view and is favored by larger fish. Because the food is dispersed, feeding is opportunistic. The screen provided by the broken currents permits you to approach each pocket and cast from a short distance, thereby keeping your line well up off of the water. Pocketwaters are particularly favorable to crawlers like the Hendricksons and Sulphurs, to swimmers like *Isonychia* and the Tiny Blue-winged Olives and a wide variety of caddis, stoneflies and midges. Beyond providing good feeding lies for fish, the rocks provide suitable sites for egglayers that crawl beneath the surface.

Large Rivers

When small rivers become large rivers, their characteristics become more uniform. Diversity of insect species decreases inversely with the size of a river as temperature, nutrient levels, lowered solubility of oxygen and flow rate reach the extremes of hospitality. Those insects that are best suited to each habitat will flourish and hatch in phenomenal numbers. With less to choose from, but in larger helpings, trout become even more selective. Fast-water dwellers like the clinging mayfly nymphs disappear, but the swimmers and burrowers appear in greater numbers. Most New England rivers, as they age, become deeper, warmer and slower. Their beds grow more silty, and the margins and backwaters support more plant life. An excess of plant life, however, especially of grasses, usually indicates an environment that is too warm for trout or salmon, even as it supports an abundance of vegetarian and burrowing insects. The trout that you do find there are usually large. They are the survivors who feed mainly on smaller fish and have themselves escaped the jaws of fiercer predators. You'll find them mainly at the mouths of cold feeder streams and over springs.

Tailwaters

The character of any river or stream is dramatically altered, usually in the favor of the fly fisherman, when it encounters any kind of impoundment such as a lake or a millpond. These stillwaters allow silt to settle as they stratify the water into warm and cold layers. They enrich the river by allowing the growth of phytoplankton, a vital part of the diet of such particle collectors as chimney-cased caddis and many swimming mayfly nymphs. The stretches of rivers below these impoundments are called tailwaters, and they provide some of the most fertile habitat for aquatic insects and the fish that feed on them. Dams that release from the top create warm tailwaters, while those that release from the bottom, where the water is much colder, can turn a warmwater fishery into good trout water. Temperatures in a tailwater usually alter the hatch calendar. The West Branch of the Farmington River in Connecticut comes out from the bottom of a ninety-foot dam at forty to fifty degrees, and when the warmer feeder streams dry up in the summer's heat, the temperature in the river actually drops. The Hendricksons arrive a week later than on the Housatonic, a warm tailwater less than forty miles to the west.

New England has no shortage of tailwater fisheries, of both the warm and cold varieties. The Connecticut River, the major artery connecting four of the six New England states, is a prime example. Just south of its source at the Canadian border it is scarcely deep enough to wet your wading boots, but it soon joins with numerous other streams flowing through a variety of ponds and into the fertile Connecticut Lakes, home to brook trout, lake trout and landlocked salmon. As it flows clear and cold out of Lake Francis it is a small river supporting brookies, browns and the occasional rainbow through miles of trophy water. A few miles below Colebrook, N.H. it begins to warm significantly and before long its progress is slowed by several large hydroelectric dams. The water above these dams is too warm and slow for much of the year to support a trout fishery, but directly below them the fishing for trophy sized trout remains fantastic throughout the year owing to cold water releases and the buildup of nutrients. As the river swells on its journey southward it continues to alternate as a warmwater fishery containing bass, walleye and northern pike, to name a few, and as a coldwater fishery below the dams at Monroe, Cummerford, Wilder and Bellows Falls. I hasten to add that these dams occasionally release large amounts of water quite suddenly, and failure to take note of rising water levels can spell disaster.

By contrast, my home water, the White River in Vermont, has no substantial reservoirs to provide enrichment, although each of its three major branches passes through at least one small, defunct impoundment where mills once stood. It is born in the granite midsection of Vermont, creating a relatively acidic habitat with sparse vegetation. It has an amazing diversity of insect orders and species and has provided most of the specimens for this book. But, except for the White Fly blizzards on the lower reaches each August, blanket hatches are uncommon, and those hatches that do bring fish to the surface may last only a very few minutes. I like to think of it as a typical New England trout stream. It has all kinds of water and a wide diversity of habitats. It is both steady and temperamental. No matter how many times I fish it, it is never the same river. It's also the home of some very large trout, which keep me coming back, again and again.

CHAPTER 2

Presentation on
New England Streams

With each trip to a new stream or visit to a favorite pool, we face a brand new set of conditions that govern how, where and on what foods its finned inhabitants are feeding. Our two most immediate decisions, based on an evaluation of those conditions, are what fly to present and how to present it. There to guide us are several underlying concepts applicable to all hatch-matching techniques, including the mechanics of insect emergence, how a fish feeds, and the forces which will affect your fly once it comes into contact with the stream. We can begin by dividing the stream into three layers—the bottom, the middle and the surface.

The surface is the membrane that simultaneously divides and unites the two worlds of water and air. It is largely the province of the dry fly. To understand its importance to feeding trout, try placing yourself in the role of an insect. Think of the surface as a large plastic drop cloth stretched tightly over a river, which is moving, plastic and all, toward the sea. Imagine also that the plastic is just barely thick enough for you to walk on, or even to run or jump on. Finally, imagine that you have six legs and wings and, for good measure, a tail. Viewed by us fish from below at an oblique angle, all that we can seen of you is the cluster of depressions created as the plastic stretches downward under the weight of your footprints. The rest of you is hidden behind the reflections in the underside of the surface in what has come to be known as the mirror effect. These depressions act as tiny lenses and focus the light as circular highlights. As you and your moving dropcloth drift directly overhead, you enter what is known as our window, where the surface no longer reflects light from underneath but refracts it from above in a circle, just the way a photographic lens collects light rays and focuses them through a single point at the aperture. The size of the window is determined by a cone, with the fish's eye at its apex and the circular window at its base. The closer the fish is to the surface, the smaller the window. At the edge of this window your feet are still little more than a pattern of surface depressions, but your upper shape now appears above the surface, and from the outline of your wings we can tell if you are a mayfly, a water strider or an egg laying caddis. Finally, when you are almost directly overhead, we can clearly see your shape and color and decide whether you are worth tasting, provided that we are not preoccupied in dining on something else.

To an insect, the meniscus created by surface tension acts just like our plastic dropcloth. It takes more energy to break through the meniscus in either direction than it does to swim in the water below it or fly through the air above it. It's what keeps an insect, or your fly, afloat. If either gets wet, the surface tension is broken. If you jump too hard or too sharply on the dropcloth, one or more feet will break through. In order to free yourself, you'll have to push against the surface with another foot, and that will probably break through as well. Now you are trapped in the surface film.

The surface of the river creates some advantages for both fish and insects. For the fish, it creates a level of protection against predators. Because all source light comes from above, glare makes it difficult for us to see into the water, whereas creatures living below it are limited (or aided, in many cases) only by the mirror and window effects. They can usually see us long before we see them. Insects that hatch on the water use it as a platform. Egg layers use the meniscus to walk upon as they either drop or rinse away their egg clusters. And surface tension allows diving egglayers to drag down with them a life saving air bubble. Just as it keeps a dry insect from falling through the surface, the meniscus provides a barrier to those trying to hatch from below it, and an opportunity for fish to feed on emergers struggling to break through. Large insects like the summer mayfly drakes have little trouble, but smaller nymphs sometimes drift for many yards before succeeding. Many expire from the effort. Once through, the nymph casing remains suspended like a slightly submerged raft as the adult climbs out on top of it, dry and ready to try its wings.

How a fish reacts with the meniscus gives important clues as to the type and the life stage of the insect upon which it is feeding. The number of different rise form descriptions is exceeded only by the number of books and articles written on the subject, but a few of the subtleties are apparent even on our free flowing New England streams. It helps to understand that the description of a fish inhaling a fly is more than a writer's cliché. It factually describes the manner in which a trout feeds, by expanding its gills so as to draw water and its contents into the mouth. It takes a great deal more energy to suck a large floating mayfly dun down through the surface film, particularly after charging up from the stream bottom, than to sip midge pupae just under the surface. In the former, a smacking or splashy rise, the nose of the fish penetrates the surface, whereas in the latter, a smutting rise, a surface dimple may be all that we see.

Another vital component of our interactions with the surface is the phenomenon known as drag. Especially in freestone streams, the water between you and your target is made up of current columns moving at varying speeds, causing line and leader to move in multiple directions. Such forces can be imperceptible. An insect drifts with the current, but the effect of drag on your line is to skim your fly across or through the water in unnatural ways, upstream, downstream or sideways. Trout flee from such offerings, just as you would if your Thanksgiving turkey suddenly danced a hornpipe on the serving platter. If a trout ignores your fly, you've probably made a poor selection. If it vanishes, the culprit is probably drag. At the same time, drag is merely a movement of the fly that's out of your control. In situations where you are the master of it, drag is a tool, an integral part of the presentation equation. These situations include wet fly fishing and some active dry fly and nymph presentations.

Trout feeding rhythmically on the surface are probably feeding selectively. They rise to surface insects with the mixed feelings you would experience in retrieving a lost wallet from a busy intersection. Fish, especially large ones, don't expose themselves to predators or to the rigors of surface currents unless there is a sufficient amount of food to make the trip worthwhile, and that rarely happens unless there are one or more species hatching or laying eggs. For big bugs the fish may wait in the relative safety of the stream bottom and then shoot up to take a passing morsel with a loud, splashy rise. But it will not expend more energy in apprehending its food than it can gain by eating it. If the insects are small, it will find a place where it can linger just under the surface and then tip up in a rhythmic sequence to sip the drifting adults. So long as there is an abundance of a single insect, the trout will be disinclined to begin feeding on another.

Selective feeding is instinctive. It is nature's way of making up for lost time. It enables a trout to gorge itself by short circuiting the relatively inefficient trial and error of opportunistic feeding. When there is an abundance of a single insect, the fish need only focus on a few key indicators, such as size, color and silhouette, rather than individually scrutinize each article in the drift. If your fly matches the criteria, the trout will strike without hesitation. The more time a fish spends in deciding to strike, the greater the probability that it will detect a fraud.

Now let's look at the part of the stream that is the furthest from us, the bottom. This is where both fish and insects spend the greater part of their time. It is the realm of the nymphs, larvae and creepers and of our imitations generally referred to as nymphs. The structure of the bottom affects the currents at the surface. What the bottom is made of, the substrate, determines what kinds of creatures inhabit it, thereby furnishing an important clue for the angler.

As hatch time nears for a particular insect the larvae migrate and gather at certain sites along the bottom in preparation for their rise to the surface. Nymphing trout will key in on the prevalent insect, and as the fish becomes more satiated, it grows even more selective. As a general rule, however, these events are isolated. Most of the time fish in New England streams are opportunistic feeders, popping anything into their mouths as long as it looks like food, and just as quickly ejecting it if it doesn't pass the taste test. This is a boon for the nymph fisherman, who is thereby liberated from the stringent requirements posed by ultra selective feeders and can instead tie on the largest nymph in the fly box that the trout will recognize as food. Much of it arrives owing to a phenomenon known as "behavioral drift", a species survival mechanism whereby stream populations are redistributed from densely crowded sections to areas where there is less competition for food. This behavior increases as larvae near maturity. The most active periods are the first few hours after dark and again during the first few hours before daylight. During these peak hours many large fish leave their secure lies to forage for exposed insects. "Catastrophic drift", in which stream disturbances cause the insects to lose their hold and be cast pell-mell into the current, occurs only randomly.

Under the surface there are no mirrors or windows to play tricks on a fish's vision. Imitations must be tied to a higher standard of accuracy. To some, this means larval and pupal patterns that duplicate anatomical minutiae in excruciating detail, but I hold the view that while a certain degree of visual accuracy is desirable, the ability of the artificial to behave like a natural, living insect is the foundation of the tier's art. If it looks and behaves like food, the fish tests it in its mouth to decide if it smells or tastes like food, or at least feels like food. The time it takes to make this decision is the time we have to set the hook.

The rest of the stream, the part that lies in between the bottom and the surface, is known as the midwater. Except at certain times, the midwater contains the least amount of food in the largest volume of water. It is the no-man's land through which fish and insects must pass on their way from the bottom to the surface and back again when the insects hatch or lay eggs and the fish feed and return to safety. It is the realm of the pupae, the hatching nymphs and the occasional victims of catastrophic drift. During times of such activity, it can be the most fertile place for your wet fly or nymph, while at other times it is the least productive.

The bulging rise is characteristic of midwater feeding. When emergers or pupae are ascending without urgency, fish take them several inches beneath the surface without actually breaking through it, but causing the water to swell. Such rises can be deceiving, as they reach the surface well downstream of the fish, especially in more rapid currents. They are also difficult to observe except when the surface is somewhat flat.

A trout is a wild animal. Equal to his instinct to feed is his instinct to avoid predators, including you and I. His reflexes are lightning fast, his vision is acute, and the lateral line along each of his sides alerts him

to disturbances in the water. You must approach your quarry exactly as a cat approaches a mouse—slowly, quietly, imperceptibly—or the game is lost. I've yet to meet a hunter who would blindly fire into the woods with the expectation of mortally wounding a deer. Each successive report from his rifle would exponentially diminish his chances of any deer remaining within range. Yet that is exactly the way many of us approach a trout stream.

Take some time when you arrive at the water to study it. Your best chances are for fish you can see at or under the surface, but you may have to settle for analyzing the stream for the best lies. When you've picked your mark, choose your optimum casting position carefully by selecting a vantage point where you can make your presentation without alarming your prey. Ideally, it is where your fly lands between the fish and the sun, where neither you nor your line will cast a shadow, and where the currents are few and simple to allow a drag free float. Most important, get as close to your target as possible without betraying your presence. For each situation, there is only one best place from which to cast your fly.

Once you've gained an understanding of the behavior of aquatic insects, and of their habitats, presenting your fly becomes almost intuitive. Start by deciding which type of fly to use—a nymph for the larval forms and the early pupal stages, wets for subsurface emergers and egglaying adults and dries for surface emergers, newly emerged adults and surface egglayers. Then decide which of three methods of presentation is most appropriate—nymph, wet or dry fly. Don't get trapped into thinking of these as mutually exclusive boundaries. Its perfectly OK to fish a dry fly in wet fly style or to float a nymph on the surface like a dry fly when the situation calls for it. Each method is subdivided into three actions: the cast, the drift and the retrieve. Because we are chiefly concerned with imitating insect behavior, we'll focus only on the last two by assuming that you can execute a few basic casts: the roll cast, the straight cast, a slack line cast, upstream and downstream reach casts. Those who are familiar with upstream and downstream curve casts have a decided advantage. The ability to throw upstream, downstream and slack mends is also vitally important. For all of the above, there is no substitute for a good clinic or one-on-one instruction followed by hours of practice.

Presenting a Wet Fly

For sheer serenity there is little to compare with the time-honored approach to wet-fly fishing. The dressings are easy to cast, and the rhythmic, down-and-across presentations, followed by swinging arcs of the fly, have a meditative effect upon the soul, at least until a sudden pull announces a fish on the line. It is the ancient approach. The earliest known fly patterns were constructed on heavy hooks and could only have been fished below the surface, where they mimicked drowned or swimming insects, including adult caddis and stoneflies. Today many forgotten wet fly methods are resurfacing as anglers discover that they succeed in situations where the dry fly and the nymph cannot.

In wet-fly fishing we put drag to work for us, using it as a force to maneuver the fly. We can narrow the method to two basic approaches, one just below the surface and the other deep near the bottom. The first provides the same approach to salmon fishing as that practiced on fifteenth century English rivers and still used on the world's great salmon streams. The wet fly is cast in a straight line, quartered down and across the stream, and allowed to swing in an arc to a position directly below the angler, who lets it hang briefly, takes a few steps, picks up the line and repeats the process until the entire pool is covered. Drag remains constant and uniform throughout the swing, which keeps an unweighted fly at a steady depth, on or just under the surface. The speed of the fly increases with the degree of belly in the line. To fish the fly deep, cast upstream and allow it to sink to the desired depth. Apply only enough tension to keep it there by following the line with your rod tip.

With wet-fly methods we are in direct control of the fly at all times to give it a lifelike movement. Beyond the basic drift, there are a variety of ways to make the fly behave like a living insect. One of the most fundamental is called the "Leisenring lift" after its originator, Jim Leisenring of Pennsylvania. Leisenring precisely pinpointed the location or likely location of his fish and drifted his fly along the bottom until it reached a spot just in front of the target. At this point he ceased to follow the drift with his rod causing, in his own words, "the fly to lift from the bottom and rise with the hackles or legs quivering after the manner of the hatching natural fly." Most of his wet-fly patterns were wingless, with soft collar hackles. Leisenring was adamant about adding no movement to the fly as it rose, and in my experience there should be no hurry in making your pickup. Instead, let the fly hang in the drift at the end of its upward swing. In apparent contradiction to all match-the-hatch logic, I've hooked many good fish through sheer patience, not only on wet flies but also on nymphs, dries and streamers. To avoid pulling the hook out of the fish's mouth, keep your rod at an angle to the line. In its most basic form the Leisenring lift is executed with the fly directly downstream from the rod tip, causing the fly to rise more or less straight up. By manipulating the rod tip away from this orientation, or by throwing a slack loop in the direction that you want your fly to travel, you can maneuver it across the current as it rises. For example, moving the rod tip or line toward the shore will cause the fly to follow in imitation of an *Isonychia* nymph or stonefly creeper preparing to hatch.

Additional opportunities to add movement to your fly come during the retrieve, which can be anything from a gradual pickup to a manipulated series of line strips. There are many techniques, but all are based on the variables of speed, distance and frequency. You can also add embellishments like an up and down or side to side motion of your rod tip. The important thing is to match your retrieve with the speed and action of the insect you are trying to imitate. The common strip retrieve allows great flexibility in all three variables and is easy to execute. Pull your line in a foot or so at a time with your line hand and pinch it with the index finger of your rod hand as you reach forward to grasp for the next strip. Keep the angle between rod and line gentle enough to minimize resistance, but sharp enough to cushion any strikes. An intermittent strip retrieve, in which you allow the fly to sink slightly between each pull, imitates insects that are awkward swimmers, like crawling nymphs. A longer, steadier strip retrieve suggests a rising caddis pupa, an egglaying caddis adult or even a swimming mayfly nymph. You can achieve real speed by tucking your rod under your armpits and stripping hand over hand, but you'll need quick reflexes to grasp your rod when you feel a sudden strike.

Except when fish have keyed on a single insect in a single size, doubling the number of flies more than doubles your chances of drawing a strike. A setup of two flies in tandem, or even three or more

flies, is traditionally called a "cast," consisting of a point fly and one or more droppers. You can easily add a dropper to the end of a long tag left on your barrel knot when you attach your tippet for the terminal or point fly. To increase the number of flies, simply add more tippets. The point fly should be the heaviest, for it controls the drift. Another method is to tie them in series, this time keeping the smallest fly on the point. Start by adding an 8- to 12-inch length of tippet to your leader in the appropriate diameter for your largest fly. Attach a similar length of lighter tippet directly to the bend or to the eye of the first fly, and tie your smaller fly to that.

If you want to add a piece of split shot, place it above the knot that joins your leader to the tippet, where it won't slip. But be wary when casting such rigs and keep your loops wide, for Queen Mab never tangled mares' manes as quickly as a single miscast will install the Gordian knot at the end of your line. If you prefer to avoid split shot, make sure that your wet flies are tied on heavy hooks, and are sparsely dressed, particularly the larger flies. Overly fluffy patterns resist your best efforts to fish them deep.

A neat nineteenth century technique called wet-fly dapping was revived by Ray Bergman and later by Leonard Wright Jr., champion of the

unorthodox. With a cast of three flies (or two, if the leading fly is bulky enough), you can cast downstream or across a pocket such that the lower, heavy flies anchor the line while the upper dry (or wet) fly daps the surface like a fluttering insect. This method requires a long rod, a light line and a short cast, with the rod held high. A strong tippet and a soft rod are recommended to absorb the violent strikes that you can expect with such a presentation.

Presenting a Nymph

Nymph fishing is the imitation of insects in their larval form. Early 20th century nymph presentations were little more than extensions of wet-fly techniques, but its modern application combines elements of both dry fly and wet-fly fishing in a whole that is greater than the sum of its parts. Its emphasis is on getting the fly down to the fish. In New England, that usually means fishing for what we cannot see, making it the most difficult of all to learn. Even today, most fly fishermen catch fish far more easily on a dry fly than with a nymph. But, once mastered, nymphing opens up hitherto unavailable opportunities. As you've undoubtedly heard many times, ninety percent of a trout's diet is consumed below the surface, and really big fish will rarely risk a trip to the surface so long as there is sufficient food down below.

The difficulty lies in learning when to set the hook. A nymphing fish blithely intercepts its drifting prey, so there is little likelihood of its hooking itself. It tests drifting objects with its mouth, spitting out anything that proves unpalatable, including your concoction of fur and feathers, in the wink of an eye. If you can see the take, you must strike immediately. If not, you must rely on secondary signals, such as the wink of white as it opens its mouth or the flash of its scales as it moves to your fly. If your line hesitates, or draws below the surface, strike quickly. Seasoned nymphers develop what seems like a sixth sense of knowing when to strike, but it is a skill that takes years to develop. For the rest of us, there are strike indicators.

For imitating crawling and clinging mayfly larvae, a drag-free dead drift is the most realistic presentation. These nymphs are capable of swimming in gentle pockets and pools, but when swept up by the moderate to swift currents of their favored habitat they remain motionless, as if stunned. In choosing a casting position, bear in mind that a fish's window to the outside world increases with depth. Cast well above the target to allow your fly to reach the desired depth before it reaches the lie, then continue the drift through the lie as it bounces along like a migrating or dislocated larva. Nymphing fish, particularly those on the bottom, rarely stray far from their feeding position, so repeated offerings might be required to get the fly within range. If your target is directly upstream, you must retrieve your line at the speed of the current to maintain direct control of the fly. If you allow too much slack, you'll be unable to strike effectively, or your fly will hang up on the bottom. Allow too little and the line will drag. By using a reach or a curve cast, you can avoid dropping the line on top of the fish. If your target is directly downstream, you must feed line at the same rate to maintain both slack and control. Meanwhile the current at the surface is traveling faster than the current on the bottom. To control drag from top to bottom, keep mending the line by throwing slack directly behind, or upstream from, the point where it enters the water, a maneuver known as the slack mend.

Drifting your fly across the current adds an additional layer of complexity. You control slack in the same way, but current drag works against you, particularly if you are trying to keep an unweighted fly near the bottom. A reach cast takes care of the problem initially, upstream if the feeding lane is slower than the intervening currents, downstream if the opposite is true. As the drift continues, you'll need to mend the line in the same direction. If you keep your rod held high and the tip pointing at your indicator or the line's point of entry into the water, you will keep better control of your slack and reduce the number of mends needed to control both current and top-to-bottom drag. The shorter the line, the quicker the response to the take.

As with a wet fly, you can add a rising motion through the midwater at the end of your drift. This is particularly useful in the early stages of a hatch, when pre-emergent nymphs and pupae are swimming to the surface or crawling to the shore. On small streams, I've often found that a twitch added to the rising motion is all that's needed to bring a hungry fish out of its hiding place. Trout in small streams may be opportunistic, but they are also extremely wary and need a little extra convincing to close the deal. You can also fish several nymphs together as a cast as described for wet flies, or add one as a dropper to a dry fly, which then does double duty as a strike indicator. Adding a big meaty staple like a yellow stonefly nymph to attract attention to your tiny hatch matching pheasant tail nymph more than doubles your chances of a strike. Three flies are even better, but only if you are less prone to wind knots than I am.

Except during a hatch, most nymph activity is on the bottom of the stream, and that's where your fly should be. With a floating line, use a leader that is twice as long as the water is deep. In gentle currents, cast well above your target to get your fly to the proper depth. For faster currents especially, it's usually necessary to put weight on the line. There are a variety of products available for this purpose, including non-toxic split shot. Start by adding about a foot of tippet to the end of your leader. Place your weight above the knot, where it can't slip, and tie your fly to the new tippet. Another method, attributed to Lefty Kreh, is to leave a long tag after tying on your nymph and crimp a piece of split shot onto the end of it. Singe or knot the end to keep the shot from slipping. It allows less movement of the fly, but in the event of hanging up you only lose your split shot. Whatever method you choose, continue adding weight until you feel your fly knocking along the bottom. It's like getting directions in rural Vermont: When you reach the fork in the road, you've gone too far. Integrally weighted flies are easier to cast and stay closer to the bottom, but many anglers feel that a weighted hook makes for a fly that behaves unnaturally.

The retrieve is as important to nymphing as it is to wet-fly methods. The difference lies in the speed. Except for the swimming and burrowing mayfly nymphs and pharate caddis adults, aquatic insect larvae move rather slowly. The slowest retrieve is the hand twist, in which you grasp the line with your line hand between the thumb and forefinger and rotate your hand up and toward you, then grasp the line with your remaining fingers and rotate your hand in the opposite direction, drawing your line in a few inches at a time. This is a great way to imitate a nymph crawling on the bottom of a slow pool. For the true swimming nymphs like *Isonychia* and *Baetis*, use a longer, steadier strip retrieve like those described for the wet-fly method.

Presenting a Dry Fly

Hardly anyone will dispute that the most satisfying event in fly fishing is the rise of a fish to the surface to snatch your dry fly. Trout take less than ten percent of their food from the surface, but this feeding activity and the insect hatches which trigger it usually occur at the nicest time to be out on the river. On warm spring or autumn afternoons or cool summer evenings there is nothing to compare with that magical convergence of insects and fish as they pierce through the membrane separating the aquatic world from the terrestrial.

In England, early experiments in dry-fly fishing began in the mid 1800s, but it was American innovation, in the form of oiled silk lines and the improved split cane rods needed to cast them, that enabled its practice to become widespread. The dead-drift presentation has changed little since then, although the dogma of the upstream cast has fallen by the wayside. Americans like Gordon and La Branche demonstrated that the dry fly could be as effective in the fast, broken waters of the Northeast as on the placid English chalk streams. Innovative tiers throughout the twentieth century have adopted new methods and materials designed to keep dry flies buoyant on our most boisterous streams.

If you've mastered the dead drift with a nymph, you can do it with a dry fly. The points to remember are to remain unseen by the fish, keep control of your line, and avoid drag at all costs. Keep the fly motionless until it is well past the range of the fish. Because the fly doesn't sink, you needn't cast quite so far upstream of the feeding lie, especially if fish are rising. For upstream or downstream dead drifts, or wherever there is a current, use a slack cast to keep the fly from immediately dragging and mend your line frequently to maintain a drag-free drift.

But dry-fly fishing goes far beyond the dead drift. A properly executed retrieve, where appropriate, can draw otherwise disinterested fish to the surface, just as a poorly executed retrieve can put them down swiftly and irrevocably. One way is to use dry flies with palmered bodies, upside down hooks or long tails and stiff, oversized hackles. These are designed to keep the hook point out of the water and avoid creating spray or a wake. Skated across the surface, these flies dance in the manner of a winged insect. Using a light floating line, a short down-and-across cast and a long rod held high, retrieve using a series of quick strips coupled with a lifting of the rod tip to bounce your fly along the water. It will perform a wonderful impersonation of an ovipositing stonefly or a large, clumsy drake trying to achieve lift off. Skating also works well in those hard-to-reach pockets.

You can skate a fluttering caddis imitation in much the same manner as a struggling mayfly. Leonard Wright, a self-styled heretic on the subject of dry-fly fishing, developed his skating technique called the Sudden Inch, a sort of pre-drift retrieve, after observing that many hatching caddis actually run across the surface while others lay eggs by

bouncing on the water. It requires either a downstream presentation or a mastery of the curve cast, made across the stream and curving in the direction of the current so that the fly faces upstream in the manner of a natural. Just as the fly alights within striking range of a good trout, and before the line has settled on the water, give a short tug to skate it forward and then let it continue to drift. The alternate twitch and drift, a modern variation, is essentially a series of Sudden Inch maneuvers during a single retrieve.

You can also pull your dry fly under at the end of a drift and retrieve it as a wet fly in imitation of either a drowned or egglaying insects. There is danger, however, in pulling a submerged fly sharply off the water when beginning the back cast, for the audible "thwop" will surely drive any surface feeders to their hideouts. By bringing the fly to the surface with a roll cast or other means you can safely start your fly on its next drift.

Tackling Tackle

The finer points of tackle, things like rod length, line weight and leader construction, are very much a matter of personal preference and depend upon your level of ability, the types of fishing that you do, even your physical stature. One of my best friends, for example, does all of his trout and bass fishing with a 5-weight, which happens to be a popular choice, and pronounces himself perfectly satisfied. For me this is a bit too much of a compromise. He accuses me of splitting hairs, but I divide almost all of my freshwater fishing between two weights, 4 and 6, and for each I choose either an eight- or a nine-footer according to the size of the water. They are all medium-action rods with which I can play a heavy fish, roll cast effectively and overcome the effects of a modest wind. The 4-weights are devoted to surface fishing where the most important factors are placing the line softly upon the water and ease of line manipulation, but in a pinch they will deliver one or two small nymphs or wet flies to the stream bottom. The six-weights carry the load of subsurface fishing including nymphs, wets and streamers, particularly in the larger sizes. After a few hours with a 4-weight my nine-foot 6-weight feels like a telephone pole, but the added muscle allows me to cast even a triplet of weighted nymphs without a hinging leader, even with split shot and an indicator on the line.

All of my floating lines are double taper, for two principle reasons. The first is that I have adopted Yankee habits of thrift, and if the tapered section gets damaged I can just reverse the line. The second is that I never seem to have enough room for a proper backcast. Roll casting requires that the rearmost part of the line lift the portion in front of it, a difficult feat if you are into the running section of a weight-forward. Weight-forward lines facilitate longer casts, but distance casting is rarely a priority. There is also less give in a double taper, an important factor when setting the hook. The weight-forward sink-tip in my kit bag rarely gets wet, and then only for deeply fished wet flies or streamers. I prefer to have my line on top of the water where I can see it and use the leader to take the fly down to the bottom.

I tried all manner of leader links, loop connectors and other widgets for attaching line to leader before settling on the good old-fashioned nail knot. It is a solid connection that transfers all of the energy from line to leader without hinging or cutting the line. I tie on a butt section that matches the line for flexibility and join it to my buttless leaders with a barrel knot. I never retie the nail knot. In fact, I seldom tie on new leaders, although I occasionally have to rebuild them, both because I use my own knotted leaders and because I divide my surface and subsurface applications between two rods. Building your own leaders takes very little time once you have mastered the barrel knot, and it creates a balanced transfer of energy from line to fly in a manner that off-the-shelf varieties rarely accomplish. My leaders are built in two sections, the taper and the tippet, with the butt residing permanently on the line. For both the butt and taper sections I use a stiff monofilament designed to ensure that the fly lands well ahead of the leader. I construct the tippet from more pliant material, not only to provide slack in my dry-fly casts but to allow a more natural motion in my nymphs and wet flies. If I change fly sizes I need rebuild only the tippet to the proper diameter.

Many formulas have been published for hand-tied leaders, but they can be distilled into two, one each for surface and subsurface presentations. The simplified version for wet fly and nymph fishing is the simple 60-20-20 formula. The first 60 percent is the butt, the middle 20 percent is the taper and the final 20 percent is the tippet. An inch or two here or there is unimportant. My own leader butts incorporate a gradual reduction in diameter. This becomes more extreme in the taper section, which brings the diameter down to the tippet in five- or six-inch segments at a rate of .002 inches per segment. For wet flies, a short leader on the order of seven feet will do nicely. Few, if any, wet-fly patterns are small enough to require overly delicate tippets, and given the savage nature of the strikes a short, heavier leader is highly advantageous. For nymphs, your leader should be at least double the depth of the water.

Dry-fly leaders must overcome two obstacles, namely unwanted surface drag and visibility. Both problems are partially addressed by using long leaders, typically 9 to 12 feet or longer. To overcome drag, they are designed for slack at the tippet by using a 40-20-40 formula. That last 40 percent, constructed of soft material, allows the leader to alight delicately and with enough squiggle to compensate for even the most minute forces of the current. Controlling micro drag is far more important than reducing the diameter of your tippet, which can never be completely invisible. Fine as they are, their presence is magnified by surface tension in the same manner that the feet of insects create tiny lenses. Not only are the resulting refractions visible at the surface, but they create an enlarged shadow on the river bottom. Wetting agents, including saliva, make short work of this problem, but keep the last few inches of tippet dry, lest they counteract the buoyancy of your fly.

Night Fishing

There are few forms of fly fishing that demand such completely focused attention and provide such intense thrills as night fishing. Many insects, including most of the very large ones, hatch and lay eggs only after dark.

This activity often coincides with the increased behavioral drift activity of larval stages. Big trout, feeling safe from many predators and eager to take advantage of both the increase in the food supply and cooler temperatures, trade their cold, deep, daytime hiding places for nocturnal feeding lies or forage in the slower and shallower areas of the stream. True night fishing, a pursuit undertaken in total darkness, can be extremely exciting and productive but is also hazardous. It requires thorough preparation and alert senses.

Before attempting to fish a given pool at night, invest an hour or two there in the daytime. Look for likely spots where the fish will be holding or cruising after dark and find the best casting positions. It is crucial to know exactly where the fish are going to be. Keep as far as possible from rapids, which mask the sound of the take with their constant noise. Familiarize your feet with the routes you will be taking to and from those spots when your eyes can no longer guide you. Make a few practice casts and see how much line you will be casting, then tie a piece of thread around the line so that you can feel it. Make a note of the trees behind you that are likely to snag your back casts or missed strikes. Finally, observe the time it takes for your line to drag and plan a system of casting and mending based on complete lack of visual contact.

The fly patterns suggested in the pages that follow are selected only to represent a range of solutions to the problems of insect imitation created by many of the region's finest fly designers, plus some of my own solutions and a few "from away." Of course, thousands of other patterns are available, and most of them will catch fish. What's important is that you choose those that closely match the naturals where you are fishing. All of my selections are filtered through my prejudices regarding imitation and fly tying. For example, there are few nymph patterns that incorporate beadheads. There's no denying that they work superbly, but I can never be sure if it isn't the bead rather than the pattern that attracts the fish. I've made a conscious attempt to offer patterns which are somewhat universal, where possible, for it is easy to become too specific and weighed down by a mind-numbing variety of fly patterns in a staggering array of sizes. Finally, where possible, I include commercially available patterns for those non tiers who have yet to experience the epiphany that comes of fooling that first fish on a counterfeit of one's own making.

CHAPTER 3

A Short Primer on
Aquatic Insect Structure

Much of our discussion of insect naturals will revolve around the anatomical details used to distinguish one from another. What follows is a brief refresher course on insect structure and, along the way, definitions for some of those odious biological terms that will unavoidably pop up in the subsequent text. At the very least, it will eliminate the necessity of adding a dictionary to your already overburdened vest.

If you imagine an insect larva or adult sitting horizontally on a rock, the underside, which we might call the belly, is the *ventral* surface, and the upper side, or the back, is the *dorsal* surface; hence the dorsal fin of a fish. The sides of the insect are the *lateral* surfaces. The head is located at the *anterior,* and the hind end at the *posterior.* Appendages, including tails, are attached at their *basal* end. As you proceed *distally* toward the outermost tip you reach the *apical* end.

If your insect is an adult mayfly, then it is easy to see the wing structure. The anterior margin of the wing is known as the *costa,* and it is defined by a lengthwise vein known as the *costal* vein. The posterior margin is the *caudal* margin, which often includes numerous tiny, separate veinlets, either singly or in pairs, known as *intercalary* veins. Biologists have names for most of the major lengthwise or *longitudinal* veins. Between them run any number of *crossveins,* which may or not be connected to the longitudinals and may or may not be darkened, providing another clue to insect identification.

Without exception, each of the insects discussed in this book has three distinct major body parts: a head, a thorax, and an abdomen, although these regional distinctions are less apparent in the worm-like larvae of the two winged or true (*Diptera*) flies. The head is a single segment, the thorax is three segmented, and the abdomen usually has eight to ten segments. It is not always obvious which end is which. Each of the segments comes with a long list of available options, the absence or presence of which is often a key indicator of order, family or even genus.

Most insect heads have antennae, mouths (lacking in some non-feeding adults), eyes, and often an additional set of two or three light-sensitive orifices called *ocelli.* Their mouths are extremely complex and include an extra set of appendages called *palps,* which act as pairs of arms for food gathering. The uppermost of these, the *maxillary palps,* are distinct for many insect families, particularly among adult caddisflies. They are visible with even modest magnification and are an important indicator used by biologists in classification. The *labial palps* make up the lower pair. A few aquatic insects have tusks used for burrowing into the river bottom.

The thorax has one pair of legs mounted laterally on each segment, for a total of six, although some *Diptera* larvae are legless. The anterior thoracic segment is called the *prothorax.* Its dorsal surface is the *pronotum,* and is often covered by a plate. If there are wings or wing pads, the first pair is attached dorsally to the middle segment, or *mesothorax,* and the second pair, if any, to the posterior segment or *metathorax.* The thorax is one of several possible locations of the insect's breathing apparatus, the *gills,* which in such cases would be found at the base of each leg.

Legs are also used as classification indicators, not only through their shapes and markings but also in how they are constructed. The basal segment, closest to the thorax, is the *coxa.* Next comes a short piece called the *trochanter* and then the largest, the *femur,* which is easiest to see without magnification. Next comes the second largest, the *tibia,* followed by a series of up to five short sections known as the *tarsi.*

Finally we come to the claw, which may be a single, in the case of mayfly nymphs, or a pair, for example on the stoneflies.

The abdomen makes up about fifty percent of an insect's body. Mayflies, caddisflies and many other orders have their gills located along the abdomen. The largest of the stoneflies have gills on the two anterior segments as well as on the thorax. Some insects also have projections known as *prolegs* attached to their abdomens, either laterally or anally. Some of these anal prolegs have claws to anchor the insect against the current. Other structures located at the posterior end of the abdomen include tails and gills or other breathing apparatus. An insect's sexual organs are also located on the abdomen. In an adult female, the abdomen may be nearly entirely taken up by the egg mass that it is her sole mission to deposit.

Stonefly and mayfly larvae, among others, pass through several *instar* stages on their way to adulthood. Because they wear hardened *exoskeletons,* they must shed these as they grow. As instars they are unprotected and, therefor, particularly desirable as food, but after a few hours their new armor hardens and they return to relative safety. The *cast skin,* both of an instar and of the transition to adulthood, is called the *pellicle.*

CHAPTER 4

Mayflies (Order Ephemeroptera)

It's easy to understand why, of all the insects consumed by trout, the mayflies embody the heart and soul of fly fishing. As subjects for imitation they are undeniably the most varied and colorful. Their upright wings make them easy to see. Floating downstream under full sail, they are poetry in motion. And the transient, *Ephemeral* quality from which their order takes its name makes them the perfect, reliable agent of dry-fly fishing. There is also a pathos about them, short lived as they are, but it is only as a winged insect that their existence is so brief. Their metamorphosis is incomplete, lacking a pupal stage, yet they are the only order of God's creatures that passes through two winged stages. Like most aquatic insects, and with few exceptions, mayflies spend a year or more in the larval stage, only emerging to a winged stage for purposes of propagation.

Stream-dwelling mayfly larvae have developed a variety of adaptive mechanisms for survival in a wide range of environments. They are roughly broken into four types: the clingers, the crawlers, the burrowers and the swimmers. Clingers all belong to one family, Heptageniidae, which includes the Quill Gordon and the March Brown. Their extremely flat profile and broad legs enable them to adhere tightly to rocks in the faster, well-aerated currents they require. Crawlers, like the Hendricksons and Sulphurs, are similar but with thicker bodies and thinner legs, preferring a slightly gentler current where they can forage with less danger of being swept away. The heavily gilled burrowers use their tusks to dig tunnels in the bottoms of slower eddies and pools where they grow quite large, giving us the midsummer drake hatches. The swimmers are built for minnow-like speed and include many important mayflies like the *Baetis* complex and *Isonychia*.

At maturity, mayfly nymphs migrate to areas of the stream where hatching conditions are more favorable. This behavioral drift usually begins several hours before hatch time and makes the pre-emergent insects available to fish, providing us with some of the best opportunities for fishing mayfly nymph imitations. Trout and landlocked salmon feed selectively on the predominant species just as they would during a hatch. You can tell a mature nymph by its well-developed and darkened wing cases. Some hatching mayflies jettison their casings on the stream bottom and swim to the surface. Others crawl out onto rocks to emerge. The majority swim to the surface, emerge, and float for some distance to unfold and dry their wings before flying off to the safety of nearby trees and bushes, where they await the next great transformation. Frank Sawyer, the famous river keeper of England's upper Avon, observed that mayfly nymphs hatching under his microscope actually burst their shucks with a kind of telescopic inflation of the legs and tails. This distension allows them to lever themselves out of their overcoats and onto the surface and will be repeated later to form the amazingly long tails and forelegs of the male spinners. I've also noticed that the tails of freshly hatched duns are short and wrinkly, but within moments they reach their more graceful, complete extension. Cool weather emergence is sluggish, and the duns' wings are slow to inflate. In warm weather the smaller insects escape quickly whereas the large drakes flutter and flop in their awkward efforts to become airborne.

As a child, I used to fashion pieces of paper into little helicopters and watch their slow, rotating descent into the stairwell of my grandfather's house. A hatched mayfly reminds me of that flight, but in reverse. When they do finally take off, with their bodies and tails hanging down and their wings seeming to spin, it is a gentle, graceful rise to the protection of nearby trees. In daylight, the translucency of their wings makes them appear lighter in color than they really are.

The dun, known to biologists as a subimago, is a pre-adult, not yet able to mate. You can tell its gender immediately by its eyes, which are quite large and vividly colored in the male, more modestly proportioned and subdued in the female. Sexual organs are generally indistinct to the naked eye except in the larger drakes. In some species, such as the Hendricksons (*Ephemerella subvaria*), differences in body color between male and female are so pronounced that it is necessary to carry two patterns for a single species (the very name Hendrickson refers specifically to the female artificial). Duns have semi-opaque or translucent wings owing to a protective outer layer that keeps them from getting wet during emergence. Winged mayflies consume neither liquids nor solids, so while the danger of getting drenched exists, their real enemy is dehydration.

There are a number of indicators or "keys" that hatch matchers can use to identify a mayfly to the genus level and which will help you when comparing your own captured specimens to those pictured in these pages. The first thing to look at is the tail, assuming they are intact, are there two or three? Then look at the wings, are they mottled? Are the veins marked? Are there any characteristic spots? Look at the shape of the hind wing, is it elliptical, does it have a slight hook on the foremargin, or is it tiny or even absent? Then the legs, are they spotted, striped or unmarked? How about abdominal markings? Finally, look at things like size and color, which are good indicators but can vary from stream to stream.

Perhaps the single greatest reason for the popularity of mayflies in dry-fly fishing is their availability and vulnerability to trout at both the beginning and the end of their brief lives as winged insects. Once they achieve their roosts, they continue to mature until the final molt that will bring them back to the stream. This process can take anywhere from a few minutes to a few days. Some females, notably the White Fly, *Ephoron leukon,* do not molt at all but are ready to mate the instant they hatch. A mayfly disrobes to facilitate mating, reducing itself to its stream-lined form, revealing its most attractive aspect to potential mates and exposing its genitalia. The dun finds a good foothold, drops its head and pulls itself forward and out, leaving an intact, spectral shell of itself, tails, legs and all, standing behind with the darker protective wing sheathing collapsed at its side. The body color of the spinner is a more saturated version of the dun's, much as the colors of a painting are restored to vividness when centuries of dust and grime have been wiped away.

Stripped of their outer casing, the wings are almost always glassy clear but distinctly veined and tinted or mottled in the manner that finger-prints their genus. The front legs of the male are elongated for grasping the female during the mating flights.

The spinners, or imagoes, in another of nature's miracles of timing, wait until conditions are favorable for mid-air nuptials and head for a rendezvous above the stream, usually a day or two after hatching but sometimes a week or more or, in some cases, within hours. The males arrive in a squadron, hovering anywhere from five to fifty feet above the water. You might never see them unless you look straight up and focus on the air space above you. They spread their tails wide apart and extend their front legs forward as they slowly migrate upstream, sometimes abruptly changing direction, then back again, sometimes dropping out of the cloud and soaring back up. Eventually the females arrive, more or less individually, and fly into the swarm to be intercepted from below by a male. The two couple in mid air, whereupon flight becomes difficult but, remarkably, they manage it.

After mating the spent males fall to the stream in sufficient numbers to bring feeding trout to the surface. Stripped of the dun's protective layer, the spinner's wings are no longer water repellent and become trapped in the surface film. The female may lay her eggs immediately or migrate upstream to lay them in the same habitat where the larvae of her generation began their life cycle. She may oviposit by landing on the water one or more times and dropping her eggs, she may lay them in a damp area in the stream bed or, in the case of some of the swimmers, she may crawl or dive underwater and lay them on a subsurface rock or other object. Voided of her eggs, her abdomen becomes quite translucent. Ultimately she, too, will join the steady stream of spent mayflies that gives us such pleasant dry-fly fishing at the end of the day.

In New England we have an astonishing variety of mayflies. Dr. Steven Burian, a biologist at Southern Connecticut State University, points to four Maine rivers that individually have over 100 mayfly species. The state is home to more species than any other. Some of the hatches, like the Green or Brown Drakes, are localized, while others occur at times of year when the fish are distracted by other, more predominant insects. In the pages that follow I will endeavor to present the most significant of our hatches at their most "fishable" stages. While there may be some omissions of locally important species, if you are

prepared for the hatches that are covered here, you should be ready for any mayfly you are likely to encounter on a New England stream.

All body measurements are for mature specimens and are taken from the head to the tip of the abdomen, excluding tails. Hatch dates are approximate, depending on location, and usually, but not always, follow a south to north progression.

Mayfly surface imitations are tied in many styles, and more are being invented all the time. Many of those styles are recommended here for specific imitations, but it should be noted that each is designed to cope with certain types of water, and the reader should exercise individual judgment in adapting recommended patterns. There is no reason, for example, why a Catskill-style Light Cahill can't be replaced by a ComparaDun of like coloration if you find it sitting too high on the surface of a pool. Briefly, some of the important tying styles are as follows:

The *Catskill* tie is a quill or fur-bodied fly with stiff hackles for the tail and legs and divided wings. It is the adaptation of the English dry fly for the rougher American waters frequented by Theodore Gordon, Jennings and many others.

The *Thorax* style places the wings and hackles away from the hook eye to get the body and tail up off the water. One early advocate was Vincent Marinaro, who tied the front and back hackles in opposing directions to better balance the fly.

The *ComparaDun* is the invention of Al Caucci and Bob Nastasi, based on the Haystack developed by Fran Betters for the Ausable. Its divided tail and deer-hair wings provide superior floatation, and there is no hackle, so the body lies flush with the surface. There are also spinner, nymph and emerger versions of the design, each using a blend of fur to match the body colors of the insects.

The *No-Hackle* style itself was revolutionary. It was pioneered by Doug Swisher and Carl Richards in 1970 and is best known through their collaboration on fly fishing entomology, *Selective Trout*. It utilizes a split tail, a fur body and a variety of upright wing styles to provide the most realistic silhouette of any design. It is ideally suited to slower pools or reaches, but is easily drowned by rough water.

Parachute versions also lie flush with the surface film but employ a hackle wound horizontally around a single upright wing or post to simulate the legs and provide stability. The post is usually light colored to make the fly easier to see. These are alternately known as Gyro or Sailwing flies.

Tiny Fork-Gilled Nymphs

Family: Leptophlebidae
Size: 6-9 mm
Genus: *Paraleptophlebia*
Species: *adoptiva, mollis, debilis*
Active: First week of May to last week of September

The first time I beheld a *Paraleptophlebia* nymph I mistook it for an immature specimen of a different family, for it had a thin, undernourished look about it. These three tailed-crawlers bear a superficial resemblance to *Ephemerella* nymphs except that they are even more slender and cylindrical, with heads that are longer than they are wide and extended antennae. Their long tails lack any obvious fringing, and, most evident, their deeply forked singlet gills are more hair-like. All of the eastern nymphs are of a warm, grayish brown to amber hue with unmarked, pale amber or cream legs, amber tails and wings pads that darken at maturity. In their immature larval stage they prefer fast flowing water where the stream bottom is composed of gravel and stone. As they mature, however, they gradually migrate to slower stretches of the stream where they subsist by day on detritus, hidden under and between the stones, and by night on algae on the upper surfaces of the same stones. *P. adoptiva* and *mollis* nymphs are attracted to more moderate flows away from the main current, whereas the late season *debilis* nymphs are drawn to slower pools, backwaters and eddies.

**Left to Right: Paraleptophlebia Adoptiva Nymph, Sawyer
Pheasant Tail
Hook Size 18**

Although they superficially resemble a *Baetis* nymph, *Paraleps* are relatively inept swimmers. As they migrate to shallow, slack waters in preparation for emergence they stay close to the bottom, crawling as well as swimming to their destinations. They also gather in schools, resulting in hatches of considerable, if narrowly located, density. Fish follow them into the stream edges, moderate riffles and transitional zones. Cast a weighted nymph from the riverbank to mid stream and use your longest nymphing rod to manipulate the fly along the bottom, back towards the shallows. Be careful to keep a low profile and stay out of the water. Once the hatch begins you can switch to an unweighted imitation and fish it dead drift through the midwater from the same position on the bank. Add a lift at the end of the swing to suggest the rising insect. Once the naturals have wiggled to the surface, they hesitate momentarily in preparation for the brief struggle of removing their larval skins. Fish taking these temporarily inert forms will pick them quietly from just under the surface film. A nymph pattern dead drifted in the surface film takes full advantage of this opportunity, but you will need to focus all of your attention on the subtle takes.

Slate Winged Mahogany Dun

Size 6-9 mm

Family: Leptophlebidae
Genus: *Paraleptophlebia*
Species: *adoptiva, mollis, debilis*
Nicknames: Iron Blue Dun, Little Blue Quill, Mahogany Dun
Active: First week of May to last week of September

The small duns of the *Paraleptophlebia* species provide a series of overlapping daytime hatches continuously from early May to late September. As the season progresses and temperatures rise, the spring hatches move into the evening hours, but by September the *debilis* duns are again on the water by noon. South of New England they are among the earliest of hatches, but here the early season *adoptiva* flies appear simultaneously with larger insects like the March Browns and spring caddis on small to medium-sized rivers and streams. Regulars of the Battenkill report that trout sip *Paralep* duns to the exclusion of other, larger mayflies. The spinner falls, by contrast, are too sparse to warrant much attention. A Mahogany Dun could be mistaken for an *Ephemerella* or even one of the many *Baetis* species that share their habitat, but it is easily differentiated by its three tails and the obvious presence of an ovular hind wing, the family crest of the Leptophlebidae; the shape of this hind wing distinguishes this family from the *Ephemerella*s. Their wings are a uniform medium gray to slate, with no markings of any kind. Long and slender, *Paraleps* are fairly consistent in their mahogany color from one eastern species to another.

(L to R): Blue Quill, Clipped Mahogany Dun, Blue Wing Mahogany
Hook Size 18

Spring hatches of Mahogany Duns can be maddening affairs, with trout suddenly going off one hatch and keying on another. Soft, sipping rises indicate a preference, however temporary, for small emerging insects like *Baetis* or *Paraleptophlebia*. Only the capture of a live sample can tell you which. Paraleps, especially the spring hatching *adoptiva,* reach their highest density on warm, overcast days. They are slow to take flight, particularly in cold weather, often drifting for many yards. Look for *Paraleps* emerging in backwaters and eddies, and along the edges of streams. Both situations present difficult casting problems given the sudden changes in current speed, which you can minimize by casting from the bank, or from directly down or upstream with a leader that is long, light and limp. As with any of the smaller insects, trout will rise with consistency only to a hatch that is sufficiently dense to reward their expenditure of energy. Nonetheless, the density of the hatch, not the size of the insect, is what causes trout to feed selectively. Don't try to fish the water, for a trout that has not keyed onto the hatch will have plenty in the way of more substantial fare to attract him. Concentrate instead on a steady feeder. After gauging his rhythm, cast your fly well ahead of him to arrive at his taking point at the moment he is ready to rise again.

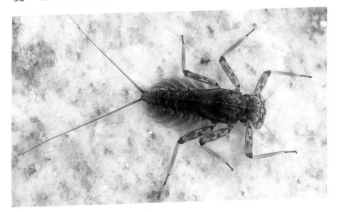

Two-Tailed Clingers—Nymphs

Size: 9-13 mm

Family: Heptageniidae
Genus: *Epeorus*
Species: *pleuralis, vitreus, punctatus, fragilis*
Active: First week in May to second week in June

Among the clingers of the family Heptageniidae are two important *Epeorus* species, *pleuralis* (the Quill Gordon) and *vitreus*. Most nymphs of this family are three tailed, but *Epeorus* have two, held wide apart. Like other clingers, they are extremely flat, with strong legs and large eyes placed on top of their heads, like a halibut. Their plate-like gills are held along the sides of their sharply tapered abdomens and serve as an airfoil against the current. Colors range from the dark olive brown of *pleuralis* to the lighter, redder brown of *vitreus*. Their legs are mottled, with a distinctive heart-shaped marking on the femur. Similar but slightly smaller species continue to hatch well into the early autumn. All of these nymphs, and many of the winged stages, are similar in size, color and shape. *Epeorus* in general and *vitreus* in particular are sensitive to pollution and silting. They spend most of their time tightly gripping the undersides of stones and require clean, fast water rushing past their gills to survive. As a result, they are rarely available to trout except during periods of behavioral drift. They also have the unique trait of hatching on the stream bottom before rising to the surface.

(L to R): 1. Gold Ribbed Hare's Ear Nymph, 2. Hare's Ear Wet, 3. Ginger Quill Wet
Hook Sizes 12-16

In many parts of New England the early mayfly hatches begin before trout are ready for surface feeding. Temperatures are still cold, there's little protective canopy, and there is a cornucopia of maturing and active subsurface insects to quickly satiate the fish. At any given time, the greatest concentration of subsurface food is usually the insect that is about to hatch, and just before a Quill Gordon hatch there are huge numbers of *Epeorus* nymphs crawling over and under the subsurface stones. But these are accompanied by dense populations of larger and more available March Brown and Hendrickson nymphs, not to mention stonefly and caddis larvae. For this reason, I always fish early spring nymphs in tandem, with at least one pattern representative of a mayfly nymph. Just about any water knee-deep or greater and of modest current can yield a fish if you keep your flies deep. Start with an upstream cast and a dead drift. At most times the flat clinger nymphs remain in the swift currents where they are impossible to pry off the rocks, but just before a hatch they migrate to slower water where they are active and swimming. Before picking up your line, work the fly to the sides and the front of any rocks where fish might be holding. The prime lies are in pockets and just below the riffles. Once the hatch begins, the fish move slightly downstream to intercept the duns.

Quill Gordon—Dun

Size: 9-12 mm

Family: Heptageniidae
Genus: *Epeorus*
Species: *pleuralis*
Nicknames: Iron Dun, Light Blue Quill, Red Quill
Active: First week in May to last week in May

In early May, as the trees begin to leaf out, the first hatches of medium-sized mayflies float skyward, led by the Quill Gordons and then, a few days later, the Hendricksons. If winter has been kind, holdover trout are there to meet them along with the swooping sparrows. It's a wonder that any survive to perpetuate the species. The Quill Gordon is the first and most famous, though not the most important, in a summer-long series of hatches of the genus *Epeorus* lasting right into September. Much of its popularity comes from the fact that it is a concentrated daytime hatch, coming off reliably just after lunch time. Once started it continues unabated through good and bad weather for a week or more. The duns are slow to become airborne due to the cold conditions under which they hatch. Both males and females of eastern *Epeorus* species bear two dark gray tails and characteristic heart-shaped femoral markings on their outspread legs. The wings are slate gray, with no real contrast to the veins. The bodies are a grayish tan to brown, really made up of a blend of olive and mahogany hues. Without close examination, they are easily confused with the slightly larger, three-tailed Hendricksons.

(L to R): Light Hendrickson, Quill Gordon, Hare's Ear Dry Hook Size 14

Preston Jennings found no direct evidence that Theodore Gordon invented his quill-bodied fly specifically to imitate the hatching *Epeorus pleuralis*. He concluded, however, that the Quill Gordon was the only fly he could present to selective trout during a heavy *Epeorus* hatch with confidence that it would be taken, and so pattern and insect are forever wedded in fly-fishing nomenclature. The natural is definitely a fast-water insect where a high-floating dry fly of the classic Catskills style is in its element. The stripped peacock quill body of the Quill Gordon accurately represents the articulated abdominal segmentation of the natural, and the light gray hackles give a good impression of a fluttering dun trying to shake out its wings. But it does a poor job of mimicking the body color or the leg markings. For this reason, I prefer another classic, the Hare's Ear, both in a dry-fly version for the floating dun and as a wet fly for the underwater emerger. Because *Epeorus* mayflies hatch on the stream bottom and swim to the surface, I have my best luck with the wet fly. Cast upstream and fish it deep with a terminal lift to imitate the ascending dun. Allow plenty of hang time before beginning your next cast. Some years I get lucky and find fish feeding on the surface. Concentrate on the heads of pools where fish gather to intercept duns floating down from the pockets and riffles.

Quill Gordon—Spinner

Size: 9-12 mm

Family: Heptageniidae
Genus: *Epeorus*
Species: *pleuralis*
Nickname: Red Quill
Active: First week in May to last week in May

Epeorus spinners manage to wait until a suitably pleasant spring evening to stage their mating rituals. The males gather late in the afternoon, high above the water where they spent the previous year as nymphs. Smaller congregations occasionally form at mid-morning. Some clouds are made up of thousands of individuals, bobbing up and down as they work their way upstream, only to drop back in the pack and begin again. They may or may not be joined by the females, and I have often witnessed their disappointment. Eventually their hopes are fulfilled, as evidenced by the congenital pairs dropping suddenly out of the swarm. The males then fall to their deaths, either on the stream banks or on the water. The fertilized females rest in the streamside vegetation to await the ripening of their eggs before returning to the surface to oviposit. The adult male Gordon Quill is a much darkened form of the dun, with large, dark brown eyes, elongated front legs and two impossibly long tails. The heart-shaped femoral markings remain in both sexes, and the veins of the glassy clear wings are much more defined than the dun's. Abdominal segmentation is even more apparent, alternating between a creamy base and bands of mahogany.

(L to R): Clipped Hackle Hacklewing Spinner, Red Sparklewing Spinner, Gordon Quill Spinner
Hook Sizes 12-16

Because mating and egg laying occur over habitat most favorable to hatching nymphs, *Epeorus* spinners gather over rapidly flowing streams with a great deal of substrate structure. A spent spinner, once its wings have made contact with the water and become trapped by the surface tension, is inert. It also presents no silhouette to a wading angler at any distance more than a few feet. The first evidence that the spinner fall has begun is the rhythmic rising of feeding fish. The current collects the spinners and funnels them into well-defined feeding lanes. Trout hold in the adjacent slower currents and rise along the current seams, lured by the steady supply of these nourishing mouthfuls. The resulting rise is an audible but unhurried smack. Study the rhythm of the rises, then cast your fly to land directly upstream and only a few feet ahead of the next anticipated rise. Keep the drifts short and absolutely drag free. To properly imitate the spent spinner, your fly must float flush with the surface. Many spinner patterns are tied with wing materials that simulate the brilliant translucency of the spent insect but float poorly. Use floatant on the wings and tails to keep the flies riding in the surface film. Other patterns are tied with a mixture of Cul de Canard, which helps to suspend the wing, but not the tail.

Gray Winged Yellow Quill—Dun

Size: 9-12mm

Family: Heptageniidae
Genus: *Epeorus*
Species: *vitreus*
Nicknames: Pale Evening Dun, Little Marryatt, Pink Cahill Female
Active: Last week in May to second week in June

Throughout New England the hatches of *Epeorus vitreus* are consistently of greater value to the angler than those of the more celebrated Quill Gordon (*E. pleuralis*). I find the nymphs of *E. vitreus* in a wider array of habitats than its more famous relative. By the time they are ready to hatch, the rivers have warmed sufficiently that trout are accustomed to surface feeding. Most important, trout are suckers for the dun's vivid colors. Its most common nickname derives from the olive and yellow hues of the male dun, but the egg-bearing female, known traditionally as the Pink Lady, is quite orange, nearly pink on the belly, for which trout show a marked preference. Both genders have translucent gray wings that appear almost white. In other respects the species resembles the Quill Gordon, with two gray tails, heart-shaped markings on the femurs and unmarked wings. Because of its size and timing, many anglers assume it to be the Gray Fox (a light *Stenonema vicarium*), but it is a very different insect both in color and in behavior. Like its more famous relative, it hatches on the stream bottom and rises to the surface as a winged insect.

(L to R): Rusty Usual, SASH, Little Marryatt
Hook Sizes 12-14

Given the warmer conditions of the *vitreus* hatch the duns become airborne rather quickly, so long dry-fly drifts are out of the question. Instead, you must deliver the fly delicately to a spot just upstream from the trout's window. Since this hatch usually occurs on swifter streams with complex currents, it is best to maneuver into a spot where you can make a short upstream or across-stream cast to a rising fish or a likely feeding lie. The orange color deep within the abdomen of the female *vitreus* is her latent cargo of eggs, and trout will often key on this element during a Yellow Quill hatch to the exclusion of the paler, more yellow-bodied males. Possibly because it incorporates both colors, or because it imitates many of the other Sulphur-bodied flies hatching at the same time, a personal pattern choice for the winged adult is the Little Marryatt, named for the late 19th century English dry-fly innovator George Selwyn Marryatt. There is also a wet-fly version to imitate the subsurface emerger, but I prefer my own Spectrumized Amber Soft Hackle (SASH), modified for this hatch from a Leisenring/Hidy pattern, the Partridge Flymph. Presented in classic down-and-across wet-fly style with an occasional twitching, or floated dead drift on the surface, it has proven itself as a searching pattern from May through June. Riffles, pocket water and small fast pools are great spots to fish this fly.

Salmon Spinner—Spinner

Family: Heptageniidae Size: 9-12 mm
Genus: *Epeorus*
Species: *vitreus*
Active: Last week in May to second week in June

During the spring there are several mayflies, including the Quill Gordon, the Hendrickson and the March Brown, which molt to a rusty brown body with medium to dark gray tails. This enables the angler to get by with one or two rusty spinner patterns in a limited range of sizes to cover several different insects. So, too, are there a number of mayflies which molt to a salmon-colored spinner, of which the female *Epeorus vitreus* is the first, to be followed by later species of *Stenonema* and *Stenacron*, all of which bear eggs of a rich orangey hue. *E. vitreus* differs from the others mainly in that its wings are unmarked, but inasmuch as silhouette and the surface patterning of light are the most important triggers of late-evening spinner falls, many patterns choose to ignore this subtle difference. *Vitreus* spinners gather later than *pleuralis*, closer to dark, but the general pattern of mating and ovipositing behavior is the same. On unusually warm evenings mating may be delayed until temperatures cool near daybreak. Females make repeated passes along the surface to expel their eggs and either rest upon the surface or return to the air during the intervals.

(L to R): Clipped Hackle Sparklewing Spinner, Salmon Parachute Spinner, Ginger Ginger Quill Spinner Hook Sizes 12-14

Epeorus spinner falls follow a pattern which becomes increasingly apparent during the early season and which remains consistent for many spinner falls thereafter. The males fall to the water or the shoreline after inseminating the females, who retire to the streamside to incubate the eggs. When the females return they first land upon the water with their wings upright or fluttering as they deposit their eggs on the surface, during which they may touch down several times before all of their eggs are released. Finally the females collapse, and as their wings fall to their sides they become trapped in the surface film, where the fish pick them off in somewhat leisurely fashion. As they proceed through each course, from the few spent males to egg-layers and back to spent spinners, the fish keep us informed by smacking loudly at upright forms and rising more quietly to the spentwings. To properly take advantage of this sequence one need arrive at the stream equipped with both upright and spentwing patterns. Standard dun patterns lack the sparkle of the wing on which selective trout key during a spinner fall, but parachute patterns tied with wing posts made of poly yarn or other sparkly material make an effective egg-laying imitation. In a pinch you can trim conventionally hackled sparkle wing patterns to lie flush with the surface when fish switch to feeding on spent spinners. Egg-layers can be mimicked with a skated retrieve, but dying spentwings call for a strict dead drift.

Crawlers—Nymphs

Family: Ephemerellidae   Size: 6-12 mm
Genus: *Ephemerella*
Species: *subvaria, invaria, rotunda, dorothea*
Active: First week in April to last week in June

It is rare that I turn over rocks or submerge my drift net between autumn and late spring without encountering the crawling nymphs of the *Ephemerella* flies. Of all mayfly genera, these are the most widespread, dwelling in every conceivable habitat where trout are found. In New England they are the larvae of the Hendricksons, the Pale Evening Duns and the little Sulphurs. I usually find them in riffles or pocket waters that run clean and cool (but not too cold) and free of rapid fluctuations in temperature. These are stout forms, but with disproportionately weak looking, banded legs. Their three tails are covered in hairs at the outer two-thirds. The gills sit above pronounced lateral abdominal spines where they flap up and down sequentially. In color the nymphs range from a deep reddish brown to olive brown or even charcoal brown against well-defined patterns of cream, light yellow or amber. The abdomens of *subvaria* nymphs are considerably lighter on the dorsal side of segments six, seven and sometimes ten. In all cases the color is unusually sensitive to variations in habitat. Emergence is a lengthy struggle beginning well under the surface and continuing until the wings finally unfold.

(L to R): Gold Ribbed Hare's Ear, Hendrickson Nymph, Gilled Ephemerella Nymph
Hook Sizes 12-18

Ephemerella nymphs move about actively as the spring sun warms the water. In climbing to the upper periphery of subsurface rocks they are exposed not only to the current but to trout picking nymphs off the bottom. This activity increases exponentially in the hours before a hatch. My experience with *Ephemerella* nymphs is limited to freestone streams with plenty of riffles and pockets. When adrift in faster water the nymphs seem to panic and remain rigid, but in slower currents they remember to swim, albeit in their awkward fashion. I've also watched them hatch in my studio tank after multiple initial trips to the surface. From this I've adopted two different tactics. The first is most effective in the hours before the anticipated hatch. Take a position directly below your target and cast well upstream to drift the nymph along the bottom, but raise and lower your rod to swim the nymph through the midwater. At the first sign of duns coming off, move quietly upstream to a position above the lie but out of the feeding lane. Cast upstream and allow the fly to bounce along the bottom. Finish the drift with a Leisenring lift, followed by a hand-over-hand retrieve, to impart a swimming action. The generation of insects that will hatch in the following spring have the entire season to mature from the egg. By late fall they have attained considerable size. Such early spring nymph imitations make great searching patterns as the season winds down in the fall.

Hendrickson/Red Quill—Dun

Size: 9-12 mm

Family: Ephemerellidae
Genus: *Ephemerella*
Species: *subvaria*
Nickname: Beaverkill
Active: Third week in April to last week in May

There is no more anticipated event in all of eastern fly fishing than the Hendrickson hatch, the first major hatch on many streams. It may be regarded as two simultaneous hatches, for the winged males and females are noticeably different in size and color. The nymphs of each gender even congregate in separate microhabitats prior to emergence, in the best parochial style. The duns also vary tremendously in color from one environment to the next, even on the same stretch of water. Their hatches are temperature dependent, sometimes beginning two weeks early in an especially warm spring. The female is the larger and more robust of the two genders, but with smaller eyes. Her abdomen, ranging from reddish to olivey cream, arcs gently upward to three finely banded tails. The male is smaller, more slender, and much redder throughout the thorax and abdomen. His tomato-red eyes are quite large. The wings of both genders run from medium tan to slate, or a mixture of both, with the male's leaning toward slate. Emergence is just below the surface, and the speed of transition from nymph to dun depends on temperature. The duns glide serenely for some time before suddenly taking off.

(L to R): Hendrickson Thorax, Light Hendrickson, Red Quill, Parachute Vertical Emerger
Hook Sizes 12-14

Frequently during a Hendrickson hatch, fish will take the emergers and ignore the duns, particularly if it is the first hatch of the season, or if warm conditions enable the duns to escape quickly. Color is extremely important with emerger bodies, which ride under the surface where fish can see them clearly. Rises to emergers are less splashy, but the differences are subtle. If other insects are hatching, your task is more complex, for it is vital to know which insects the fish are taking, and in what stage. Really selective fish concentrate most often on the larger females, but males are not entirely ignored. When Hendrickson duns drift calmly on the water, rises to them are confident, creating sharply defined rings as the insect is sucked under. The hatch takes place without urgency, with fish inspecting each morsel at leisure. Cast well ahead of any rise forms. As the hatch progresses, fish develop a feeding rhythm, which slackens as they become satiated. Adjust your own rhythm accordingly. Look for rises on either side of the current tongue and float your fly between the current and the fish. On blustery days, watch the stream edges where these little slate-winged sailboats, lacking keels, are easily blown. The Light Hendrickson was designed to imitate the female *subvaria,* with the Red Quill corresponding to the male. Because *Ephemerella*s ride a bit higher on the water than duns of the clinging nymphs, a thorax tie is helpful when fish get really picky.

Red Quill Spinner

Family: Ephemerellidae   Size: 9-12 mm
Genus: *Ephemerella*
Species: *subvaria*
Active: Third week in April to last week in May

Beginning a few days after the first emergence, and lasting until as many as five days after the final hatch, Hendrickson spinners return en masse for a rousing evening reprise. Even if the trout have ignored the dun hatch, they will rise freely to egg-laying and dying spinners. This early season spinner fall occurs while there is still enough light to tie on a fly, as early as 4 or 5 o'clock, making it one of the best opportunities in the young dry-fly season. The shift from duns hatching to spinners falling is often seamless. Should the weather turn cold the mating flight may be delayed until the following morning. If it warms up the spinners won't gather until 6 or 7 p. m. Hendrickson spinner clouds form just downstream of the water where they began their lives the year before. Male spinners are dark, with variegated bodies of tan and mahogany or brownish red. Their elongated forelegs and tails are dark, and their large eyes are a deep, brownish red. Soon the females join the swarm. After mating, the exhausted males fall quickly to the stream or streamside while the females fly upstream. The rust-colored, fertilized females are easily recognized by the yellow egg clusters carried at the tips of their downward curving abdomens. Soon after dropping to the water to deposit their eggs on the surface they are overcome by the effort and collapse.

(L to R): Red Quill Parachute Spinner, Semi-spent Henwing Egglayer, Rusty CDC/Antron Spinner
Hook Sizes 12-14

The Hendrickson spinner fall begins shortly after the females enter the mating swarm and the spent males begin dropping to the stream. I like to start with a spent-wing configuration for this first act of the play. As the fish key onto this suddenly available food supply they increase their range to left and right, but in a particularly heavy hatch this extra expenditure of energy becomes unnecessary, and your casts will have to pinpoint the center of their feeding lanes. They will also be at their most selective, forcing you to match the rhythm of their rises. The second act introduces the fertilized females bearing their yellow egg sacs. Their wings remain upright as they vigorously move to dislodge their now fertile eggs. On their arrival my spent pattern suddenly stops producing, so I replace it with an upright or semi-spent pattern with a bit of yellow or chartreuse dubbing at the base of the tails. For the final act, which brings together the entire cast, I find it necessary to change back to a spent wing pattern. I use a floatant on synthetic wings (but never, never on CDC) and let the body settle into the surface film in the manner of the dying mayflies. With spent patterns it is vital to maintain a drag-free float, for once trapped in the surface film the spent spinners are powerless to move. Fly pattern books still offer more spent-wing patterns for the Hendrickson than any other spinner.

Pale Evening Dun

Family: Ephemerellidae
Size: 8-11 mm
Genus: *Ephemerella*
Species: *rotunda, invaria*
Nicknames: Eastern Sulphur, Yellow Dun
Active: Second week in May to third week in June

As the Hendrickson hatch declines, the Pale Evening Duns begin to appear. These are slightly smaller mayflies of the same genus, but larger than yet another, still to come *Ephemerella*, the Sulphur. Pale Evening Duns hatch when numerous other insects, including the much larger March Browns and Green Drakes, are making their appearance, with trout showing a preference for the more numerous smaller insects. The two most prevalent eastern species, *rotunda* and *invaria,* are treated here as a single hatch, not only because their emergences coincide, but also because they are nearly identical in appearance and behavior. The only obvious difference is size with *invaria* running slightly smaller. Both have pale yellow to olive bodies, never as intense in color as the Sulphurs. Their wings are light tan to blue gray, with considerable variance from stream to stream, both in hue and in saturation. Their unmarked legs nearly match the body color, as do their lightly banded tails. The female's eyes are small and dark, the male's large and deep orange. I've never found these hatches to match the Hendricksons for sheer numbers, but warmer temperatures and the presence of other insects usually mean more rises to the duns and emergers.

(L to R): Parachute Vertical Emerger, Tufted Wing Sulphur, Parachute Sulphur
Sizes 12-16

The Pale Evening Duns, like the true Sulphurs that follow, are one of the few early season hatches in which trout readily take the floating duns in preference to emergers. Any number of appropriately sized patterns designed for yellow-bodied mayflies will serve in a pinch, but truly picky trout hold out for the paler body and darker gray wings of *rotunda* and *invaria*. Many patterns labeled Sulphur are actually better suited to the earlier, larger Pale Evening Duns. You can expect hatches of this group of mayflies on the same waters that you find the Hendricksons, especially in the pockets and riffles where there is plenty of oxygen, but they also tolerate wider extremes of temperature. Hatches begin later in the day, around 3 or 4 o'clock, but are more spread out during cold spells. As the weather warms the delay between hatching and takeoff is shortened, leading fish to rise more aggressively and to pay greater attention to emergers than to the duns. Plan on a shorter drift than with the Hendricksons, but be thankful that your imitation won't be as subject to lingering inspections. Even more care is needed with this mayfly to ensure that fish are rising to it and not to a different insect altogether.

Pale Evening Spinner

Family: Ephemerellidae
Size: 8-11 mm
Genus: *Ephemerella*
Species: *rotunda, invaria*
Active: Second week in May to third week in June

As summer approaches, warm evenings become less rare, and spinner falls, like those of the Pale Evening Spinners, begin later and later, even as the sun extends the day. Given the pale yellow hues of the dun one would expect yellow spinners, but they are surprising in the richness of their orangey-brown hues, although not so deeply colored as the rusty browns of the female Hendricksons. The mating and egg-laying activities of *invaria* and *rotunda* adults are quite different from those of their predecessors. The swarms gather above the stream as before, but actual mating occurs closer to the stream bank, so very few males fall into the current. The females return to the cover of nearby trees and shrubs for roughly half an hour to incubate the eggs, then return above the stream to drop their eggs into the water. As a consequence, only some become trapped in the surface film, and the spinner falls are less spectacular than those of *subvaria.* The success of the angler's evening is therefor dependent on the overall density of the spinners and the numbers of fish that are there to meet them.

(L to R): Rusty CDC/Antron Spinner, Clipped Hackle Hacklewing Spinner, Parachute Invaria Spinner Hook Sizes 12-16

When clouds of spinners collect overhead, it is time to approach the reach or head of a pool where trout are likely to intercept the dead and the dying insects. Soon enough the females arrive, and the cloud moves closer to the surface and away from the center of the stream, only to disappear entirely for a brief interval. By the time the individual spinners land on the surface darkness is fast approaching. You will have time to land one, at the most two, worthwhile trout. The first feeders are likely to be smaller fish, and as their activity increases they arouse the interest of their larger neighbors. Resist the temptation to fish for the small ones, for should you hook one the ensuing hubbub will turn off the grownups. As soon as a good fish pokes its nose through the surface, make your offering, as it is most likely to take your fly at the outset when it is least satiated and before it has established the breadth of its feeding lane. As the spinner fall continues, and particularly as it begins to thin out, a fish will range further from side to side, and you should follow its example by placing your fly alternately and increasingly to the right and left of the center of its feeding lane, a practice developed by Vincent Marinaro and which he dubbed "bracketing."

Sulphur—Dun

Family: Ephemerellidae
Genus: *Ephemerella*
Species: *dorothea*
Nicknames: Pale Evening Dun, Pale Sulphur Dun, Pale Watery Dun
Active: Second week of June to first week of July

Size: 6-8 mm

Hatches of the diminutive *dorothea* duns are among the most challenging during the height of dry-fly season. They are the smallest of the major hatches, preceded by the larger Hendricksons, March Browns and similarly hued *rotundas,* and with the truly large summer Drakes still to come. The fish have had plenty to chose from, and although they have long become accustomed to surface feeding, they have also grown more selective. Sulphers also hatch in slower water than the previous *Ephemerella*s. At least these bright mayflies hatch in large enough numbers to draw the attentions of even the most jaded trout. And it often happens that Sulphur emergence peaks when other late-spring hatches are waning. The *dorothea* males are a full hook size smaller than the females. Their gender is easily recognized by their ridiculously large tomato-colored eyes. Body color ranges from cream to yellow depending on habitat, with paler, creamy legs and tails and warm gray wings. The larger females are of a purer hue, ranging from pale to rich yellow with either an olive or orange cast. Their legs and tails are light cream, and their wings the palest of yellow grays.

(L to R): Loopwing Vertical Emerger, Sulphur Dun, Parachute Sulphur
Hook Sizes 16-18

In gathering samples of Sulphurs I've found an unusually high incidence of crippled duns with bedraggled wings. To this do I attribute the fact that my most consistent producers during a Sulphur hatch have been emerger patterns fished with a downstream, and slightly across, presentation. I make a slack line cast only far enough above a rising trout that the line tightens just as the fly reaches the taking point. Immediately I shake out enough line to continue the drift. The resulting twitches simulate a struggling emerger, which no self-respecting trout can resist. The bulging rise form is quiet and unhurried, but as long as I control the slack, they simply hook themselves. But fish are just as happy to go after the fully hatched duns, and if the rise forms are splashy, a surface pattern is called for. My preference is for a body with a well-saturated yellow, even more so than the Catskill style Sulphur pattern suggested here, the George Harvey classic. But Harvey's experiments showed that a bit of orange in the hackle increased the fly's effectiveness. Parachute patterns are easy to see and stay upright in the pocket waters where these flies are common. These complex currents call for sharp eyes and plenty of slack in the long tippet section of your leader. It seems unfair to have to resort to very small flies and gossamer tippets when so many large insects are hatching, but these Sulphurs provide consistently good fishing throughout the region.

Sulphur—Spinner

Family: Ephemerellidae
Genus: *Ephemerella*
Species: *dorothea*
Active: Second week of June to first week of July

Size: 6-8 mm

Spinner swarms of *E. dorothea* are delayed by the heat of midsummer to the hours just before nightfall, when the air and the water have both cooled. This can be quite late in northern regions. Mating occurs quickly once the females arrive, but a brief rest is required for the eggs to ripen, and since the spent males don't always fall upon the water it can be quite dark before fish start feeding on spinners. A few females will wipe their eggs against the water's surface, but most drop their eggs from several feet above the water before falling spent upon it. All of this activity is concentrated over the riffles and reaches where *dorothea* nymphs are found. Both male and female have supersaturated yellow to butterscotch abdomens with shades of orange dorsally in the thorax, extremely pale gray legs and tails and clear, unmarked wings. At the risk of confusing the issue, I should note that not all of the Sulphur dun specimens I have captured have molted to the same intensified yellow. Some look like smaller versions of the chestnut-colored spinners of *invaria* or *rotunda,* leading me to conclude that we must contend with more than one species of small Sulphur.

(L to R): Wingless Sulphur Spinner, Polywing Sulphur Spinner, P. E. D. Parachute Spinner
Hook Sizes 16-18

Because of the possible variations in body color, this is one of those cases where obtaining a live sample is imperative before selecting an imitation from your fly box. Fortunately, the range of possible spinner colors falls well within the spectrum covered by a few standards, and a modest selection of sizes in both Sulphur and rusty spinners should fill the need. Some spent males may appear on the water, but unless the spinner fall is unusually heavy they won't merit much attention from the fish and you're better off not creating a disturbance in advance of the main event. Soon enough the females will begin arriving, some with upright wings as they skid on the surface to dislodge the more stubborn egg balls from their abdomens. It may test the limits of your patience, but on all but a few New England rivers the challenge will be to wait until a fish begins rising before making your first cast. Searching, even with small flies, can only reduce your chances, and you won't have many between the first soft but confident rise and the onset of darkness. Once you've selected your target move carefully into position, gauge the time between rises and at just right moment deposit the fly a few yards ahead of the expected rise and exactly in the center of the feeding lane. Where hatches are heavier the need for such precision in both timing and placement diminishes but, as with any spinner fall, spent forms must be fished on a dead drift.

Common Clingers—Nymphs

Family: Heptageniidae   Size: 10-16 mm
Genera: *Stenonema, Stenacron*
Nickname: Flatheads
Active: First week of March to last week of June

The larger nymphs of the Heptageniidae family, the closely related *Stenonema* and *Stenacron* genera, are extremely common in eastern waters. They include the larvae of the well-known March Browns and Light Cahills and many other species that appear very similar in normal viewing conditions. Like the *Epeorus* nymphs of the same family, the bodies of these larvae are amazingly flat, with hefty outstretched legs and heads with eyes on top. It is difficult to imagine that the mighty March Brown dun could rise from such a flattened form. They have rapidly moving leaf-shaped gills along the sides of their abdomens, and some have lateral spines on the last few segments. The gills of *Stenacron* nymphs are more pointed. All have mottled legs and heads, and most have an obvious banding of the abdominal segments. Whereas *Epeorus* has two tails, *Stenacron* and *Stenonema* nymphs have three, which they hold wide apart at nearly a right angle, particularly in moments of stress. When threatened they move backward or sideways, like a crab. Their coloration is warmer, with more vivid yellowish to reddish browns, when compared to the olive tones of *Epeorus*.

(L to R): 1. March Brown Nymph, 2. Solomon March Brown Floating Nymph, 3. American Pheasant Tail
Hook Sizes 10-16

Common clingers are sensitive to reduced levels of oxygen and prefer the undersides of stones in the riffles or in gravelly streambeds, but I have found mature specimens in surprisingly slow water. They feed on algae and detritus, for which they can forage without great danger of losing their tenacious grips on their subsurface supports. If caught in the drift, they alternately freeze in a slight upward curve and swim clumsily by waving their abdomens and tails up and down. Both *Stenonema* and *Stenacron* are surface emergers who swim upwards in the same dolphin-like manner. A good imitation of the clinging nymphs must duplicate the extremely flattened profile of the natural. For weighted nymphs, this means lashing a length of lead wire to each side of the hook before applying the dressing. Store bought flies can easily be tailored by carefully trimming the dubbing from the dorsal and ventral surfaces and by picking the fur out and away from the sides, both to increase the width and emphasize the gills. When cold weather retards the process of emergence, trout may key on any of a number of sub-stages. Use the weighted flies only just before, or in the early stages, of the hatch when fish are working the bottom, but as the hatch progresses you'll need to drift an unweighted pattern just below the surface or switch altogether to a surface emerger.

American March Brown—Dun

Family: Heptageniidae   Size: 12-17 mm
Genus: *Stenonema*
Species: *vicarium*
Nicknames: American Brown, Gray Fox
Active: Third week of May to last week of June

A trio of large, two-tailed *Stenonema* mayflies hatches in the late spring. Fly fishers know them as the March Brown, the Gray Fox and the Light Cahill. During a single month I photographed specimens of all three, ranging from a large, dark form to a smaller tan and yellow insect. Although varied in appearance, they had so much in common that I sent male spinners to Dr. Steven Burian for identification. He pronounced them all the same species, *S. vicarium*, which he went on to describe as having a "variable morphology." It appears in a spectrum of sizes and hues, and the markings on their legs and abdomens, ranging from ginger to dark brown, vary in intensity. They share a pale yellow base color and darkened crossveins on their wings. Their eyes shift from dark brown to pale green after exposure to light. Like most fast-water dwellers they swim to margins or pools to emerge, choosing calmer water than the Quill Gordons or Hendricksons. Upon reaching the surface, they struggle somewhat before fully emerging, and take off only after a few false starts. Even though their numbers are usually disappointing, their size, noisy emergence and prolonged availability make them tempting targets to trout.

(L to R): American March Brown, March Brown Henwing Emerger, Gray Fox ComparaDun
Hook Sizes 10-12

Whether or not they are the same species, differences between the March Brown and the Gray Fox remain real to anglers, and so does the necessity of carrying patterns for both. The insect takes its nickname from a Preston Jennings pattern, but Art Flick's version is most widely used today. Flick made his adaptations to match the *vicarium* hatches on his Catskill river, the Schoharie. You'll have to choose the pattern that best suits your local hatches. Another Jennings patterns, the original Gray Fox, is bereft of its mythical natural, S. *fuscum*, but nonetheless useful for S. *vicarium* hatches. This is another struggling fast-water insect, but your imitation should not ride too high, because all *Stenonema*s keep a low profile against the surface. ComparaDun and parachute constructions not only give a low-riding silhouette but also float well in fast and choppy currents in the manner of the hatching dun. Long, drag-free floats suit the lingering tendencies of the emergers. Once out of the shuck, these heavy duns flop a bit before take-off. You can imitate this action by throwing just enough slack to cause a hackled fly to bounce upon the surface. It is important to keep in mind, when purchasing ready made imitations, that our eastern fly was dubbed the American March Brown to differentiate it from the mayflies of Britain and the American west which go by the same name. Another eastern species, S. *ithaca*, resembles a smaller, lighter *vicarium* and can be fished in the same manner.

American March Brown—Spinner

Family: Heptageniidae   Size: 13-17 mm
Genus: *Stenonema*
Species: *vicarium*
Nicknames: Ginger Quill Spinner, Dark Cahill, Great Red Spinner
Active: Third week of May to last week of June

Like the dun, the spinner of the March Brown comes in a range of hues, from deep mahogany to ginger, but always with a noticeable banding of the abdomen. It is easily recognized in the air by virtue of its two tails, spread at a 90-degree angle, and its size, the largest spinner so far of the season. Like the Hendrickson spinners, it is the more reliable phase for bringing fish to the surface. The males gather in a dense cloud while other insects, including the smaller Pale Evening Duns, are still coming off, and while still others, like the Cinnamon Caddis, are laying eggs. The females join them over the faster riffles and pockets that will provide suitable habitat for their young, but you'll find the trout in the heads of pools and in slower currents where the duns hatch. They seem to know that the *vicarium* spinners will reach them soon enough, and they need waste no energy in pursuing them. The entire sequence of mating, egg laying and dying upon the water takes place before dark, and even if fish are feeding on other insects they collectively switch to the March Brown spinners when the spent flies blanket the water.

(L to R): Clipped Henwing Spinner, Great Red Sparkle/CDC Spinner, Red Parachute Spinner
Hook Sizes 10-12

I've enjoyed some of my best spring fishing during March Brown spinner falls, but only after I learned to construct large spentwing patterns that would stay afloat after the first few casts without gallons of floatant, that would melt into the surface film and that had wings that sparkled like a spinner's. The combination of CDC and Antron wings, the preference of naturally water-repellent materials like clipped hackle or certain furs over synthetics solved many of these problems. Parachute flies have an added advantage in their usefulness during the upwinged egg-laying stage. *Stenonema* females lay their eggs in the riffles by making multiple descents to the surface and releasing a portion of their red-orange eggs each time. When trout are on to March Brown spinners it almost seems that you can do no wrong, as long as you keep your fly in the fish's feeding lanes and avoid abrupt and unnatural movements. Put plenty of slack in your leader to handle the rougher currents. As the line goes taught at the end of the drift resist the temptation to lift for your next cast and instead be prepared to set the hook. I've caught some large fish in this manner, despite the obvious paradox of imitating a dying insect that appears to be fighting the current. The best places to fish the spinner fall are slow to moderate pocket waters and the heads of pools just as the entering current begins to soften.

Cream Cahill—Dun

Family: Heptageniidae
Genus: *Stenonema*
Species: *mediopunctatum, modestum* and others
Nicknames: Olive Cahill Quill, Cream May, Summer *Stenonema*
Active: First week in June to second week in September

Size: 9-12 mm

The Cream Cahills are a group of widely distributed species of the *Stenonema* genus and of similar size and color. They are found in a much wider array of habitats and for longer periods than the larger, darker spring hatching species. I regularly encounter them on streams that support few other clinging or crawling mayfly nymphs. The Creams begin to appear on the downward side of the March Brown hatch and remain in varying densities throughout the dry-fly season. They are characterized by pale gray wings with lightly marked crossveins, delicately banded cream to pale tan tails, and yellowish or creamy white bodies with small, brown slash markings located dorsally on the abdomen. Some females have a distinctly orange cast, especially in the thorax, while some males have darker, browner tones at the thorax and the last two abdominal segments. This brown color will become very apparent in the spinner stage. Males also have ridiculously large eyes, which are quite black until exposure to light causes them to fade. The summer *Stenonema*s hatch at twilight and return two or more days later for the spinner falls. They spend the intervening time shaded from the harsh sun by clinging under the leaves of streamside shrubs and trees.

(L to R): Cream Cahill Parachute, Cream Wulff, Usual
Hook Sizes 12-16

In my experience, the Summer *Stenonema*s seldom amount to a major hatch east of the Hudson River. Still, they are rarely absent during their season, and there are evenings when they constitute the only hatch worthy of note. Additionally, their season is so extended that they offer a good place to start when summertime fish are feeding opportunistically. By late June the spring runoff has ended and streams have settled into clearly defined areas of riffles, runs, reaches and pools. Conditions are more demanding, and care must be taken to match the pattern to the type of water and the behavior of the insect. In currents, for example, a Wulff pattern may be more visible, but unless the mayflies are actively fluttering their wings, a lower riding ComparaDun or an emerger like the Usual would be a better choice. In slower water the classic Catskill tie imitates an active insect, whereas a No Hackle or Parachute gives a better silhouette of a more serene mayfly. Clear, low water also calls for extremely fine tippets and greater stealth, not only because we are more visible to our prey but also because opportunities for dry-fly fishing become fewer as the summer wears on and before the fall feeding binge. Avoid downstream presentations, especially in deeper water where the fish's window is enlarged, and any direct upstream casts where there is a danger of lining the fish.

Cream Cahill Spinner

Size: 9-12 mm

Family: Heptageniidae
Genus: *Stenonema*
Species: *mediopunctatum, modestum* and others
Active: First week in June to second week in September

At the height of summer the *Stenonema* flies hatch at the onset of darkness and lay their eggs a few days later under cover of darkness. After prolonged exposure to light their eyes have faded to a ghostly green. The subdued orange cast of early season females becomes slightly more saturated in the spinner stage. But by mid August the spinners become paler, approaching a bleached white. They also appear on the water much earlier as late-summer evenings grow cooler. It is only during these later spinner falls that I notice them in any real density, occasionally mistaking them for the beginnings of a White Fly hatch. I seldom see the males, because their spinner flights are comparatively dispersed and the males fall to the water directly after copulation. Several species produce male spinners with the familiar Jenny Spinner pattern. Females rest to incubate the eggs and then fly upstream to scout out riffles and pocket waters to lay their eggs. These reconnaissance flights are the first tip-off that a spinner fall is about to begin. Once devoid of their eggs the spent females on the surface appear all the more pallid.

(L to R): Light Cahill Parachute Spinner, Cream Egglayer Spinner, Polywing Jenny Spinner
Hook Sizes 12-16

Some mayflies, like the *Ephemerella*s and *Isonychia*, extrude their eggs to form a ball and drop or dip them all into the water at once. Most adults of the clinging mayflies, including the numerous species of *Stenonema*, make repeated descents to the water's surface and push out a few clusters of eggs each time. Trout have multiple chances to feed on upwinged egg-layers in advance of the spent insects. The rises are quite splashy in the manner of a fish chasing a furtive target. But active egg-layers don't touch down for long, and the best chance of interesting a fish in an upwing spinner imitation is to drop one directly on its nose or skate the fly in front of it. Note the feeding rhythm of the fish and allow it to return to its feeding position before you present your offering. These egg-laying flights are relatively short-lived, and before long the trout go off of the upwings to concentrate on the increasing number of spent forms as characterized by sipping rises. Before changing flies, try clipping the hackle of your egg-laying pattern on the top and bottom to reduce its profile. Like other *Stenonema*s, male spinners are equally important for the angler. Although scattered as they fall to the water, the current quickly collects them until they cluster in the eddies and seams. If possible, scoop up a sample before choosing your imitation, because not all have the two-toned Jenny coloration. Rusty spinners are also a common appearance of some males.

Light Cahill—Dun

Family: Heptageniidae   Size: 9-12 mm
Genus: *Stenacron*
Species: *interpunctatum*
Nicknames: Little Yellow Fox, Orange Cahill
Active: Third week in June to first week in August

Among the potpourri of Heptageniidae hatches that follow the March Browns are the Light Cahills. Of these the most distinctive are of the genus *Stenacron*. Early texts refer to it as *Stenonema canadense,* but it is now recognized as a separate genus, based on the structure of the nymphs' gills. In the winged stage, with two tails, lightly marked cross veins, well-marked abdomens and banded legs, it bears a passing resemblance to the lighter *Stenonema* flies. Variegated yellow to orange abdomens and salmony thoraxes are coupled with a distinct yellow cast to the dun's wing. Many of the females exhibit the same deep orange, egg-laden hues of the female *E. vitreus.* What distinguishes *Stenacron* adults from *Stenonema* is a telltale series of spots running up along the costal wing vein. Cahills are surface emergers, cracking the exoskeleton just under the meniscus and climbing through to the top in about half a minute. The duns emerge in slow water, but usually where they are quickly picked up by the current and carried downstream. The nymphs prefer a slightly slower current and a siltier substrate than the somewhat larger *Stenonema* larvae, but the two genera are difficult to differentiate in this stage without magnification.

(L to R): Rusty Usual, Yellow Ginger ComparaDun, Light Cahill Hook Sizes 12-14

Stenacron interpunctatum got its nickname from the Light Cahill, a classic Catskill pattern belonging in every fly box. The hackled construction helps the fly maintain its buoyancy in faster waters. Light Cahill hatches coincide with those of the Creams, and the same demanding fishing conditions apply. Like the summer *Stenonemas*, *Stenacron*s squat low on the water, and they emerge in water that is less boisterous than that of the earlier hatches. By trimming a V from the bottom of the hackle, you can recreate the lower profile needed for smoother surfaces. My own pattern is a ComparaDun based on the same blend of body colors used in my *E. vitreus* emerger. I use it for a reliable evening hatch just below a short rapid, which tails out of an extremely large pool. The water is well aerated, but not particularly fast or turbulent. Trout stack up on either side of the current tongue and pick off the just-hatched or emerging insects as they pass by. I can stand near the river's edge and make an up-and-across cast with a downstream reach to the fish on the near side of the current. Then I stroll fifty yards downstream and quietly cross the river to fish the other side. It's such a textbook situation that I've used it to teach fly fishing to my children. The spinners resemble those of *Epeorus vitreus* but with faintly yellow, marked hyaline wings. We don't wait for the spinner fall, which happens long after bedtime.

Leadwing Coachman—Nymph

Family: Isonychiidae   **Size: 12-17 mm**
Genus: *Isonychia*
Species: *bicolor*
Active: Third week of March to last week of October

Whenever I use my kick net to sample the drift the first things to catch my eye are the *Isonychia* nymphs. These energetic creatures wiggle frantically in their efforts to escape, creating flashes of light with their dark, wet forms. They are built for speed and are among the fastest swimmers of all aquatic insects. Compared to other mayfly larvae their bodies are streamlined, rather like a modern submarine with thickly fringed front legs, prominent, plate-shaped lateral gills and three fringed tails that serve as a paddle. Some of our eastern species have a bold light stripe down the middle of their backs. *Isonychia* are found anywhere in the northeast where there is clean, well-oxygenated water. They emerge all season long, so on any given day specimens can be gathered in a whole range of sizes. They favor moderate to fast currents where they cling to rocks or bravely swim in open water. They are semi-predatory, occasionally dining upon smaller larvae, but their characteristic feeding tool is their front pair of legs, with heavily fringed anteriors, brought together in front to form a basket for gathering food particles from the drift.

(L to R): Isonychia Nymph, Leadwing Coachman, Zug Bug
Hook Sizes 10-12

The greatest testimony to the importance of *Isonychia* nymphs is the number of patterns that have been developed to imitate them, like the popular Leadwing Coachman and the Zug Bug, a favorite in New England. Nearly all of them work, but with *Isonychia* the pattern is far less important than how you fish it. These nymphs are never helpless in the drift, and when they move they move quickly. Shortly before emergence they migrate to shallower, slower waters and particularly to stones upon which they can climb above the surface to doff their shucks. Alert fish will follow them in search of an easy meal. Although most of the duns hatch during the late evening and early morning hours, they continue throughout the day. During peak emergences in the spring and the fall it is always a good idea to include an *Isonychia* nymph pattern either with another swimmer like a *Baetis* or a streamside emerger like a stonefly. Because they might be anywhere—gathering food on the stream bottom, swimming in open water or migrating to the shallows— it's a good idea to try a variety of presentations, beginning with the nearest water where a fish is likely to be. High stick a nymph, a wet fly or a combination through the shallows before entering the stream. Then, after drifting your flies along the bottom and through the midwater, swing your rod tip toward the stream bank to migrate the flies back to the shallows, allowing enough time for the fish to follow before finishing with a hand-over-hand retrieve.

Leadwing Coachman—Dun

Family: Isonychiidae   **Size:** 12-17 mm
Genus: *Isonychia*
Species: *bicolor*
Nicknames: Slate Drake, Chocolate Drake, Dun Variant
Active: Second week of June to second week of October

Two points of controversy surround the *Isonychia*: first, that the dun hatches not from the water, but by crawling onto the rocks like a stonefly; and second, that the early and late-season species are one and the same. The first is partially true, for the duns hatch where they can. In low water I see hundreds of their shucks on protruding stones, but at the same time I have always found surface imitations of *Isonychia* to be effective when the fly is hatching. The second is a red herring, for in selecting a fly pattern, appearance matters a great deal, and classification matters very little. Both species have the characteristic dark pair of front legs ahead of two pair of cream-colored legs, as well as prominent hind wings and very dark eyes. On the White, the spring duns are large specimens, at least a size 10, and quite as dark as rich chocolate. By October they are leaner, lighter, and smaller, rarely larger than a 12, with much less mottling of the wings. Emergence is in the evening during warmer weather but, as temperatures decline in the fall, they begin hatching as early as noon. The most concentrated hatches occur during June and late September.

(L to R): Dark Hendrickson, Dun Variant, Adams
Hook Sizes 10-12

Few insects are as important to New England dry-fly enthusiasts as the *Isonychia* mayfly. They hatch throughout the region, and whenever they hatch, fish will take them. In regions where they emerge throughout the season, they do so sporadically and often mixed with other hatches of caddis, small stoneflies or smaller mayflies like *Baetis* or *Leucrocuta* where they really stand out. Whether the duns hatch on the water or on stones is largely a moot point on New England waters, because a well-tied imitation will take fish both above and below the surface. For the big, dark, mottled-winged *Isonychia*s of the early season, the gray muskrat body, brown and grizzly hackle and grizzly wings of the venerable Adams pattern make it a pretty convincing impostor. A skated fly like Art Flick's Dun Variant imitates the clumsy *Isonychia* drakes trying to take off. Cast along the slow edges of riffles and runs, especially those with protruding rocks that might make good hatching platforms. For some reason, imitations of the *Isonychia* have always provoked strikes when fished wet at the end of a dry-fly dead drift, especially where riffles collect and run into pools. Fish gather just outside the current to intercept cripples as they struggle in vain to become airborne. Cast right into the current and mend your line downstream to keep up with the progress of your fly. Pause at the end of the drift to let the current pull the fly under, and wait. Finally, retrieve your fly with short, quick strips to remove any lingering doubts on the part of the trout.

White Gloved Howdy—Spinner

Family: Isonychiidae   **Size:** 12-17 mm
Genus: *Isonychia*
Species: *bicolor*
Nicknames: Great Red Spinner
Active: Second week of June to second week of October

The famous nickname of the *Isonychia* springs from the habitual "prayer" position of the spinners, who hold their light-tipped forelegs out in front even while at rest. The final molt occurs within 48 hours of emergence, but since many areas experience season-long hatches a spinner flight can happen on almost any evening into October, with most activity occurring after dark. Late spring and early autumn offer the greatest densities of spinner swarms. The males stage their parade relatively high above the stream or over vegetation where females await their cue. After fertilization, the males fall spent to the water while the females returns to protective cover to extrude a green egg mass from the tips of their abdomens. My reference texts describe the females as releasing their eggs by flying low over the surface of the stream to repeatedly dap their abdomens until the egg mass is dragged off. They are also reported to release the egg ball from several feet above the water. But I have watched egg-laden females land in the damp spots between streamside rocks, release their precious loads and then fly off to their inevitable end.

(L to R): Bent Body Spinner, Red Parachute Spinner, Great Red Sparkle/CDC Spinner
Hook Sizes 10-12

I have found solitary *Isonychia* duns and spinners miles away from any suitable habitat. On summer nights, many females collect under lights at the local mall with their eggs balls attached to the arched tips of their abdomens. Mating and egg laying can occur many miles apart. The densities of the spinner falls are thereby dissipated, rendering them of somewhat less significance than the hatches. Still, many spinners, both male and female, do end up on the surface of the water, where they are sucked under either by opportunistic trout, who cannot pass up an insect that is both large and easily recognized as food, or by selective feeders. Such events often coincide with hatches and spinner falls of other insects, especially the Olives of autumn, when the emergence and mating sequences become more concentrated. The louder and more erratic rises are likely to be those to *Isonychia* spinners. If I see active egg-layers disappearing into splashes I'll respond with a skated Dun Variant or a drifted Parachute spinner. But once the spent forms appear in the surface film I'll fish much as I would in any spinner fall, with drag-free drifts of a spentwing pattern placed accurately in the fish's feeding lane and timed to the rhythm, if any, of the rises. Opportunistic feeders present a greater challenge, for they are more easily put down. To meet it, place yourself carefully to attain the longest possible drag-free drift and consider fishing a smaller dun or spinner in tandem with your *Isonychia* imitation.

Gray Drake Spinner

Family: Siphlonuridae   **Size: 9-15 mm**
Genus: *Siphlonurus*
Nickname: Brown Quill Spinner
Active: Last week of May to first week of July

One of the most mysterious mayflies is the Gray Drake, actually an overlapping series of hatches of the "two-tailed" genus *Siphlonurus*. The northeast distribution of *Siphlonurus* is uneven, but substantial populations inhabit well-known rivers like the Battenkill, the Swift in Massachusetts and the Saco in New Hampshire, where Dick Stewart and friends have been studying their singular habits for years. Dun sightings are rare. Emergers are thought to crawl out of the water, but on the Saco duns have been observed, albeit from a distance, to hatch directly from the surface, so sporadically that it seems a miracle when darkness approaches and spinners convene over the current by the thousands. Males are easily identified by their banded abdomens of dark walnut alternating with the palest of yellows, and by the white bands encircling the bases of their large eyes. Females appear similar except, as expected, in the eyes, forelegs and genitalia. Fertilized females migrate upstream to oviposit in habitat suitable for the nymphs, leaving the males to expire. Sometimes, if the air temperature dips below 65 or conditions are otherwise imperfect, the females fail to appear, and the entire event is postponed to early the following morning or to the next warm evening.

(L to R): Siphlonurus Spinner, Bent Body Spinner, Mirus Spinner Hook Sizes 10-14

In terms of behavior, there is little difference from one *Siphlonurus* species to the next, but colors vary wildly from one species to another, and between environments. *Mirus* spinners, in particular, have a unique brown hind wing for which special patterns are tied. Some species are smaller than others, all of which makes it necessary to capture a sample before selecting your pattern. In addition to the spent patterns, many anglers opt for a Quill Gordon or a Red Quill to imitate the egg-layers. Peak hatches are in June, but overlapping species emerge well into the season. To take full advantage of the spectacular spinner falls one has to be in place before nightfall and be prepared to make well-placed casts in nearly total darkness. Males gather directly over the current, and fish align themselves on either side to dine on the casualties. After laying their eggs upstream in slower water by dapping their abdomens repeatedly on the surface, the females eventually succumb in the current as well. To avoid drag, position yourself to cast to the near side of the current. Strangely, the best time to fish a nymph is during the spinner falls. These are the peak hours of behavioral drift, when nymphs move through the current and into the shallows to hatch. Dick Stewart speculates that the spinners bring the trout to the table where they opt for the meatier larvae. Because the light is subdued, swimming patterns like the *Isonychia* make acceptable nymph imitations.

Common Burrowers—Nymphs

Family: Ephemeridae   Size: 13-40 mm
Genera: *Ephemera, Litobrancha, Hexagenia*
Active: Last week of May to first week of September

Tunneled into the substrate are all of the members of the Ephemeridae family, giants of the Mayfly kingdom. For stream fishing east of the Hudson, the most important of these are the *Ephemera* larvae, including the Green (*guttulata*), Yellow (*varia*) and Brown (*simulans*) Drakes, and *Hexagenia*, the largest of the North American mayfly genera. These nymphs are easily recognized by their long, slender bodies, by their outwardly curving tusks, and by their long, wavy double gills which attach laterally to their abdomens but flow up over their backs as they undulate. This motion forces oxygen through their burrows and past their gills to prevent their suffocating in the sediment. Body colors range from a pale grayish cream for *Hexagenia* nymphs through a golden yellow for the *varia* larvae to the darker mottled browns of *simulans* and *guttulata*. They feed on the rich organic goop that settles in slow backwaters and eddies to support incredible densities of these large insects. They must leave their burrows regularly during their two- to three-year life cycles to molt. Ephemeridae nymphs are found in trout stomachs even in winter. They are extremely agile swimmers. Art Flick lamented that Green Drake nymphs surfaced and emerged so quickly that fish couldn't take them, but during a full-blown drake hatch many of the largest fish feed exclusively on nymphs as they leave their protective burrows.

(L to R): Burk's Hexagenia, Kennebago Emerger, Wiggle Nymph Hook Sizes 4-10

Some Ephemeridae are associated with lakes and ponds, but they are important players in the life of trout rivers as well. And though we associate these mayflies with fantastic dry-fly fishing, the larval forms are extremely important, as year-round patterns and especially during a hatch. Their dolphin style of swimming has given rise to numerous variations on the wiggle nymph, in which one hook is tethered to another to form the base of the fly and one of the points is removed. It is an ideal pattern to use when imitating the nymph rising to the surface. Where trout are steadily feeding from a fixed position, cast a few feet ahead to let the fly settle on the bottom, then allow it to rise in front of the feeder. Add a swimming motion either by gently wiggling the rod up and down or by tugging with your line hand. Sometimes fish cruise the slower pools and backwaters where these nymphs proliferate. By patiently studying the cruiser's circuit you can anticipate its arrival at the point where you want to cast your fly. Retrieve the fly with short strips, rapidly enough to keep it rising to the surface as the fish comes into range. In waters densely inhabited by multiple species of burrowing mayflies it is productive to fish nymph imitations during non-hatch periods to opportunistic feeders. The instar stage, one of the few circumstances under which immature nymphs leave their burrows, requires a pattern several shades lighter than normal.

Green Drake—Dun

Family: Ephemeridae   Size: 17-25 mm
Genus: *Ephemera*
Species: *guttulata*
Nicknames: Green May, Large Gray Fox Variant, Black Drake
Active: Last week of May to last week of June

The Green Drake is one of those mythical "Super Hatches" which is in some need of deflating. This beautiful mayfly attracts more fishers than fish, especially on large rivers, a consequence not only of its emergence behavior, but also of the prevalence of other insects. Hatches begin as early as sunup, and continue all day, one or two drakes at a time. It appears in southern New England around Memorial Day and works its way northward, reaching the Adirondacks two weeks later. Its appearance in Maine is well documented, but there the name Green Drake is reserved for *Litobrancha*, a different and even larger genus of the same family. *Guttulata* is big in every way. Its overlong, heavy abdomen offers a creamy preview of the famous waxy white abdomen of the spinner, but with a darker gray dorsal shading. The enormous forewing is well marked with dark crossveins and purplish-brown splotches. The head and mesothorax are yellow, and the legs are cream to yellow with dark markings on the front pairs. Its three brown tails are banded with black. It leaves the water with much flutter and fuss, but it glides serenely up to the trees, where it can be found hanging under the leaves as it molts to its famous spinner, the Coffin Fly.

(L to R): Eastern Green Drake, Gray Fox Variant, Green Drake Parachute Vertical Emerger
Hook Sizes 6-8

Many of America's famous fly-fishers have lamented their frustrations with the Green Drake hatch, noting both the difficulty of accurately imitating so large an insect and the abundance of alternative foods during their period of emergence. Fish seem to prefer concurrently hatching caddis like the Dark Blue Sedge or the prolific Sulphur mayfly duns. As a result, it is most productive to fish New England's Green Drake hatch in places where it has little competition from these insects. These include smaller streams, where food is scarce, or impoundments and long, slow pools and reaches that are ideal for burrowing mayflies. Tailouts of pools also provide slow pockets where fish collect to intercept insects as the current funnels them overhead. But they are nightmarish when it comes to controlling drag. Plenty of slack in your tippet will compensate for the accelerating current. There is also an old George La Branche trick, which is to cast your line from downstream, but over a rock, thus keeping your line from accelerating away from your fly. Green Drakes are fast-moving emergers, and fish are forced to make their commitment long before they have a chance to scrutinize your imitation. Variants and other heavily hackled flies land softly despite the larger hook. But they also twist leaders when you cast them, especially with undersized tippets. Green Drake is another name that is applied to more than one insect, something to consider when choosing flies from the bin.

Coffin Fly—Spinner

Family: Ephemeridae   **Size: 17-25 mm**
Genus: *Ephemera*
Species: *guttulata*
Nicknames: Brown and White Spinner, Black and White Spinner
Active: Third week of May to last week of June

My introduction to the Coffin Fly came on a small, wooded stream, just below an impoundment. Duns had been hatching all day, but as it grew dark I had nearly given up hope of seeing any spinners. Finally, I saw their dark forms near the treetops, high against the clear sky. A male suddenly glided down to the stream, as easily as a paper glider, rested briefly, then shot skyward again. Soon more males descended by the hundreds as the egg-laden females joined them on the stream. I netted my specimens while my companions pulled 2- and 3-pound rainbows and browns from below the spillway. The transformation from dun to spinner is so radical, so striking, that it defies belief. Gone is the vibrant green of the wings, although the dark patterning and a greenish tint remain. The male has long, darkened legs and three banded tails, each more than twice the length of its body. Nearly black eyes and a dark chocolate thorax are a stark contrast to the milky white abdomen. Females share the ghostly abdominal pallor, especially after extruding their twin cylinders of yellow eggs, but their heads and legs are yellow, and their tails and forelegs more modestly proportioned.

(L to R): Hairwing Spent Spinner, Coffin Fly, AuSable Coffin Fly Hook Sizes 6-10

Unlike the dun hatch, the spinner falls of the Coffin Fly are concentrated events, packed into an hour's time with a few minutes of peak activity at the onset of darkness. By this time the air is also likely to be full of stoneflies and *Stenonema* spinners as well as hatching Sulphurs, *Isonychia*s and caddisflies. Once a critical mass of spinners is on the water, the fish, including those normally reticent lunkers, will rise to them eagerly. In the early stages, the male spinners are landing and taking off, and the females are laying eggs by dipping their abdomens on the water, so a hackled, upright-wing pattern will provoke the greatest response. These are designed to be skated across the water in the manner of the active egg-layers, but those incorporating clipped hackle bodies will also float well if you prefer a dead drift. Soon the dying spinners will achieve a majority, at which point you should switch to a spent-wing imitation, either without hackle or with the hackle clipped on the bottom to allow the pattern to lie flush in the surface film. As with any spent spinner, they must be presented in a dead drift, but because of their size even large fish will be coaxed from their feeding lanes to intercept your offering. The major difficulty with any of these large patterns is their tendency to twist the leader as you cast them. To combat this problem, use the stiffest leader that the surface of the water will allow.

Brown Drake—Spinner

Family: Ephemeridae   Size: 13-18 mm
Genus: *Ephemera*
Species: *simulans*
Active: Second week of May to the last week of June

Like the spinner of the Green Drake, the Brown Drake spinner is the
most fishable stage of this mayfly. Its emergence roughly coincides with
that of its green relative. It is only slightly smaller, and it is more widespread, tolerating a wider range of habitats. Unlike the Coffin Fly, its
transformation from the dun stage is less dramatic, for the Brown Drake
retains most of its color as a spinner. It is, in fact, quite creamy on the
ventral surface, but the overall impression to the fish is of a brown insect
with clear, spotted wings, amber legs and three absurdly long banded
tails, especially on the male. Brown Drakes hatch continuously throughout the day, seldom in any concentration, and the duns immediately fly
to the safety of the trees, climbing ever higher until they find a roost.
There they can be found hanging from the leaves, frequently with their
shed pellicles beside them, as they wait for evening. Just about sunset
their mating swarms begin high up in the treetops. They slowly spiral
downwards until the first spinners swoop to the water, first the males
and then the females. There they remain upwinged until their business
is complete and they litter the surface with their spent forms.

(L to R): Loopwing Hatchmatcher, Sparkle Paradrake, Brown Antron/Poly Spinner
Hook Sizes 8-10

Like those of many insects that hatch in late May and early June, Brown Drake spinner falls commence in the hour of waning light and face stiff competition from other hatching and ovipositing aquatic insects. The advantage to the fly-fisher is that they are not only the largest insect available, but often the most numerous, at least above the surface. If fish are rising, they are most likely taking the big brown spinners. The event is a two-stage affair, beginning with the arrival of the active, upwinged males and egg-laying females and ending with the flattened spinners who provide such a large and easy meal for the fish. (I've often thought that nature designed the return of the spent males to the river as a decoy to ensure that a sufficient population of females survives to complete the delivery of their yellow eggs). Rises to the upwinged flies are loud and aggressive, while rises to the spent spinners are quieter, more rhythmic and more confident. Your ears may be your best guide, for the spinner fall continues long after it is too dark to see, and many of the biggest fish wait until nightfall to venture to the surface. Currents in Brown Drake habitats tend to be on the slow side, and feeding fish are on the move. Treat the occasion as an adventure in night fishing by establishing a good casting position with a known exit route and cast patiently to the spot where you know a good fish ought to be.

Yellow Drake—Spinner

Family: Ephemeridae   **Size: 13-18 mm**
Genus: *Ephemera*
Species: *varia*
Nicknames: Cream Variant, Yellow May
Active: Second week of June to the last week of July

The last of the *Ephemera* mayflies to appear each season, and one of the most widespread east of the Hudson, is the Yellow Drake. I've seen only a very few duns, which resemble the female *Hexagenia* except for the three tails, smaller size and mottled wings. These have come off the water so sporadically that they could hardly constitute a hatch. They pop up on rivers so disparate that I would be hard pressed to define their habitat. I find the best populations on medium-sized streams where the current is slow to moderate and where some silt is available for the burrowing nymphs. The spinner falls, though less dense than those of the Green or Brown Drakes, still bring large trout to the surface. Mating occurs discreetly, high up in the treetops. Just after sunset the large females suddenly appear, dropping to the surface of the stream, their abdomens carried low as if weighted down by their yellow egg sacs. Their glassy wings are dotted with purple spots, and there is just a hint of yellow remaining in their creamy legs and abdomens, with enough sepia markings to distinguish them from the larger Coffin fly.

**(L to R): Cream Haystack, Cream Variant, Hacklewing Spinner
Hook Sizes 8-10**

The summer of 1999 was hot and dry, and the first Yellow Spinners came weeks earlier than anticipated. I watched the big females touch down on the water to dislodge their yellow eggs, again and again over the shallower water along the banks and on either side of a current tongue where it enters a large pool. Soon a fish began to rise steadily in front of a ledge that forced the weakened current off its course. By a happy coincidence, I had just purchased a pair of beautifully tied Cream Variants from a variety store in the Catskills. It was also my first night with a new rod, which helped me to deliver the fly precisely a foot in front of my target. The Variant quickly disappeared, and when I drew tight a large rainbow shot across the pool, leapt in the air and bolted downstream. It had taken the fly for an active, egg-laying female. Alas, failing to trust my new rod I played the fish too delicately and lost it. Later, as the spinners completed their task, their spent forms littered the surface. Other fish continued to rise downstream just ahead of the large rocks that dotted the pool. I switched to a spentwing pattern, and when my first cast landed with too little slack and dragged, the feeding temporarily stopped. When it resumed I caught two lesser trout, played them confidently, and brought them to the net.

Great Leadwinged Drake—Dun

Family Ephemeridae   **Size: 18-40 mm**
Genus *Hexagenia*
Nicknames: Michigan Caddis, Fishfly
Active: Third week of June to third week of September

Of the big summer drakes, the two largest genera are two-tailed as adults. Of these, the great *Hexagenia* is familiar on still waters but is also important on rivers in every state in the region. Of the several species, one is transcontinental and has achieved distinction as the largest of all North American mayflies. A female *Hex* looks like an overgrown *Ephemera varia*, but with one less tail and unspotted wings. Like most mayflies, *Hexes* come in a range of colors, from bright yellow to reddish brown with tan to slate wings. Males are consistently smaller and darker than females. Emergence and growth are temperature dependent, taking longer and occurring later as you head north. Peak hatches surround the Fourth of July, but in Maine the hatches continue throughout the summer. At home on the White River I've seen spinners in early September. Heavy midsummer hatches begin just as its getting too dark to tie on your fly, a bit earlier on very overcast days. Spinner falls occur at the same time. Predictably, the spinners are more saturated, clear-winged versions of the duns. The females land on the water with upright wings, but eventually fall spent to the surface.

(L to R): Yellow Haystack, Deerhair Spent Hex, Hexagenia Hatchmatcher
Hook Sizes 4-8

Even the largest trout and bass throw caution to the wind during a *Hex* hatch, but it is foolhardy to think that they are not selective. Given the smooth currents where *Hexes* thrive, fish get a good look at your large imitation, even in dim light. I recall a late-season hatch when I cast a *Hexagenia* Wulff pattern squarely between two naturals. The real McCoys vanished simultaneously in twin vortexes while my impostor, poorly matched to the smooth water, remained unmolested. Switching to a sparser pattern, I hooked a fine brookie on my next cast. Veterans of the midsummer hatches will stake out a familiar piece of water just after sunset when it's still so quiet that an imminent feeding frenzy seems impossible. It is vital to know where the fish will be feeding, since most of your casts will be in the dark, with only your ears to guide you. Previsualizing the currents will help you to keep a drag-free float. All the cautions, rules and methods of night fishing apply, like pre-measuring your casts, marking your lines and keeping your casts short. It helps to have at least two pre-rigged rods, one with an emerger and the other with a dun pattern so that you can, in effect, change flies without the use of lights and avoid spooking the fish. Loop-to-loop leader to tippet connections also save time and trouble in the dark, especially if you are prone to "wind knots".

Fringe Gilled Nymph

Family: Potamanthidae   **Size: 10-16 mm**
Genus: *Anthopotamus*
Species: *distinctus*
Nickname: Hackle-Gill
Active: Last week of June to the second week of August

Most mayfly larvae fit neatly into one of the four physical types, but the unique hackle-gilled nymphs of *Anthopotamus* literally fall through the cracks. These dirty brown and yellow, distinctly patterned larvae look like burrowers, with their spiny, inward turning, bison-like tusks, their luxuriant wavy gills and richly fringed tails, and in fact the immature nymphs do settle somewhat in the substrate. But even when fully developed they are smaller and more compact than the common burrowers and spend most of their time crawling around rocks and submerged sticks, more on the substrate than actually in it. I usually find them in rivers and large streams where the current is slow to moderate, and they definitely prefer slower currents when they hatch. They migrate to the river's edge just before emergence, but it isn't unusual to find them in shallow water at any time. Anglers in the Northeast need to know only one species, *distinctus,* although others have recently been discovered in the region, and the genus ranges everywhere in the eastern half of the U.S., except Florida.

(L to R): Light Cahill Nymph, Speckled Hen Nymph, Soft Hackle Hare's Ear
Hook Sizes 10-12

Anthopotamus populations are usually found only on higher order streams where warmwater fish like bass can be found. Their high capacity gills endow them with tolerance of slower water, but they are equally at home deep in the riffles. These are usually places where trout fishing is fast and furious in the early season but slows down after mid-summer, except in cooler tailwaters or near springs or coldwater tributaries. As with the Quill Gordons, *Anthopotamus* nymphs are presented here more as an indicator of an impending hatch than for their actual value as a fish catcher, but at times they are the only game in town. Although they hatch on the surface, they are usually crawling where fish can't get at them except for the short interval before emergence. They are also somewhat solitary and hatch sporadically. I've watched one of them swim around indecisively, then suddenly bolt downward. The increased leg and tail action attracted two small fish, who converged upon it. If you find fish feeding on them, keep your fly in motion during the drift with frequent, brief pauses as you follow the line with your rod tip. Plenty of soft hackle or teased out dubbing adds to the impression of leg, tail and gill action. Because the duns hatch all day, an *Anthopotamus* nymph fished in the shallows and eddies succeeds as a searching pattern, especially in tandem with a small stonefly or *Baetis* nymph.

Golden Drake—Dun

Family: Potamanthidae   **Size: 13-16 mm**
Genus: *Anthopotamus*
Species: *distinctus*
Nicknames: Evening Dun, Golden Dun, Cream Variant, Cream Drake
Active: Last week of June to the second week of August

Of all the winged mayflies, the Golden Drakes are to my eye the most striking—the seasonal climax of color. Many texts describe them as having a pale hue from white to cream, but on my local streams the females, at least, are a canary yellow throughout their abdomens, wings, three tails and the two rear pairs of legs. The thorax and front legs are a salmony pink. These showy colors seduce trout, and artificials continue to attract long after the naturals have ceased hatching. Many of these long-bodied duns escape the notice of coldwater fish because they hatch on slower reaches and in eddies of medium to large rivers when the water is not only low, but reaching midsummer temperatures inhospitable to trout. But great dry-fly action can be enjoyed in the marginal areas where warm and cold water mingle, and where fish and mayfly interact. Peak emergence is at dusk as the semi-burrowing nymphs migrate to these slower waters before rising quickly to the surface. Takeoff is slow and clumsy. Spinner falls occur at the same time of day. The spinners are a more saturated version of the dun, with wings that, although transparent, retain the deep yellow color.

(L to R): Cream Variant, Anthopotamus ComparaDun, Anthopotamus Emerger
Hook Sizes 10-12

In July, large trout seek refuge in spring-fed pools and near riverbanks where cold feeder streams provide relief from the lethal summer heat. In the evenings they cruise the shallows and backwaters in search of emerging insects like the Golden Drake. Alas, who among us has not surprised a large trout in these productive areas with our hasty efforts to cast our dry fly into the main current? It pays to search the banks with an emerger or dun pattern before wading into the river. Emergers should be fished in a dead drift, but like all of the summer drakes, Goldens need a few trial hops before achieving liftoff. For this reason, skating patterns like Art Flick's Cream Variant (from which the *Anthopotamus* derives its early nickname) were developed to lure unseen trout. In choosing your casting position, remember that currents in shallows and eddies are not always aligned with the main flow. Fish rising near the main current could be grabbing duns or sipping spinners. Determine which stage these fish are taking by observing the rise forms and the behavior of the insects. Active presentations are apt to spook the steady risers, so start with a dead drift regardless of the insect stage. Both the hatch and the spinner fall are drawn out affairs, lasting well into the night, and much of the best hot weather fishing comes in the cool hours before sunrise when fish are still cleaning up the previous night's spinners.

Blue-winged Olives—Nymphs

Family: Ephemerellidae   Size: 6-10 mm
Genus: *Drunella*
Species: *cornuta, cornutella, lata,* **others**
Active: First week of May to first week of August

As June gives way to the hot days of July I find less and less in my drift net, even when raking up the substrate. Olive caddis larvae are always there along with the usual mixture of cranefly, fishfly, stonefly and beetle larvae, but most of the major mayfly hatches have come and gone. One notable exception is the genus *Drunella*, the daytime-hatching little Blue-Winged Olives of the same family as the Hendricksons and Sulphurs. The nymphs are crawlers with three fringed tails, and look like the larger, earlier *Ephemerellas* except that they are rather plain, usually quite dark, and the front femurs look like the product of daily upper-body workouts. Colors vary from chestnut brown to black, and some species sport a light thoracic collar. Some also have a dash of crimson in the light areas, and most species have small horns projecting from their heads. The notable exception to this is *D. walkeri*, an olive/brown-bodied species that looks like a piece of moss. They are widespread, from western Connecticut to northern Maine, with warmer rivers experiencing hatches of *D. cornuta* as early as the beginning of May. A similar, related mayfly, *Attenella attenuata,* is also important on our New England streams.

(L to R): 1. Dark Crawler, 2. Wet Black Gnat, 3. American Pheasant Tail
Hook Sizes 16-18

In terms of behavior and habitat there's little difference between *Ephemerella* and *Drunella* nymphs. I find them both in moderate to fast currents, of which there is less and less in the dog days of summer. *Drunella* nymphs are good to imitate when searching riffles and pockets during non-hatch periods, particularly in July, when fish stubbornly remain in the cool depths and are less prone to take surface flies. I like to fish them on the point of a tandem nymphing rig, with about a foot of leader tied to a weighted stonefly or caddis nymph with split shot on the leader. The actual choice is made only after carefully checking the stream to see which species predominate. Because they are clumsy swimmers, *Drunella* nymphs leave the bottom only in the hour or two before emergence. Because the duns hatch at midday, the most productive time to offer the nymph is during the early morning migrational drift just before sunrise. This is the coolest part of the day, especially in the water, and fish are most likely to be working the riffles and pockets just upstream of the deeper pools before the rays of the sun expose them to predators and heat up the water. As hatch time approaches at midday, drift a nymph on the bottom and through the midwater at the shallower edges, for it is there that the nymphs are headed in search of a suitable place to emerge.

Blue-Winged Olive—Dun

Family: Ephemerellidae   **Size:** 6-8 mm
Genus: *Drunella*
Species: *cornuta, cornutella, lata,* others
Nicknames: Little Blue Dun, Small Dun Variant
Active: First week of May to first week of August

The eastern species of the genus *Drunella*, collectively known as Little Blue-Winged Olives, are the diminutive cousins of the western Green Drake. Their chief attraction to eastern anglers is that they hatch smack dab in the middle of the day during the hottest days of the year. Fish are reluctant to rise when the sun is at its brightest, but on cloudy days, or on small streams or cold tailwaters, *Drunella*s are a midsummer boon to dry-fly purists. They are readily distinguished from the similarly nicknamed *Baetis* flies by three pale, flaccid tails. Their modestly proportioned rear wings stand in contrast to the imperceptible or absent rear wings of the Baetidae, and they retain the broad femurs they displayed as nymphs. *Drunella* emergence is a sort of dead man's float. Aided by internal gases, they rise to the surface and remain there, motionless, until the wings appear and, in the blink of an eye, the dun is completely out of the shuck. If cooler conditions prevail, they float indefinitely, even as they are picked off by passing ducks and rising trout. I've also noticed a high rate of cripples, which renders them even more appetizing to the fish.

(L to R): Blue-Winged Olive, Attenuata CDC Emerger, Blue-Winged Olive Parachute
Hook Sizes 18-20

In July, the Farmington River runs clear and cold, and its fish rise to hatches of tiny caddis, *Baetis*, *Ephemerella*s and *Drunella*s. Regulars from the Farmington River Anglers Association meet every morning to catch fish on tiny dry flies delivered on 8X tippets and 2-weight lines. They know their insects and, together with fly shop owner Dave Goulet, have designed Lilliputian imitations to match the hatches. Hot weather forces the rest of us to head for canopied smaller streams that remain cool in midsummer and where opportunistic feeders respond to dry flies of any kind served up in the middle of the day. But the best places to fish the Little BWOs are cold tailwaters where the hatches come off slowly and linger until late in the day. On cool, overcast days you can look upstream on a smooth reach to see them floating placidly towards you. Under these conditions, a low-riding dun or emerger gets the most attention. In hotter weather the duns are more impulsive, and fish are quicker to take the classic, high floaters that appear poised for flight. In either case, use plenty of slack on the smallest tippet you can cast, and select a fly that you can see. Takes are often subtle, and your eyes are your only guide. Note also that body colors in the *Drunella*s are very deceptive, because as soon as they emerge they begin to darken from an apple green to a dark olive, even before they take flight.

Blue-Winged Olives—Spinners

Family: Ephemerellidae   **Size: 6-8 mm**
Genus: *Drunella*
Species: *cornuta, cornutella, lata, walkeri*
Nickname: Dark Olive Spinner
Active: First week of May to first week of August

It is widely proclaimed that spinner falls of the Little BWOs are of little importance to the angler, owing to competition from other insects and to the fact that mating and egg laying occur in the dark. I would argue that it is foolish to dismiss any spinner fall, if only because we know that weather can shift both hatching and mating to other times of the day, and no two trips to the river are alike. The noted exception is the single species *Drunella lata,* a July emerger, which stages its mating dance an hour before dusk or early the following morning. Upon molting to the spinner stage, *Drunella* adults darken considerably, not only in their bodies but also in the now duller, chocolatey eyes and in the tails, which lose their former waviness as they telescopically extend. Their wings become glassy clear, and there is also an exaggerated banding in the abdomen.

(L to R): BWO Sparklewing Spinner, Olive CDC Spinner, BWO Parachute
Hook Sizes 18-20

The spinner falls of the *Drunella*s are a warm up to the better-known tiny mayflies of late season, the *Baetis* and Tricos. One principle difference between these and the later mayflies is that they hatch and lay their eggs on faster water, which requires a more buoyant imitation but allows for a slightly coarser leader. A second is that there is nowhere near the insect density that one experiences with the tinier Baetid flies, with the increased likelihood that trout will give your imitation some serious consideration. Look for the spinners to gather over riffles, pocket waters and the heads of pools in the late evening or early morning. Concentrate on the small-eyed females, who must rest during a brief period of incubation before returning to touch down and lay their eggs on the surface. The males, by contrast, can fall just about anywhere after mating. Trout rise with a splash to the active egg-layers until a preponderance of spent spinners leads them to sip more quietly from the surface film. Imitations should be carefully placed only a few feet ahead of the rises and allowed to drift motionless only for short distances. Evening spinner falls come at a time of the season when few other insects are available to compete for the trout's attention. Morning spinner falls may coincide with the season's early Trico hatches, and anglers should take care to determine which insect is actually on the menu.

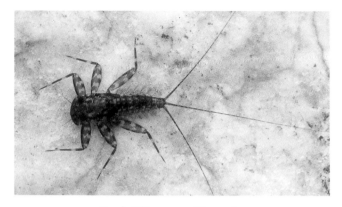

Dark Clingers—Nymphs

Family: Heptageniidae   Size: 6-8 mm
Genus: *Leucrocuta*
Species: *juno, minerva, aphrodite hebe*
Active: First week of June to third week of September

One of a trio of genera known as the *Heptagenia* group, *Leucrocuta* is an often overlooked but locally important genus on New England freestone streams. Nymphs of this group are typical of the clingers with wide, flat profiles, large heads, well-marked legs and long, fragile tails. They are generally more slender and invariably darker than *Stenonema* nymphs. Their gills are slightly different, too, but unless you tie your nymphs in excruciating detail, the difference is unimportant except for identification. I have noticed, for example, that they undulate their gills all at the same time, rather than sequentially. Colors vary from chocolate to dark olive, but they appear black. Only by capturing local samples can you ensure a good match with your artificial. The nymphs grip tenaciously to the undersides of streambed rocks and are available to trout only during their migration to calmer waters, prior to emergence. Early season species are hardly noticeable relative to the abundance of other insects in the stream but then, beginning in July, they suddenly seem to be everywhere. Like other clingers, they like moving water, but they are more tolerant of the slower currents and warmer temperatures that prevail when they are most active.

**(L to R): Dark Clinger, Black Gnat Wet, Sumner's Secret
Hook Sizes 16-18**

I haven't figured out why, in Nature's grand design, both the clinging and crawling mayfly nymphs of high summer are so dark compared to their early season counterparts, but it does explain why dark imitations with some degree of sparkle or sheen are so effective during that time of year. Summer trout seem to be on the lookout for these modest-sized, dark forms, and anglers equipped with appropriately dark nymph patterns have the odds stacked in their favor. In contrast to the crawling *Drunellas* that are around for a relatively short period, clingers of the *Heptagenia* group are active for most of the season. They are also of more importance to the angler than the duns, which spend very little time on the water. One reason given for their quick emergence, particularly in the case of *Leucrocuta* duns, is that they split their shucks a few inches under the surface and are ready to fly the instant they penetrate the meniscus. During a hatch, look for fish rolling beneath the surface as they feed on emergers. Cast a soft-hackled fly well upstream of these feeders and allow it to drift along the bottom until it reaches the fish, then use the Leisenring lift to raise your fly into the feeding area. Allow it to linger for a full minute before withdrawing it for your next cast. For non-hatch situations, use a dead-drift nymph presentation to keep your pattern moving along the bottom.

Little Yellow Quill—Spinner

Family: Heptageniidae   Size: 6-9 mm
Genus: *Leucrocuta*
Species: *juno, minerva, aphrodite hebe*
Nicknames: Little Evening Sulphur, Evening Yellow Dun
Active: First week of June to third week of September

They are the goddesses of summer: Juno, queen of the gods and name-sake of the season's first month; Minerva, the wise warrior goddess; Aphrodite, goddess of love and beauty, and Hebe, Juno's daughter, goddess of youth. Their seemingly continuous emergence from June to October are actually a series of overlapping hatches, occurring with such frequency that spinners and duns are often on the water simultaneously. Early hatches receive scant attention from fish or anglers distracted by other insects. Come August, the larger and more abundant mayflies have all but disappeared, and the diminutive *Leucrocuta hebe* provides plenty of dry-fly action when there otherwise would be none. The duns' distinctive wings are the palest of grays, with barred cross veins like their *Stenonema* cousins but with more pronounced costal markings on the forewings. Their bodies and unmarked legs are nearly the same color, ranging from pale cream to an almost canary yellow with light olive to dark brown markings along the dorsal surface of their abdomens. After molting the yellowish hues of the females get richer, and the markings on their clarified wings become more sharply defined, with a propensity toward rainbow-like refractions. Some darker late-season males molt to the familiar Jenny Spinner pattern.

(L to R): 1. Polywing Sulphur Spinner, 2. Wingless Sulphur Spinner, 3. Parachute Sulphur
Hook Sizes 16 -18

My first experience with the summer goddesses began disappointingly. The duns were emerging, but the trout were ignoring my flies. When the spinners, who had been making reconnaissance flights over the water, touched down, fish began rising indiscriminately adjacent to the main current tongues. Without even changing my pattern I began to catch fish at a steady pace. As it turns out, emerging *Leucrocuta*s leave the water with such astonishing speed that trout waste no energy in pursuit. But egg-laying females come briefly to rest before flying off a short distance and repeating the process several times. Trout capture them with the splashy rises we associate with active winged insects. Dry flies tied with hackles but without wings accurately suggest an insect whose clear wings are in motion. Clingers of the *Heptagenia* group inhabit waters that are not so fast as those of *Epeorus* or *Stenonema*. The adults lay their eggs in the faster sections of pools and reaches that also make good summer feeding lies for trout. Position yourself to cast to fish rising on the near side of the current and to make your presentation within an arc ranging from up and across to down and across. Add plenty of slack to compensate for the differential between fast and slow water. You can cast across the current if you position yourself on the near edge and throw an upstream reach or mend. When active egg laying has ceased, switch to a spent pattern as fish mop up the spent insects drifting downstream.

White Fly—Nymph

Family: Polymitarcydae   Size: 11-14 mm
Genus: *Ephoron*
Species: *leukon, album*
Active: Second week of August to second week of September

Just as we've grown accustomed to summer's easy pace we are awakened by a sudden explosion. The White Fly hatch fills the air with millions of frantic mayflies for an hour between dusk and dark. For the rest of their yearlong cycle, *Ephoron* nymphs dig into the silt of warm, slow, slightly alkaline rivers, rarely venturing into the open except to migrate, molt or hatch. They look like the burrowing Ephemeridae except for their size, and for their weak legs, unmarked abdomens and differences in the gills and tusks too small to see without magnification. Mature females have three short tails that are the same vanilla color as their bodies, which already reveal the yellow of the twin egg clusters within. Their heads and wings cases are an amber brown. Gray, doubled filamentous gills wave continuously. The male nymph is less yellow, and his outer two tails are longer. Based on the samples I have found, the genders appear to segregate in the weeks leading up to emergence. An hour before hatch time they leave the safety of their burrows and scurry furtively on the bottom. At the appointed hour, they bolt to the surface and escape quickly into the air.

(L to R): Light Cahill Nymph, White Fly Nymph
Hook Sizes 12

I think it is important to check the stream bottom for nymphs, particularly in unfamiliar territory, to be sure that I am in a good position for the hatch to come. With the White Fly, establishing gender can be especially valuable, because the females travel to meet the males, who are the first to hatch. Imitations of the furtive nymphs themselves are of questionable value. They only appear in the drift during the hatching period, and even then it is only for a few moments as they dart to the surface to hatch. While it seems pointless to do nothing while waiting for the hatch to begin, it is even sillier to sabotage the entire evening by spooking the water. If you're determined to try nymphing, rig up a second rod and keep your dry-fly stick ready for the hatch. Emergence takes place in slow water at any depth, but unless the water is unusually cool for late summer you can ignore the shallows and concentrate on the heads of the deeper pools where fish will be holding. You won't find *Ephoron* in cold tailwaters or spring fed streams. Start by drifting a weighted nymph along the bottom, but, as you halt the progress of your rod to raise the fly, strip the line in quickly and continuously in short intervals of a foot or so. *Ephoron* nymphs are good swimmers, and they are loathe to remain at rest for any length of time.

White Fly—Dun/Spinner

Family: Polymitarcydae   Size: 11-13 mm
Genus: *Ephoron*
Species: *leukon, album*
Nickname: White Drake, White Mayfly
Active: Second week of August to second week of September

If you've ever stood in a blizzard, you have an idea what it's like to experience a White Fly hatch. The first August hatches fill your pockets with mayflies, and they continue into mid September with decreasing density. The males hatch first, just after sundown, popping off the water here and there until they seem less to hatch than to materialize in a hurricane of small white blurs. They immediately secure a foothold on vegetation, porous rock or even your clothing to molt. The instant their wings are free the spinners fly off with shucks in tow, leading some to believe that they molt in mid-air. The male dun's feeble legs barely support him as he molts. Amazingly, the spinner's front legs are quite long and capable of grasping the female. Her legs are so weak that she must fly immediately upon emergence and never rest until she lays her eggs on the water. Females never molt, but fly directly into the male swarm. The two storms collide, and pandemonium ensues. For a half-hour the insects mate, lay eggs and die on the water by the thousands. The yellow abdomens of the female becomes translucent once she releases her twin, sausage-shaped egg clusters. Females have three short, weak tails, as distinct from the male's two long tails. Both have dark leading edges on their pale wings.

(L to R): Usual, White Spinner, Harold's White Fly, White Wulff Hook Sizes 12-14

Preparedness is the key to the White Fly hatch. It happens so quickly that there is little time to change flies, and much of it happens in the dark. Target the feeding fish while there is light enough to do so, and have your emerger pattern ready at the first appearance of the male duns. Fish begin working the surface as soon as the hatch begins, taking emergers as they briefly struggle with their shucks. As the emerger activity subsides, the male spinners begin to die and the females land on the water to extrude their eggs. Ovipositing females are in a constant flutter best imitated with a well-hackled or hairwinged pattern. Because they lay their eggs in the dark, profile is more important than color. The males quickly fall to the spentwing position. All of this activity is concentrated near the shore or in wadeable water, so don't worry about long casts into the darkness. Focus all your senses on the whereabouts of the fish. Given the short period in which White Flies must accomplish their task, their behavior is, understandably, frantic until, suddenly, it's all over. An hour after the first males emerged, the skies clear and the river is blanketed with spent spinners. Females often travel great distances before ejecting their eggs, with spinner falls occurring wherever they happen to land. As the current clears away the carnage, fewer naturals remain to compete with your imitation. Now you can switch to your spentwing pattern, and cast just ahead of the rises.

The Tiny Swimming Nymphs
Family: Baetidae   **Size: 4-9 mm**
Active: First week of March to last week of November

Frank Sawyer, the great English river keeper and amateur entomologist, believed that swimming mayfly larvae offered the greatest sport for devotees of subsurface presentations. Sawyer's observations reflect the fact that swimming nymphs, particularly the small swimmers of the family Baetidae, are plentiful during the daily periods of behavioral drift which peak in the hours just after sundown and just before sun up. These foragers have many haunts, including the stream bottom, underwater vegetation, among detritus or moving to and fro in backwaters, eddies and the calmer margins of the stream. I can usually find them by shaking underwater plants upstream of my drift net. Research has shown that they are the most prevalent component of behavioral drift. The Baetidae family is extremely large and includes both three-tailed genera, whose center tail is shorter than the outer two, and two-tailed genera. All of the species are quite small and have somewhat long, evenly tapered bodies, legs that tuck neatly under for swimming, modest, single plate-like gills and eyes mounted at the sides of their heads. The best populations are to be found on medium to large streams that support aquatic vegetation.

**(L to R): 1. Floating Baetis Nymph, 2. Sawyer Pheasant Tail,
3. Flashback Hare's Ear
Hook Sizes 16-22**

There is never a poor time of day or year for drifting small nymphs on rivers with healthy populations of Baetid mayflies. But the most productive times are the peak hours of behavioral drift and the hours leading up to a hatch. Circumstances dictate whether to fish patterns actively or in a dead drift. During periods of migration, the nymphs release themselves into the current to ride it, legs dangling, until they arrive at their destination. At hatch time they swim rapidly to the surface to emerge, but many are unable to penetrate the meniscus and hang there, resting, either to try again or to be devoured. Frank Sawyer designed his slender Pheasant Tail nymph without legs and used an induced take to suggest a swimming insect. Patterns incorporating legs, or at least a suggestion of legs, are better suited to dead drifts. For non-hatch periods, keep the nymph drifting passively along the bottom. In the hour or two before the hatch, when the larvae are active, fish the nymphs more like a wet fly, both on the bottom and through the mid-water. Whether you fish your pattern in a dead drift or by actively swimming it, it is always more productive to couple it with a larger nymph, if only to draw attention to your tiny Baetid imitation. Once fish begin rising, keep your fly motionless and just under the surface, either by dousing it with floatant or by adding it on the point with a dry imitation.

Tiny Blue-Winged Sulphurs, Rusts and Olives—Duns

Family: Baetidae   **Size: 4-9 mm**
Nicknames: Little Blue Duns, Little Quills
Active: Middle of April to last week of November

The chalkboard outside the Housatonic River Outfitters listed BWOs among the day's hatches in early November, so I strolled in and asked Harold McMillan just what insects were meant by this often-misleading nickname. The roll of the eyes above his polite smile betrayed his thoughts: "Spare me the Latin." "There are upwards of six different kinds on a given day," he replied aloud. "Just pick one." Of all the Mayfly families the Baetidae are the most taxonomically unsettled, with names shifting more than the sands of the Sahara. The term "Blue-Winged Olive" includes the autumn emerger formerly called *Pseudocloeon* as well as *Baetis*, *Diphetor*, *Acentrella*, *Acerpenna*, *Procloeon*, *Centroptilum* and others, with a range of colors to match the hues that line our rivers in autumn. What differentiates all these genera, besides color, are the number of intercalary wing veins, the absence or presence of a minute hind wing and other details too minuscule to be of real significance in designing an effective imitation. Habitats also vary. What the winged stages have in common are their small size, a graceful taper, their apparent lack of a hind wing, and twin tails that they wag from side to side like a happy dog. Capturing a sample is essential.

(L to R): BWO CDC Emerger, BWO Catskill, Double U
Hook Sizes 18-26

These diminutive flies emerge all year long, but rises to them during our chilly New England winters are negligible. In midsummer I've found tiny Sulphurs gathered under the fluorescent lights of a riverside shopping mall by the thousands. But primarily we fish them in early spring and fall as afternoon hatches, especially on chilly, overcast days when they emerge in the greatest numbers. They hatch in all kinds of water, but you'll find most fish taking them where the current is mild, not only because the rises are easier to see but because it is inefficient for fish to hold in fast water. When sipping small duns like the Olives a fish lingers near the surface to conserve energy. Watch for a rhythm in its feeding, and time your cast accordingly. Using a long and very fine tippet for your tiny fly and as short a line as possible, cast just upstream from the fish's nose. If it refuses your offering, but continues to feed, change to a smaller pattern and keep trying. Because they are so near the surface, fish don't get much of a look at the fly until it is almost on top of them, so they may drop back with the current to prolong their scrutiny. Members of this mayfly family lie low on the water, and a well-tied parachute or emerger presents an accurate silhouette. But in faster water, such as the head of a pool where the current enters, I've had better luck with a higher riding pattern.

Tiny Blue-Winged Sulphurs, Rusts and Olives—Spinners
Family: Baetidae   **Sizes: 4-9 mm**
Active: Middle of April to last week of November

Like most mayflies, members of this family molt to reveal a streamlined version of the dun, with a more saturated body color, elongated tails and clear, unmarked wings. Because Baetid hatches are so dependent upon weather conditions, and because spinners don't mate until at least a day after they hatch, a sparse hatch of duns is not necessarily a harbinger of a weak spinner fall. I've spent sunny fall afternoons waiting for a hatch that never came, but as the afternoon progressed the spinners began to gather, not so much in a cloud as in heavy traffic of males and females cruising up and down the edge of the stream. In less than an hour the traffic slows down as the impregnated females allow their eggs to ripen, but before long they return to the stream, now laden with tiny, and rather sticky, pale green spheres extruding from their abdomens. Many of these will find a spot in the stream where they can dislodge their eggs into the water. But some Baetids are unique among mayflies in one major respect. Adults of many species swim underwater to paste their eggs on the bottom of the stream, much like a caddis.

(L to R): 1. BWO Parachute, 2. BWO Sparkle Spinner, 3. Blue Dun Wet Sparkle
Hook Sizes 18-26

One prerequisite to successfully fishing Olive spinners is to determine whether the females are ovipositing on or below the surface. Unfortunately, neither an underwater insect, nor a spent spinner lying flush in the surface film, is easy to see. Olives are also subject to a variety of masking hatches of mayflies and caddises. Anglers must pay special attention to the character of the rises. The best indicator is the gentle but deliberate rising of fish feeding on apparently invisible insects. If egg-layers are abundant, but rising fish are few, they may be feeding below the surface. Make your presentation to surface feeders as you would during any spinner fall, with drag-free drifts on light tippets and with dry spent or egg-laying patterns delivered accurately into the feeding lane. Time your casts to coincide with the rhythm of the rises. Most underwater egg laying occurs in relatively calm, shallow water where actively fished wet flies are effective, but even subsurface egg-layers eventually end up in the drift. To cover all bases, drift two flies, with a wet fly on the point and a dry fly above it to double as a strike indicator. If fish consistently spurn your imitation in favor of the naturals, switch to a smaller pattern. As insect sizes diminish, matching color becomes secondary in importance to matching size and profile. It bears noting, however, that male and female spinners of a given species are usually different in appearance, and males of several genera fall upon the water after mating.

Trico—Dun

Family: Leptohyphidae   Size: 3-5 mm
Genus: *Tricorythodes*
Species: *stygiatus*, **others**
Nickname: Tiny White Winged Black Dun, Pale Olive Dun
Active: First week of July to second week of September

One of the great pleasures of summer's second half is the extended hatch of the tiny Tricos. Their well-regulated hatching and egg-laying sequence provides three to four hours of nearly continuous surface fishing between the emergence of the female duns at daybreak and the last sipping rises to the spinners. The males hatch before first light but will become important as spinners. The nymphs look like miniature Hendricksons with wing flaps extending over each side of their abdomens and are too tiny to be of any value. Region wide, the hatch continues for months, and as the weather cools the entire sequence moves to later in the morning. The female duns are extremely robust looking with a thick thorax and stubby abdomen, three flimsy, pale gray tails and a single pair of oversized, opalescent wings with a dark vein on the leading margin. They are not so much black as varying shades of olive to dark brown, with the abdomen appearing quite green against a darker thorax and light greenish gray legs. They hatch below the riffles and near the heads of slower pools.

(L to R): Trico CDC Emerger, Hairwing Trico, Wingless Trico Hook Sizes 22-28

They're called the White Winged Curse. The flies are tiny, and they often emerge on calm surfaces where a dragged hook looks like a water skier. Trout can be rising everywhere, taking everything but your fly. All it takes is a little skill and lots of patience. Most people wait for the spinners, but early risers who arrive in time to catch the hatching females find it equally rewarding. Tricos emerge both on the surface and just below it, where tiny, unweighted nymphs, emerger patterns or even drowned flies all produce well. Approach slowly and stealthily to well within your optimum casting range. Use a light line and a long tippet, 7X or finer, depending on the smoothness of the water, and be careful not to drop your line over the fish. Large trout must find a quiet spot near the surface to sip the tiny duns efficiently. This limits their visibility, and they are more easily spooked by physical disturbances than by anything else. As with any heavy hatch, expect many casts per hookup. Don't try to cover all of the rises, but concentrate on a single target with a series of short drifts. Think of it as a lottery, and eventually your number will come up. The best Trico populations that I've encountered are on water that doesn't overheat in summer and has a slightly silty bottom and a modest current capable of sustaining the crawling nymphs. These include sections of the Farmington, the Battenkill and the upper Connecticut.

Trico—Spinner

Family: Leptohyphidae   Size: 3-5 mm
Genus: *Tricorythodes*
Species: *stygiatus,* others
Nickname: Reverse Jenny Spinner
Active: First week of July to second week of September

I rarely encounter Trico mating swarms over open water. Instead, I find them along the calm edges of reaches or pools and at the downstream tips of midstream islands. At the outset the clouds consist entirely of males which gather even as the females are still hatching. The swarm persists while the females fly off to molt. It begins to dissipate only after fertilization, when the spent males fall to the water and the impregnated females once again fly off. Once the eggs have ripened the female spinners migrate upstream and congregate on the edges of the riffles to release their progeny. Each carries her impossibly large, forest green globe of sticky eggs at the tip of her collapsed, whitish abdomen, giving her body a hooked appearance. Freed of her burden, she appears much shorter than the spent males. The male, by contrast, is virtually black except for the light posterior edges of each abdominal segment. His white, translucent tails are about three times as long as his body. He holds his elongated forelegs straight out in front of him both in flight and in death. The spent spinners lie not so much in the surface film as on it.

(L to R): Foam Trico Spinner, Head to Head Spinner, Spent Trico Female
Hook Sizes 22-28

It's a good thing that Trico spinners fall over relatively flat water. Otherwise we'd never be able to see the subtle sipping rises of fish feeding on the tiny spent mayflies. The sips are louder than rises to the duns, yet still so gentle that the fish rarely break the surface. This preserves the option of making a downstream presentation with a slack-line cast, directly to the feeding lane, with little chance of dragging the fly or lining the fish, and close to our target, where it can't be ignored. Trout are never more selective than when there are many naturals on the water. You'll find the fish where there is just enough current to carry food to them. You will need two patterns to properly fish the Trico spinner fall, one each for the males and females. The males fall first, immediately after mating. Meanwhile keep one eye open for the females as their swarms at streamside begin to dwindle, for upon laying their eggs they provide a second wave of spent spinners. Tiny flies are difficult to see even in the mildest currents, and there's no overlooking the fact that Tricos are damnably small. Anything larger than a size 24 is too big. But there is a way around it. A Cluster Spinner has double the amount of white wing and can be tied on a larger hook for greater visibility. Currents gather the dying insects into clumps, and fish feeding on tiny insects favor these more efficient mouthfuls.

Caddisflies (Order Trichoptera)

If the Mayflies are the aristocracy of the fly-fisher's insects, then the Caddisflies are the working class. The drab, earthy Trichoptera cannot compete with the colorful Ephemeroptera for sheer majesty, but when it comes to satisfying the appetites of hungry trout it is the caddis that bear most of the load. There are over 1200 species in North America, double the number of mayflies, but once you learn to recognize the important genera, they are as easy to identify. I have found an abundance of caddis larvae on several New England streams where there were few signs of other insects. Especially here in New England, caddis larvae, pupae and adults make up the greater portion of insects in a trout's diet, yet many of us persist in trying to fish their imitations like mayflies. Many of the great Catskill fly fishermen failed to perceive that most caddis, even adults, are taken by trout below the surface. As a result, they became thoroughly frustrated during caddis hatches.

Caddis, also known as sedges, are of a more highly evolved order than either mayflies or stoneflies in that they undergo complete metamorphosis, passing through a transitional pupal stage between the larval and adult stages with a more profound morphological change. To most of us, there seem to be few differences between the adult caddis families beyond the obvious traits of size and color. But there is enormous variation in the larval stage, ranging from free-living forms to those which house themselves in elaborate cases made of silk and either rocks and sand, vegetable matter or both. As a result, caddis have adapted to a wide array of aquatic habitats.

Often referred to erroneously as worms, caddis larvae are clearly segmented, with six legs and a distinct head. Some segments have dorsal plates, and the last segment terminates in a pair of prolegs with hook shaped claws. They have neither wing pads nor tails, but do have gills in varying degrees. Adult caddis resemble moths, except that at rest they hold their two pair of wings down in the shape of an old-fashioned pup tent rather than flat. The outer wing is usually semi-opaque over a more translucent inner wing, so that they appear much lighter in flight than when their wings are folded. Instead of the scales found on moth wings, caddis wings are covered with minute, water-repellent hairs from which the order takes its name, which means Hairwings. They have a pair of antennae (roughly the same length as the body and wings in most families, with notable exceptions), short bodies relative to wing length, no tails, and a mouth. They can sustain themselves on liquids for as long as two months. They are further equipped with a pair of compound eyes and up to three light-sensitive ocelli.

As a rule, a fully mature caddis larva is 20-25% larger than an emerging pupa. With few exceptions, they have a one-year life cycle and pass through five instar stages before the transition to adulthood. For practical purposes, the larvae are divided into five types—the free-living caddises, the net spinners, the saddle case makers, the purse case makers and the tube case makers. They can also be classified by feeding types as shredders, scrapers, foragers or predators, and it is important to consider both case-building and feeding characteristics when determining which caddis genera are likely to thrive in a particular habitat. They range greatly in size, anywhere from a few millimeters to about 40mm at maturity. All of them spin a silk as the mortar for their case building, to trap food or to tether themselves to rocks. From time to time they appear in the drift, swimming with their heads down. Fortunately for the angler, behavioral drift of many caddis species takes place during the day.

Because of their distinctive and often fixed cases or retreats, Caddis larvae are not difficult to find or identify. Turn over any rock in a fertile stream and you will find samples of the predominant genera to imitate with nymphs. Stir up the stream bottom and you will release numerous worm-like larvae into the drift. These will include not only the net spinners and free livers but also those capable of abandoning their cases and building new ones. Portable case makers share an ability to breathe by forcing water through their cases and are more adaptable to low current and warmer habitats where levels of dissolved oxygen are reduced. They are also free to forage for food among detritus and sand. Caddis larvae with fixed retreats are much more dependent on the drift.

At maturity all caddis enter a pupal stage. They begin by sealing themselves inside their cases, sometimes with silk, sometimes with a small pebble. Unlike mayfly nymphs, which migrate to more favorable hatching environments, the caddis remain in or near their larval habitats. Even the free-living varieties build crude retreats and remain there until metamorphosis is complete, much like a moth or butterfly in its cocoon. Hatching is a two-stage process. First, the pupae cut their way free from their retreats. At this stage they are known as pharate adults, fully formed but still sealed in a membranous pupal skin with their wings compressed to 1/3 of their body length. There is a momentary pause as this skin inflates with gases that will buoy them to the surface, and fish are on the

prowl for them at this vulnerable period. Even at this stage, the pupae are capable of lightning quick movement by using their middle pair of legs in a powerful oar-like motion, both in the water and on the surface.

Their ascent is rapid, and although fish can and do chase them it is far more efficient for them to wait until the caddis have reached the surface. The pharate adults must break through the meniscus and arch themselves so that a relatively brittle section of the skin splits open to allow them to climb out onto the top of the water, completely dry. Some, like the Grannoms, accomplish this feat very quickly but, for most, this final emergence takes several minutes, during which they are defenseless. Once free, their escape, from fish at any rate, is all but assured. Some may run across the water, others may flop and hop, but only rarely do they ride placidly in the current in the manner of mayflies. Not all caddis emerge on the surface. Some pupae rise to the meniscus, break through and then run across it to the streamside, still encased in their pupal skins. Others crawl along the bottom to reach the banks. Climbing out onto the rocks, they extract themselves from their wetsuits and

shake out their wings. Such emergences are invisible to the untrained human eye, but they rarely escape the notice of the fish.

Because Caddis adults emerge near their larval habitat, they remain there to lay eggs as well. Their frenzied courting flights and dances are wilder than teenagers on prom night, but actual mating occurs in more private streamside surroundings. Some females lay their eggs in damp streambeds or in the leaves of overhanging trees, but the majority return to the water to lay their eggs in a variety of ways. Eggs are extruded either as a single, ball-shaped mass or as a string of smaller clusters. Some species lay their eggs on the surface. Others flit across the water, or slam themselves down upon it and dap their eggs as they go, and still others crawl or dive, then swim down to the stream bottom to oviposit on the rocks. These either swim back to the surface or release themselves into the drift. For trout, this is the last great opportunity to feed on adult caddis. Knowing the egg-laying habits of each genus is important in determining how to present your fly. Unlike mayflies, most caddis die away from the stream, but female mortality during egg laying can be significant. Those that survive will mate and oviposit several times before expiring.

Most adult Caddis activity, including emergence, egg laying and larval drifting, takes place in the subdued light of morning and evening. Many of the species that are important to anglers have attained that status because they hatch and oviposit during daylight hours in the coolness of spring and autumn. Other hot weather emergers are active at only at night. The Caddis genera listed on the following pages are a sampling of the most important for New England fishing. Adult measurements are from head to wingtip.

American Grannom—Larva

Family: Brachycentridae   Size: 8-14 mm
Genus: *Brachycentrus*
Nicknames: Shadfly, Little Black Caddis, Olive Dun Caddis
Active: Third week of March to last week of May

Grannoms are among the most geographically widespread caddisflies. Because of its daytime hatches, long emergent drifts and surface egg laying, *Brachycentrus* is also one of the most important genera for fly-fishers. They emerge, sometimes in incredible density, on spring afternoons, and lay their eggs in the early evenings. Their larval cases are singular and easily recognized. The square cross-section constructed of tiny sticks or plant fibers resembles a tapered chimney. This dynamic design enables them to inhabit the riffles of cool, swift rivers and streams. Removed from their casings, the bright green larvae have no apparent gills and lack the dorsal or lateral humps on the first abdominal segment that characterize all other case builders. These are scrapers, who attach the lips of their cases to rocks and harvest nearby algae. At other times they protrude far enough to sift both plant and insect food particles from the drift with their legs, retreating in a flash at any sign of danger. A peculiar and, for the angler, useful trait of the Grannom larva is its ability to migrate along the stream bottom by using its fine white silk as a rappelling rope. It shares this ability with several of the non-cased varieties of caddis larvae.

Left to Right: 1. Herl Cased Caddis, 2. Dark Cased Caddis, 3. Fur Peeping Caddis
Hook Sizes 12-14

Owing to their habit of dangling into the current, *Brachycentrus* are among the few cased caddis larvae upon which trout can dine without having to pick them off the rocks. Trout have little trouble digesting the larva and simply excreting the cases. As they mature in the fall and as other food sources grow scarce, cased caddis make up an increasingly large part of a trout's diet. Before fishing a larval pattern, examine one of the cases to be sure that it is neither sealed nor empty. Then use Gary LaFontaine's trick of whitening the first six inches of your tippet to suggest the Grannom's silk tether. In swifter water where trout are holding their ground, dead drift your fly through, and well past, the best holding lies. Keep at it until you have covered the entire width of the feeding lane with drifts separated by no more than six inches while watching for even the slightest hesitation in your line. If you can pinpoint a fish or its feeding lie, attach a piece of split shot a few inches above the whitened portion of your tippet, heavy enough to rest on a rock while your unweighted nymph hangs and undulates with the current. Then lift your rod just slightly to hop the weight downstream toward your target a rock or two at a time. The periodic movement not only duplicates the migration of the cased larva but provides enough motion to arrest the attention of the fish.

American Grannom—Pupa

Family: Brachycentridae   Size: 7-12 mm
Genus: *Brachycentrus*
Nicknames: Shadfly, Little Black Caddis, Olive Dun Caddis
Active: First week of May to the last week of May

I've had the rare good fortune to have a *Brachycentrus* pupa hatch in my photography tank. It swam about, using its fringed middle pair of legs in a breaststroke, while I prepared my light. Suddenly, I noticed that it was floating just under the surface. Within seconds, it had slipped from its thin skin. Quickly shaking out its wings, it flew away. Too stunned to record either the pupa or the adult on film, I did notice that the visual effect of gases trapped under the sheath was less pronounced than I'd expected, and that in many respects the body of the pupa and of the adult appeared the same. The pupae of *B. americanus* have pale green bodies with brown heads and wings. Those of *B. lateralis* are olive bodied, with a tan lateral stripe, and a nearly black head and wings. The trailing shuck is wispy, but certainly noticeable. In the wild the pupa, or pharate adult, cuts its way out of its casing and lingers briefly to generate enough gas to aid its rapid swim to the surface. Once there, the struggle to shed its sheath is somewhat hampered by the roughness of the current, increasing its chances of being eaten.

(L to R): Deep Sparkle Pupa, Grouse and Flash, Emergent Sparkle Pupa
Hook Sizes 14-18

The Deep Sparkle Pupa and the Emergent Sparkle Pupa are two patterns developed by Gary LaFontaine, based on his underwater studies of this life stage. According to his observations, caddis pupae are all structurally similar and differ only in size and color, and one need only vary those two properties to match the hatching species. It's an oversimplification, but his two patterns are ideally suited to the Grannoms. The Deep Pupa represents the pharate adult, newly freed from its casing, and is designed to be fished on the bottom and through the midwater. The Emergent imitates the adult escaping from its pupal sheath on the surface. In Vermont, Nick Yardley developed the Grouse and Flash for his home river, the Winooski, but has also found it effective on the waters of the American west and in his native Yorkshire, where soft-hackle flies feel right at home. It's use of Krystal Flash as an outer skin follows the same principle as the LaFontaine patterns, but it is designed to cover both stages of the pupal ascent. Using a dead-drift nymphing technique, guide the imitation to a point just upstream of the feeding fish, then allow it to rise to the surface. Because pupae are such speedy swimmers, movement against the current appears quite natural. If the fish are taking at or near the surface, keep your fly there in a dead drift. Grannom pupae cannot swim while slipping out of the pupal membrane.

American Grannom—Adult

Family: Brachycentridae;   Size: 8-13 mm
Genus: *Brachycentrus*
Nicknames: Shadfly, Little Black Caddis, Olive Dun Caddis
Active: First week of May to the last week of May

Several species of *Brachycentrus* provide the first major caddis hatches of the season. New England has both tan and black varieties of Grannom adults. What appears tan in flight is actually a brown, semi-translucent wing over a thinner underwing, a pale green abdomen and ginger head, thorax and legs. The smaller, darker species have nearly black wings with wavy bronze highlights over a green to olive body with a pale lateral stripe. Ovipositing females carry a huge round egg ball, as green as a shamrock. They bounce across the water just before sunset and slam themselves down to dislodge their eggs, without penetrating the surface, and moving in an upstream direction. On the streamside, others crawl below the surface to oviposit. Hatches move gradually upstream each day. In contrast to just about all other caddisflies, adult Grannoms seem to be in no hurry to leave the water. Hatches begin each day in early to mid-afternoon, occasionally overlapping with ovipositing activities of females hatched in prior days. Most of the egg-laying flights occur in the early evening and provide the better opportunity for dry-fly fishing. Their rather violent egg-laying technique leads to a high mortality rate, and the surface becomes littered with spent females.

(L to R): Henryville Special, Quad Wing Spent Caddis, Dette Caddis
Hook Sizes 14-18

When caddis are in the air the first step in selecting the right pattern is always to note whether they are newly hatched adults or egg-layers. One trick is to fish a surface egg-layer such as a Henryville or Dette Caddis with an unweighted pupal imitation. Simple observation will tell you the same thing, for if the winged adults are a uniform size and are dropping heavily onto the surface, they are egg-laying adult females. For a true hatch the best bet is always a pupal imitation, but the hesitance of these caddis to take flight allows you to indulge in an alternately twitched and drifted adult pattern. When egg laying is the game, switch to a downstream presentation or use a curve cast or an upstream mend to keep your pattern facing upstream as you skitter it along the surface. Allow the fly to rest only briefly before you move it. This is also a good time to try anchoring your line with a wet fly, such as a diving caddis, and adding a dry pattern tied above it as a dropper. With your rod held high, let your dropper flutter on the surface. The pocketwater habitat of *Brachycentrus* is ideally suited to this method. Only when spent caddis blanket the surface should you attempt anything like a dead drift. The fish will announce by their more casual rises when it is time to switch to a spent-wing pattern.

Saddle Case Maker—Larva

Family: Glossosomatidae   **Size: 6-9 mm**
Genus: *Glossosoma*
Active: First week of May to first week of September

At first glance, the unique cases of *Glossosoma* larvae, known as saddle cases, resemble those of several fall-hatching pebble case builders. These are often found together in cool, turbulent streams where tiny bits of sand and gravel are available for the construction of their houses. What separates the saddle cases is that they are constructed of the most wafer-like pebbles and are dome-shaped, rather than cylindrical. If you pick them up, you will see the larvae poking out the bottom at each end. You'll have to pry them off with your thumbnail, for they adhere as tightly to the stones as barnacles to a ship's hull. This keeps the larvae safe from foraging predators, even as they crawl over the exposed upper surfaces of rocks to graze on fine food particles. However, as they out-grow their domed houses they must abandon them to construct new ones. At such times the creamy white to smoky pink larvae are available in the drift. Their favored habitat is cool running mountain streams but I've also found domed larvae and hatching adults during the spring on larger rivers that run warm in the heat of summer.

**(L to R): USD Cream Caddis Larva, Brassie, Pink Caddis
Hook Sizes 16-20**

As long as *Glossosoma* larvae remain in their cases, firmly glued to the rocks, they are relatively free from predation, but nature has provided the angler with a window of opportunity to angle for trout as they feed on these larvae. As if by pre-arrangement, *Glossosoma* larvae engage in a coordinated migration during which, having outgrown their shelters, they abandon them to build new ones. This collective resettlement occurs most often during major growth periods in the summer and fall. Lacking advance notice, we can only take advantage of this opportunity by habitually taking drift samples to discover the presence of the uncased larvae. When their numbers are high, trout feed on them selectively. Their synchronicity is also confined to a single brood, so it is imperative that you match the species for size as well as color. The chubby larvae cannot swim, and once adrift they are at the mercy of the currents until they regain their footing. Drift your larval imitation along the bottom with weight on the leader but none whatsoever on the fly. During high-density migrations you can employ two identical imitations in tandem. But if the larvae are a small percentage of the total drift, then a cast of two distinct patterns takes better advantage of opportunistic feeding, especially if the larger fly is weighted and allows the smaller caddis larva to drift free.

Saddle Case Maker—Pupa

Family: Glossosomatidae **Size: 5-8 mm**
Genus: *Glossosoma*
Nickname: Little Short Horned Sedge
Active: First week of May to first week of September

Shortly before pupation, the *Glossosoma* larva builds its final structure. This differs slightly from the larval saddle in that the dome-shaped pupal case is open on the underside, and the pupa itself is encased in a sheath that resembles a gelatin pharmaceutical capsule. The emergence behavior of *Glossosoma* played out dramatically when I first attempted to photograph a pupa. Two weeks after discovering a cluster of newly pupating saddle makers I returned to collect a pharate adult. Carefully removing my specimen from its protective capsule, I placed it in my photography tank. Air bubbles threatened to mar my picture, so I removed the pupa from the water. Suddenly the poor creature became frantic, and when I replaced it in the tank it ricocheted across the surface and from edge to edge, searching for the stream bank. As soon as I provided a rock for it to climb upon it crawled out and became calm. I had only a few minutes to observe that its head and wing cases were dark brown, its abdomen shaded from a ventral pale yellow to a dorsal pink, and its legs and antennae a translucent brown. Then it pulled free from its pupal suit and shook its wings.

(L to R): Tan Caddis Emerger, Foam Caddis Emerger, Ginger Partridge SLF
Hook Sizes 18-22

I learned to fish *Glossosoma* pupae by watching the Church Pool regulars during the summer hatch of *Dolophilodes distinctus* on the Farmington River. Although they are of a different family, *Dolophilodes* is similar to the *Glossosoma* both in size and in its emergence behavior. It swims to the surface and then runs, still in its pupal skin, to the streamside to crawl out onto the rocks. There the similarity ends. Early in the hatch, fish will take pupae along the bottom in pockets and deep riffles and as they rise to the surface, but once they begin surface feeding a dead-drifted imitation produces no response whatsoever. An active twitch, however, not only calls attention to the fly but successfully imitates the surface sprint of the natural. Look for rising fish near the heads of pools and along the quieter margins downstream of the riffles. Keeping a short line, cast both upstream and across the feeding lane of a rising fish. Then, by raising your rod, stripping line or both, drag the fly across the surface. Add a side-to-side wiggle of your rod tip to make the motion even more lifelike. Keep a sharp eye on the fly, because rises to running pupae are not nearly as splashy as those to surface emergers. If you continue dragging the fly during the take, you are liable to pull it right out of the fish's mouth.

Saddle Case Maker—Adult

Family: Glossosomatidae   Size: 6-10 mm
Genus: *Glossosoma*
Nickname: Little Short Horned Sedge
Active: First week of May to first week of September

Among the very first caddis adults that I see in the young season are the *Glossosoma* as they crawl or flutter at the edge of the stream. They coincide with the emergence of the Grannoms and of the Hendrickson mayflies. What sets them apart is that they will continue hatching throughout the season, with an early peak in May on warmer rivers and a second wave from August through September, especially on colder mountain streams. Their wings are very much like the darker species of *Brachycentrus* in their teardrop profile, but longer and less rounded, and run from brown to almost black with a subtle patterning of lighter shades. They are also slightly smaller than most *Brachycentrus* species, but just as energetic when in motion. Their bodies are yellow to tan, and their legs and antennae are brown. In spring the hatches begin in the late morning. You'll first notice them not in the air but crawling or basking in the sun on streamside rocks. As the season progresses emergence moves to later in the day, even to after dark. To lay their eggs, females dive under the water and paste them to the rocks before floating or swimming back to the surface.

**(L to R): Diving Caddis, Deer Hair Caddis, Black Caddis
Hook Sizes 18-20**

If you see *Glossosoma* milling about on the rocks while fish are surface feeding it is probable that a hatch is still in progress. At this stage, fish are feeding exclusively on pupae. But caddis that are in the air and tapping the surface are laying eggs. Few caddis are as energetic or swim more capably than *Glossosoma*. Dead-drift presentations during egg-laying flights are fruitless, for these hyperactive creatures are never still until they die on or off the water. To imitate them on the surface, use an active retrieve like the sudden inch or the alternate twitch and drift. Trout and salmon react to moving insects with startling speed. Up-and-across presentations draw the most strikes, but require so much arm motion to retrieve with the current that it is nearly impossible to set the hook. A direct downstream presentation carries with it the danger of pulling the hook away from the fish unless you can pinpoint the rises and anticipate the strike. The most effective method is to cast across the current and slightly downstream a few inches beyond a rising fish so that the first twitch brings the fly directly into its window. Many strikes come when we least expect them, compelling us to guard against overzealous movements of the fly. Some will come beneath the surface, either as you retrieve your dry fly or as the result of a wet-fly presentation. Study the rise forms to determine the level at which fish are feeding.

Common Net Spinners—Larvae

Family: Hydropsychidae   Size: 8-14 mm
Genera: *Hydropsyche, Ceratopsyche, Cheumatopsyche*
Active: All year long

It is impossible to overstate the importance of the netspinning Hydropsychidae as a fish food and to the fly-fisher. By virtue of their widespread distribution, availability to trout and season-long emergence, they are by far the most important of northeastern caddisflies. Gary LaFontaine calls them overall the most important trout stream insect of any type in North America. The most striking features of the larvae are their generously branched gills, curved bodies ending in hair-like filaments and the dark dorsal plates covering all three thoracic segments. Their bodies range from bright green through olive to brown. These are the common netspinners, who seine the drift for food particles, both plant and animal, with their tiny silken traps, built on the surfaces and in the crevices of stones. The adjacent shelters, usually an extension of the nets, constructed of silk and camouflaged with sand, pebbles and leaf litter, are readily apparent. If disturbed, the larvae can become dislodged from their retreats and forced to seek or construct new ones. Their habitat is widespread, but they are most plentiful in tailwaters where the drift contains a high density of food particles. At any given time, you might find a half-dozen species in the same riffle.

(L to R): Simple Caddis Larva, Glass Bead Caddis Larva, Netspinner Larva
Hook Sizes 12-18

Netspinners need running water, not only for its higher oxygen content but to bring them their food. Pick up a stone in a riffle or pocketwater that is densely populated with these caddis worms and you'll find it encrusted with their silk-mortared refuges. The characteristic nets will collapse, but you'll find the larvae in the remaining debris. Examine the prevailing body colors closely. Given the large number of possible species, care is needed in selecting your fly. Bound to one location by their food-gathering apparatus, netspinning caddis have little need of migration except to relieve overcrowding, when they become part of the behavioral drift. Fish must either pick them off the rocks, find them dangling at the end of their tether or catch them when they are riding the currents. When completely adrift they hang head down in order to grasp the next available foothold. For this reason, many patterns are tied inverted. Like the cased *Brachycentrus*, common netspinner larvae are equipped to move downstream from stone to stone by means of their fine, white silk. The nymphing method used with Grannoms of adding split shot above a whitened tippet also works with the net spinners. Even during peak migration you should keep your fly close to the bottom with weight, an upstream cast or both, and keep a drag-free dead drift. Fish feeding on netspinners may hold just below a riffle, but they also venture into the riffle itself, especially in low light.

Common Net Spinners—Pupae

Family: Hydropsychidae   **Size: 8-13 mm**
Genera: *Hydropsyche, Ceratopsyche, Cheumatopsyche*
Active: First week of May to last week of September

The pupal case of a netspinner is a rudimentary affair, little more than
an oblong pile of sticky gravel on the surface of a rock. If you remove it
with a knife, the developing pupa is revealed on the underside. The
spotted *Hydropsyche* and the plainer, tan-winged *Ceratopsyche* appear
very similar in the pupal stage with their cinnamon-colored abdomens
and ginger legs and antennae. They also share the same habitat and
emerge at the same time. I've seen no evidence that trout distinguish
between one and the other. Like most current-loving caddis, netspinners
pupate in their larval habitat. But the emergent pupae commonly drift
near the stream bottom for long distances before rising to the surface,
and they can take quite a long time to struggle free from the pupal skin.
By the time they take flight, they have migrated downstream and into
the open currents of mid stream, even into slower pools. Consequently,
the hatch is spread out over the course of the stream and the length of
the day, and fish are liable to feed on them at any time. Later in the
season, in warmer rivers, you'll find the smaller, olive-bodied pupae of
Cheumatopsyche, the Little Sister Sedge, another important genus
of this family.

(L to R): Yellow Caddis Emerger, Teardrop Emergent Pupa, Grouse and Flash
Hook Sizes 12-16

Because this hatch is both physically and temporally scattered it can be especially difficult to guess whether the fish are feeding on emerging pupae or on diving and resurfacing egg-layers. Adults flopping on the surface indicate that egg laying is in progress, but both activities routinely occur at the same time. One answer to this dilemma is a two-fly rig. When fish break the surface with telltale splashy rises, begin with a buoyant dry-fly pattern to which is tied a surface emerging pupa. If the fish are bulging just beneath the surface, substitute a wet fly for the adult and either a soft hackle or Teardrop Pupa for the emerger. In either case, the fish will solve your dilemma by choosing between the two flies. You can then eliminate the inappropriate fly or continue to fish two flies to match the colors of multiple species (or genera) that often hatch simultaneously. Pay particular attention to eddies and other places where flotsam collects, for the slowly emerging pupa collect there as well. If adults are flying over the water but there is no surface activity, fish your soft hackle or deep pupa down along the bottom. Allow for the longest drag-free drift that you can manage, because the naturals travel a great distance before surfacing, and there is no need for the fish to chase them. Include a lift at the end of each presentation, particularly just ahead of places where you think fish might be holding.

Cinnamon/Spotted Caddises—Adults

Family: Hydropsychidae   Size: 8-13 mm
Genera: *Hydropsyche, Ceratopsyche*
Active: First week of May to last week of September

I live near the Connecticut River where, within a five-mile stretch, it joins three other medium-sized Vermont and New Hampshire rivers. From May to September, there is not a single night when I cannot find Spotted or Cinnamon caddis secreted in the foliage along the riverbanks or swarming under the lights at the local mall. Peak hatches are from early May to late July, but they continue intermittently throughout the season. Cool weather sees day-long, sporadic hatching activity, but as the weather heats up emergence is delayed until evening or the cool hours before sunup. Some early season adults have tan to light brown bodies, richly spotted gray to brown wings and cinnamon to light brown legs and banded antennae. As the season progresses the grayish brown and cinnamon-colored bodies and plainer tan to brown wings become more prevalent. The females' return to the stream for egg laying is well coordinated. They flop on the surface or swim to the bottom, where they paste a strings of eggs on just about anything solid before releasing their grip to float back to the surface. There they either remain spent and inert or gather strength to return to the bushes to await another episode of egg laying.

(L to R): Hare's Ear Caddis, AuSable Caddis, Cinnamon Caddis Hook Sizes 14-16

Wherever and whenever caddis are hatching, Spotted and Cinnamon caddis are likely to be part of the mix. Wherever you fish east of the Hudson, wet and dry adult imitations of these ubiquitous caddis should be part of your fly assortment. Some good fish come when I least expect them, and I'm convinced it is because of the egg-laying habits of Spotted and Cinnamon sedges. When fishing wet flies, I often use a water haul to flick my fly back upstream. The fly hangs briefly in the current while I raise my rod and pivot my upper body. As I start to bring the rod forward, the sudden movement triggers a strike. Fish take it as a diving caddis. When a female swims under water to lay her eggs she carries along a supply of oxygen trapped by the tiny hairs on her wings. Well-designed imitations of caddis adults make use of this phenomenon. Jack Pangburn's Cinnamon Caddis uses shiny raffia wings to suggest these air bubbles, while the rough body of the Hare's Ear Caddis actually carries the bubbles with it in the manner of the natural. It also skates well, so you can begin with an active surface presentation before dragging your fly under. The most vulnerable moment for the subsurface egg-laying adult comes as she releases herself into the current. Match this with a subsurface dead drift terminated with a Leisenring lift. If necessary, add weight to your leader to bring the fly down to the subsurface rocks.

Little Sister Caddis—Adult

Family: Hydropsychidae   Size: 6-9 mm
Genus: *Cheumatopsyche*
Nickname: Little Olive Sedge
Active: First week of July to third week of September

Everything I've read about the Little Sisters touts them as second in importance only to the Cinnamon and Spotted caddises. That may be true west of the Hudson, or even on some of the larger, warmer, southern New England rivers, but I haven't found them in anything approaching the numbers of the two larger genera, and certainly not in any quantity before the first of July when the streams really heat up. Like their bigger cousins, they inhabit most streams that support trout populations but display a particular fondness for the riffles of warm tailwaters. They are more populous in larger order streams. The Little Sisters are annoyingly small and dark, but they cannot be ignored when fish won't take anything else. Perhaps it is their bright green to olive brown bodies that make them so attractive. They have the sleek, flat-ended wing shape characteristic of larger Hydropsychidae, but their wings are dark brown to deep chocolate with a few stray tan to whitish spots, especially on the top edge. Their legs are ginger brown. As summer rushes toward autumn, their wings become noticeably lighter, and emergence shifts from mornings and evenings to midday.

(L to R): Solomon Caddis B, Spent Polywing Caddis, Olive Hare's Ear Caddis
Hook Sizes 18-20

The methods employed in fishing the hatches of the Little Sister caddis are the same as those used with the Spotted and Cinnamon caddises with a few notable exceptions. The first, and the most obvious, is size, closely followed by color. During the earliest appearances of the Little Sisters there is likely to be considerable overlap with the larger members of the family, and it is in the angler's best interest to determine which genera are receiving the selective attentions of the fish. The third major difference is habitat, for although the larger caddises are fairly ubiquitous, the Little Sisters are found mainly on big water where the nutrient levels are sufficient to support them. Bring a big stick to deliver your fly, but plan on light tippets to camouflage the tiny imitations and plenty of slack for the long drifts needed when fishing pupal imitations. Peak hatches can develop either late in the evening or early in the morning with sporadic emergences any time in between, thereby doubling the likelihood of egg-laying flights occurring at the same time. Little Sisters can either sprawl on the surface or dive below to deposit their eggs. Perhaps because of their diminutive size, they are subject to high rates of mortality during and after the egg-laying process, and one should be prepared with a spentwing pattern much as one would during a mayfly spinner fall. Once again, trout may key on any one of these stages, from active swimmers to females released into the current to spent caddis lying in the surface film.

Dark Blue Sedge—Larva

Family: Odontoceridae   **Size: 12-15 mm**
Genus: *Psilotreta*
Species: *labida, frontalis*
Active: First week of October to last week of June

Among the first caddisflies described in American fly fishing entomologies is the Dark Blue Sedge. Its hatches on the rivers of the Catskills are legendary, but it is also important east of the Hudson on a more modest scale. All of my specimens have come from small brooks and the upper reaches of medium-sized streams, but the two Eastern species, which differ only slightly, are reported to be equally at home on larger, free-flowing rivers. The worms themselves bear a superficial resemblance to *Brachycentrus*, especially in the bright, almost iridescent green color, and in fact, they are found in many of the same habitats. But the gently arched cases are made of fine, smooth, dark stones and with a cylindrical cross section that renders them extremely crush resistant. The larvae have dorsal and lateral humps on the first abdominal segments. They remain unattached to stones, but roam freely across them, especially on the sides protected from the current, searching through silt and debris for bits of plant and animal matter. This habit leaves them exposed and easy to spot, but they are quite shy, and if threatened will drop into crevices or into the current.

(L to R): Sparkle Yarn Caddis, Fur Peeping Caddis, Herl Cased Caddis
Hook Sizes 10-14

They have many unusual traits. One is that they spend much of their lives burrowed into the sand and gravel of the substrate. I used to accept the prevailing gospel that they are rarely available as fish food. But I would see them in the early spring, months before their scheduled emergence, roaming over the rocks, just outside the main current. Once in late October, on the final day of Vermont's season, their populations were conspicuous, each solitary larva grazing on its own boulder, in exactly the same places where I saw them in the spring. That they were almost of mature size was evidence of their two-year life cycle. I have no direct evidence that fish were eating them, but it became clear that, like many cased caddis, *Psilotreta* larvae are among the foods available to fish during the relative famine between late autumn and early spring. In summer they vanish into the substrate. Many patterns designed for Grannom larvae serve equally well as *Psilotreta* imitations, and are doubly effective for their shared habitats. Even so, it is always wise to fish them in tandem with a much larger or much smaller nymph, and with enough weight incorporated into the fly or added to the leader to keep the flies near the bottom. This is especially true when only *Psilotreta* larvae are present, as they are apt to be foraging on the edges of deeper reaches and pools than one would normally expect to find Grannom larvae.

Dark Blue Sedge—Pupa

Family: Odontoceridae   **Size: 13-16 mm**
Genus: *Psilotreta*
Species: *labida, frontalis*
Active: First week of June to last week of June

Yet another unusual trait of the genus *Psilotreta* is the behavior of its species just before, and upon completion of, pupation. In middle to late May, following two years of solitary behavior, the larvae stage a mass migration towards selected large or small rocks, like the faithful to their chosen temples, and attach themselves securely to the undersides, sometimes stacked several layers thick. The water in these areas is, if anything, a bit faster and shallower than the larval habitat. Concentrations of pupae will be dense in one section of the stream but nonexistent just around the bend. Locating these pupae is the first step in preparing to fish the hatch. Examine them carefully, even to the point of inspecting the larvae inside. Each larva seals its tube with a single pebble. Inside, the bright chartreuse worms transform into dark, gray green pupae with charcoal gray wing cases and long antennae. Because of their unusual concentration and the synchronicity of their emergence, they issue forth in a steady stream from isolated spots within the pool or reach. As the hatch progresses, fish also become concentrated as they line up just downstream of these hot spots.

(L to R): Crow's Nest Soft Hackle, Emergent Sparkle Pupa, Deep Sparkle Pupa
Hook Sizes 10-12

Even more than other early season caddisflies, Dark Blues hatch in an eruption. The first sign of a hatch is the sudden appearance of the dark flies in the air as both large females and smaller males seek shelter without touching down on the water. Center stage of the drama is still well under the surface where the pharate adults are cutting their way out of their cases. While they generate the gases that elevate them to the surface, the current conveys them to run the gauntlet of fish gathered downstream. If I know the water, or read it correctly, I'll cast my pupal pattern up and across so that it sinks to the bottom and then rises at the end of a dead drift. Working my way downstream, I cover each possible feeding lie. Most hookups occur just as the fly begins to rise, or as it reaches the surface. But throughout the drift I watch the line, not the surface or the fly. Occasionally I'll see it suddenly move and lift my rod to the overwhelming satisfaction of finding a fish attached. As the hatch peaks, the action moves to the surface and the number of rises increases. The temptation to switch to an adult pattern grows unbearable, but resist it. Fish have little chance of catching the adult once it's out of the shuck, but they will pursue an emerger fished in or just under the meniscus in a drag-free dead drift.

Dark Blue Sedge—Adult

Family: Odontoceridae **Size: 13-16 mm**
Genus: *Psilotreta*
Species: *labida, frontalis*
Active: First week of June to last week of June

No single caddis species has done more to provoke thoughtful fly designers into action than the Dark Blue Sedge. Preston Jennings, Art Flick, Leonard Wright and Gary LaFontaine all wrote of their frustrations with *Psilotreta*, which for Wright and LaFontaine formed the basis of a life-long preoccupation with caddis imitations and techniques for presenting them. Its hatches are fairly predictable, often dense, but not widespread. It arrives in the early evening when we do most of our fishing, and it distracts fish away from the more celebrated, concurrent hatches of the Green Drake and the March Brown. It will drive you mad if you persist in trying to entice a fish during a hatch with anything like an adult surface pattern. I've never witnessed the blizzard hatches of legend, but on some June nights they are unquestionably the predominant insect over the water. No other large eastern caddis is nearly as dark. They range from a satiny black to a dark smoky gray, depending on the species, with either black or brown legs, respectively. The antennae are nearly black, and are half again as long as the body and wings. The abdomen is a dark but pasty green gray.

(L to R): Solomon Caddis D, Dancing Caddis, Black Deer Hair Caddis

Hook Sizes 12-16

As with any adult caddis, the initial step is to decide whether the Dark Blues are hatching or laying eggs. Trout prefer pupae during emergence. The females return in the evening to oviposit by repeatedly skimming the surface to drag the egg mass off the tips of their abdomens. Your presentation should be just as noisy. Leonard Wright Jr. developed the Fluttering Caddis for fishing the Dark Blue Sedge with an active retrieve he called the sudden inch. He threw an upstream curve cast across the stream and added a short upward twitch of the rod just after the fly touched down, causing the fly to hop upstream. He then let it continue its drift into the jaws of a goaded trout (the Solomon Caddis substitutes a deer-hair wing where Wright used spade hackle or mink guard hairs). Gary LaFontaine's Dancing Caddis has similar properties with the advantage of an upside down hook, and it skates beautifully. If you can't manage a curve cast, try a downstream slack cast, then feed line through the guides for the drift. Don't use too fine a tippet, as you will be directly upstream of the fish. Strike firmly but gently. The wet-fly dapping method also imitates the floppy behavior of *Psilotreta*. Many females become too exhausted to fly off after ovipositing, but trout much prefer active egg-layers to spent females.

Green Caddis—Larva

Family: Rhyacophilidae   Size: 11-18 mm
Genus: *Rhyacophila*
Nickname: Green Sedge, Rock Worm
Active: All year long

If the Michelin Man had a personal caddis larva, it would be *Rhyacophila*. These turquoise to bright green or olive worms have exaggerated body segments that expand and contract as they move. Like an inchworm, the larva uses its anal claws to grasp at one position while the front end reaches for the next as it roams among the stones in search of food. Some species have dark rings to each segment. All have a single dorsal plate on the prothorax and on the posterior abdominal segment. A mixture of species may be present in a single habitat. They are predatory, and each species has distinct dietary preferences. I've found them dining on the contents of pupal casings. Because they build no shelters until pupation, they are defenseless against fish and other predators. *Rhyacophila* are an important component of behavioral drift, at dawn and at dusk, and are a major underwater food source in early spring. Their gill structures are simple and minuscule, restricting them to fast, cool riffles and pocket waters. They are especially abundant in tailwaters that are rich in food particles and oxygen. Because the hatches are sporadic and usually mixed with other similar adults, the larvae are more important than any other stage.

(L to R): Rhyacophila Larva, Glass Bead Caddis Larva, Simple Caddis Larva
Hook Sizes 8-16

On an early June trip to the Ausable River, I raked up the substrate ahead of my drift net to find little else besides a quantity of Green Rock Worms. The river was getting too warm, and it appeared that many of the major caddis and mayfly species had either hatched or entered the pupal stage, while others clung securely to the rocks or remained burrowed in the silt and gravel. Later that morning I put my observations to use. I tied on a Catskill Curler stonefly nymph with a green Glass Bead Caddis Larva on the point and drifted it through the riffles. While several anglers vainly pounded the pools above me with dry flies, I hooked two strong browns in the fast water, both taking the smaller caddis imitation. I didn't bother with the pools or slower reaches. These worms need the fast, well-oxygenated water that many coldwater fish seek on hot days. Like *Brachycentrus* larvae, Rock Worms use their silk to tether themselves to rocks, but it is light brown instead of white. A fine piece of Maxima Chameleon tied to a clear tippet of the same diameter imitates this rappelling rope. Add a piece of split shot above the knot to keep it down near the bottom and allow plenty of hang time at the end of your drift. Hot spring days aren't the only good times to fish *Rhyacophila* patterns. They are active during the cold months, and are especially important for diehards who fish warm tailwaters in the winter.

Green Caddis—Adult

Family: Rhyacophilidae   **Size: 10-16 mm**
Genus: *Rhyacophila*
Nickname: Green Sedge
Active: Second week of May to last week of June, then sporadic through September

With the exception of their telltale bright green bodies and vivid chartreuse throats, *Rhyacophila* adults look very much like Spotted Caddis. Indeed, I recall an evening on the upper Connecticut when the air was filled with female caddis slamming themselves upon the water in an effort to break the surface. Their legs were ginger, and their wings were a dark gray peppered with tan spots and with an overall sheen, like a sharkskin suit. On closer examination of a half dozen samples, I discovered that half of these were a species of *Hydropsyche*, otherwise looking and behaving just like *Rhyacophila*. Green Caddis have distinctly green bodies and a lighter splash of green at their throats. Not all species have shiny wings. Hatches can occur any time during the season while there are leaves on the trees, especially in the afternoon or early evenings of late spring and early autumn. They last a month or longer in a given location. As a result, the population emerges intermittently, usually mixed with caddis of other genera, and the emerging adults have developed a reputation, perhaps undeserved, as being less important than the larvae.

(L to R): Henryville Special, Brown and Green Diving Caddis, Quad Wing Spent Caddis
Hook Sizes 12-16

Green Caddis hatches may warrant scant attention with adult or pupal imitations, but the egg-laying flights are another matter entirely. Like the Spotted Caddis, the females crawl or swim unhurriedly to bottom, lay a string of eggs, and then blithely release themselves into the current. Drifting, without trying to swim, they take their time pushing back through the surface. Most of the action happens below the surface or in the film and never in slow water, which would be inhospitable to the new larvae. To give the impression of an active, rather than drowned, insect, use a wet-fly presentation with a stiffly hackled dry fly such as the Henryville Special, an old English pattern renamed for a section of the Brodhead in Pennsylvania. Begin by aiming your cast directly toward the water so that the fly lands hard, like the natural. Let the fly drift just over the fish's head before beginning your gentle strip retrieve. Keep your rod tip up to cushion the take. The casual return of the females to the surface is suggested by the Leisenring lift. Sometimes the trout pursue them as they attempt this second emergence, but more often they lie in ambush, especially in deep pockets and runs just below the riffles, watching for spent females to pass by in the stronger current. They indicate this preference by their sipping rises, the signal to switch to a spent-wing pattern, like the Quad Wing, drifted drag free, motionless and squarely in their feeding lanes.

"Alder Fly"—Larva

Family: Hydropsychidae   **Size: 13-18 mm**
Genus: *Macrostemum*
Species: *zebratum*
Nickname: Zebra Caddis
Active: First week of October to last week of June

New Englanders have nicknamed the caddis *Macrostemum zebratum* "Alder Flies" owing to their habit of roosting under the leaves of alders, a nearly ubiquitous streamside tree or shrub. Known elsewhere as the Zebra Caddis, the larvae are structured much like others in their family Hydropsychidae with several important distinctions. They are of a much brighter green, they are quite stout, and their retreats, a gooey network of tunnels formed of their silk and whatever materials are at hand, are quite extensive. Their nets are of the finest mesh of any Hydropsychid. They gather in clusters on the undersides of small to medium-sized streambed rocks in the fast-water riffles where they strain plankton from the drift. Endowed with a profusion of gills to survive reduced levels of oxygen in the heat of summer, *Macrostemum* larvae thrive in warmer trout streams like the Housatonic and particularly in food-rich tailwaters and lake drainages like the upper Androscoggin and the Newfound, both in New Hampshire. They frequently share this habitat with other netspinners and with large predatory stoneflies. For the record, true alderflies are members of the order *Megaloptera*, whose larvae bear little resemblance to netspinning caddis.

(L to R): Bright Green Caddis Larva, Simple Caddis Larva, Glass Bead Caddis Larva
Hook Size 12-14

Assuming you've found the proper habitat, *Macrostemum* larvae are easy to locate. Their gelatinous tunnels coat the streambed rocks, even to the point that wading over their slippery surfaces becomes difficult. Alder Flies lay their eggs in early summer, and by late fall the larvae have already grown in size and number. This makes them valuable for winter and early spring fishing, particularly as their fast, warm tailwater habitats rarely freeze over. Because there is little else available during the cold months, trout will not only intercept the larvae in the drift but pick them off the rocks. In either case, they remain on the bottom of the stream where the water is warmest and food is most prevalent. Energy-conserving fish are reluctant to move to anything that isn't directly in front of them. Fishing during the cold seasons is confined to dead drifts through deep pools and pockets with the fly or leader heavily weighted to keep it on the bottom. As always, a tandem rig is doubly effective. Try a large golden stonefly nymph on the point. Keep your eyes on your line or use an indicator to detect any strikes, and set the hook immediately. In late spring, when fish are more active, cast your flies upstream into the riffles and let them bounce along the bottom.

"Alder Fly"—Pupa

Family: Hydropsychidae   **Size: 13-15 mm**
Genus: *Macrostemum*
Species: *zebratum*
Nickname: Zebra Caddis
Active: Third week of June to second week of July

In early June the *Macrostemum* larvae abandon their tunnels for new positions on the lower edges of rocks to construct more rigid, if crude, pebble casings and begin their pupal metamorphosis. If you pick one off the rocks, you can view the pupa through a window formed by the transparent lining of its enclosure. As its wing pads and long antennae develop, its bright green color fades to a more subdued olive, capped dorsally and ventrally by a much darker shade and banded with yellow. The large, relatively weak pupal cases of "Alder Flies" make them easy targets for roving predators like the large stoneflies that share their habitat. They survive largely through the density of their populations, one of many reasons they are so important to New England fly-fishers. The pupae emerge from the swifter riffles that they inhabited as larvae by cutting free from their shelters, crawling to the tops of the rocks to which the cases are attached and, if necessary, swimming to the surface, even though, by virtue of their robust size, they are clumsy swimmers when compared to other Hydropsychidae. They are most vulnerable as they drift just under the meniscus while shedding their pupal skins.

**(L to R): Olive Partridge SLF, Alder Fly Pupa, Golden Maple
Hook Sizes 10-14**

When the "Alder Fly" is hatching, the fish settle in fast-water pockets to take advantage of the increased levels of oxygen and the abundance of these fat, juicy pupae and adults. In general, there is little difference in emergence behavior between *Macrostemum* and other genera of the family Hydropsychidae. This calls for a pattern that drifts well along the bottom and rises to the surface when its progress is halted. There is, however, some speculation that many *Macrostemum* pupae emerge by crawling to the surface on large streambed rocks. I suspect that, being too large to swim well, the pupae make use of any available footing to assist with emergence, which large boulders in the current are well situated to provide. In fact, properly dressed pupal imitations, fished wet-fly style and guided around larger stones in reaches and fast pocket water, succeed not only because they accurately imitate the behavior of the emerging Alder Flies but because such places are the best lies for feeding trout. Later in the hatch, when fish are surface feeding, present an unweighted and lightly greased pattern in a drag-free surface drift. Not to be overlooked is the fact that the Alder Fly hatch occurs at a time of year and in the type of water where smallmouth bass are beginning to replace trout as the most active game fish. Smallies are as likely to attack an actively presented caddis pupa, and are no less reluctant to submit to the angler's net.

"Alder Fly"—Adult

Family: Hydropsychidae   **Size: 16-17 mm**
Genus: *Macrostemum*
Species: *zebratum*
Nickname: Zebra Caddis
Active: Third week of June to second week of July

There is a stretch of riffles and pockets on the Newfound that I frequently have all to myself, even when the pools above and below it are crowded with anglers. It is lined with alder trees, and in mid to late June they are full of the large, zebra-patterned caddis that earned their New England nickname from this favorite roost. The river is the outlet of Newfound Lake, so the water is warm by trout stream standards and full of nutrients. Its faster stretches are perfect Alder habitat. Although the larvae are very like the other netspinners in the Hydropsychidae family, the adult bears no resemblance either to its cousins or to the true alderfly, an oafish, brown-black insect. *Macrostemum* owes its other famous nickname, the Zebra Caddis, to the vivid dark purplish gray and tan camouflage pattern of the adult's wings. It's other distinguishing feature is its black and extraordinarily long antennae, up to three times the length of the insect. Freshly emerged adults have ginger-colored legs supporting dark green bodies, which quickly darken to almost black with a greenish yellow banding. "Alders" hatch in dry-fly prime time, those warm late afternoons and evenings of mid summer.

(L to R): Brown and Olive Diving Caddis, Pheasant Wing Caddis, Deer Hair Alder
Hook Sizes 10-12

Adult *Macrostemum* are available to fish primarily during the ovipositing activities of the females and more rarely during actual adult emergence. During a hatch the fish are more likely to take pupae as they wrestle with their skins just under the surface, but in the event that they break the surface to take the fresh adults you should be ready with an olive-bodied adult pattern. Later, when fishing the egg-layers, a dark olive to black body color provides a closer match. Study the behavior of both the insects and the fish to determine the best presentation. Hatching "Alder Flies" head for the bushes. Egg-laying females are bat-like in flight as they touch the water to replenish moisture. Although strong enough to fly in a brisk wind, they swim less well than the Cinnamon or Spotted Sedges. To compensate for this deficiency, fertilized females rise skyward and then hit the water like a Kamikaze pilot to penetrate the surface and deposit their eggs below. Some don't make it, and instead release their eggs while sprawled on the surface. Quite expectedly, they have a high drowning rate. A dead-drifted spent-wing or deer-hair pattern, delivered with an overpowered cast, accurately mimics this behavior. At the end of the drift, pull the fly under and retrieve it like a wet fly by stripping quickly, roughly eight inches at a time. Finally, release your line and allow the fly to swing back up to the surface like a spent female.

Northern Casemakers—Larvae

Family: Limnephilidae   **Size: 18-25 mm**
Genus: *Pycnopsyche*
Active: First week of April to last week of June

Some casemakers hibernate during summer's hottest months and only begin to pupate when fall weather arrives. They are leaf-shredding larvae who build portable houses of sticks, leaves, gravel, or whatever is handy. The cream-colored worms slip easily in and out of their cases. Among the most common, the largest and certainly the most recognizable, are the *Pycnopsyche*, the nearly ubiquitous inch-long bundles of sticks and/or stones seen crawling over rocks and along the stream bottoms each spring. They breathe by a process of undulation that forces water to pass through the case. This adapts them to life in relatively slow pockets and pools of small tributaries and slightly acid wild, North Country streams where brook trout feel at home, like the headwaters of the Connecticut River or the Allagash in northern Maine. Caddis of this family are also numerous in coldwater ponds and lakes. Eggs hatch as the leaves fall in autumn and grow through winter, spring and early summer when their food is most plentiful. When hot weather arrives, they attach themselves under rocks in safe locations, which remain under water, particularly in feeder streams where temperatures remain cool. It is then that they enter a period of stasis.

(L to R): Chopped Deer Hair Caddis, Fur Peeping Caddis, Sparkle Yarn Caddis
Hook Sizes 6-12

It might seem unlikely that foraging fish would relish a meal encased in so much masonry or lumber, but, in fact, they have little trouble digesting the sizable larva within and excreting the remainder. A sure sign that fish are after these larvae is the swish of a tail as they work to keep their snouts down on the bottom and pick off the roaming caddis. Even when attached to rocks the cases are easily pulled free during the larval stage. In the spring they seem to be nearly everywhere, but as the waters warm their populations become concentrated near springs and the influxes of cold feeder streams. Not surprisingly, they are slow and clumsy and will drift for quite a distance if they lose their footing, which is probably why I almost never find them in fast water. Your presentation should be equally deliberate. Keeping your fly down on the bottom is essential. An unweighted pattern drifts more naturally, but an imitation dragged slowly across the bottom behaves more like a natural if the weight is built into it. I eschew the former in favor of the latter, because I only find it worthwhile to fish large-cased larvae when I know the fish are actively looking for them. Cast ahead of the fish, and use a hand-over-hand retrieve to walk the imitation slowly along the bottom. Fish cruise these slower habitats. Rather than try to get the fly to the fish, let the fish come to the fly.

Northern Casemaker—Pupa

Family: Limnephilidae   **Size: 14-18 mm**
Genus: *Pycnopsyche*
Active: First week of August to last week of October

During the hottest summer months, the stream-dwelling casemakers of the Limnephilidae family are dormant, in a sort of summer state of hibernation. Beginning as early as July they seek safe thermal refuges where they seal their cases of rocks and sticks with silk or a pebble and begin to pupate. Once metamorphosis is complete, pharate adults emerge from their houses to crawl along the bottom and out onto stones or deadfall to emerge. The wide diversity of temperatures and flow rates from one stream to the next at this time of year provides hatches that last for over a month. The ginger coloring of the pharate adults is most evident in the head, legs and wing pads, with evidence of the larval cream color remaining in the abdomen. The ginger antenna is banded with brown. There is also a dark, semicircular fringe of hairs around the last few segments of the abdomen. Unfortunately, the vast majority of the large, brightly colored adults hatch at night, but pupal activity begins in the early evening and continues into the early hours of the morning, providing some exciting angling opportunities on warm fall nights when large trout come out to feed.

**(L to R): SLF Bird's Nest, Pumpkin Caddis, Partridge SLF
Hook Sizes 10-18**

Many pupae of large tube casemakers are eaten by fish who pick them off the bottom. A few get caught in the drift as they initially pull free of their cases and drift for some distance until they regain their footing. Those remaining achieve relative safety in emerging out of the water. By the time the autumn caddis varieties begin to appear, the supply of edible insects is dwindling. Nevertheless, fish are still feeding aggressively and opportunistically on insects, crayfish and minnows to store energy for spawning and for the long winter ahead. The best way to learn if autumn caddis are hatching is to seek the adults under building lights the night before your outing. If that isn't possible, turn over rocks in the margins of woodland rivers and streams to inspect the large pupal cases glued underneath. Pupal patterns should be constructed on heavy hooks and fished deep, but too much weight built into the pattern will cause it to snag frequently on the bottom. Cast your fly upstream, into the current, and allow it to sink. Then, crawl it along the bottom with a hand-over-hand retrieve. You can also let drag do the work for you by keeping just enough tension on the line to maneuver your fly towards the stream edge as it reaches the end of the swing, or around the protruding rocks where pupae crawl out to emerge, and where fish will be looking for them.

Northern Casemaker—Adult

Family: Limnephilidae   **Size: 18 to 24 mm**
Genus: *Pycnopsyche*
Nicknames: Giant Red Sedge, Great Brown Autumn Sedge
Active: Last week of August to last week of October

The largest of all the eastern stream-dwelling caddisflies are among the last to appear. Caddis season at our house is in the fall, when adult caddis from nearby small, upland streams and beaver ponds congregate on our screen doors. Many of them are the color of a ripe pumpkin, from the tips of their antennae to the posteriors of their abdomens and wings, with variations of brown mixed in. These markings are more pronounced in some specimens than others, even within the same species. Early fishing entomologies referred to this and several other genera collectively as *Stenophylax*. I rarely see them during the daytime except in the far north, where their size in flight makes them easy to mistake for moths. Because so much of their activity is nocturnal, they are a subject for much confusion. For example, there is an entrenched belief that adults lay their eggs at the water's edge, either in overhanging vegetation or in damp locations where subsequent rains wash the eggs into the stream. There is also anecdotal as well as scientific evidence that females lay their eggs directly into the stream by crawling or swimming underwater.

(L to R): Golden Demon Hairwing, Ginger Deer Hair Caddis, Ginger Diving Caddis
Hook Sizes 8-12

In my studio tank, *Pycnopsyche* adults have emerged on the water's surface when no other footing was available, but most crawl out onto protruding rocks to shed their pupal skins. Even if, as the preponderance of my reference texts suggest, females return to the water to lay their eggs on the bottom, they rarely do so over open water. So I stick to pupal patterns during a hatch. For the egg-laying adults I concentrate my efforts on the slack waters in the eddies and at the stream's edge where I found feeding larvae the previous spring. These are prime lies for brown trout in the fall, and cruising fish explore these areas as well. A wet fly like the Diving Caddis, fished actively around rocks and other obstructions, makes a good imitation of the ovipositing female. In fact, I strongly suspect that some streamer patterns like the Golden Demon are so effective during the fall because they are taken for swimming *Pycnopsyche* or similar caddis. Although most large fall caddis hatch and lay their eggs at night there is still enough dawn and dusk activity to provide good fishing with adult imitations. Night fishing in familiar waters with a large surface imitation is especially thrilling. You can trust a well-palmered dry fly to stay afloat in the dark, and it makes a lot of fish-attracting noise when you pull it under for a wet-fly style retrieve with quick, short strips of the line.

CHAPTER 6

Stoneflies

At first glance, stonefly larvae appear similar to mayfly nymphs, but they are easy to tell apart by the rule of two: two distinct pairs of wing cases, two tails and two claws on each leg. Only the very largest stonefly larvae, also called creepers, have abdominal gills, and then only on the first two sections, whereas the gills of mayfly nymphs are always located on the sides of the abdomen. Like mayflies, stoneflies undergo an incomplete metamorphosis, lacking the pupal stage, but they have only one winged stage. Stonefly creepers are strong crawlers but extremely poor swimmers. If dislodged into the drift they curl their abdomens but keep their legs outstretched in an effort to regain their foothold.

Stonefly larvae hatch from the eggs in anywhere from a matter of hours to three or four months and will pass through 10, 20 or more instars over a period of one to three years before emerging as adults. They are intolerant of sustained water temperatures above 77 degrees and require clean, well-oxygenated water to survive. Because most species feed on detritus during at least the early stages of development, and because agricultural runoff is often responsible for reduced oxygen levels in streams, stonefly larvae are most likely to be found in wooded areas and away from pastures. They can be very picky about their diet.

Some will eat only the leaves of certain trees, while others will eat only leaves that have become host to the fungi that accelerate leaf decay. Still others are carnivorous, searching out hapless insects and even small minnows on the stream bottom. Like many aquatic insects, stoneflies have additional light sensors called ocelli, which appear as tiny holes behind their clearly defined eyes. These organs help to regulate the insects' daily and seasonal clocks.

For anglers the most important taxonomic keys in the larval stage are the presence (or absence) and location of gills, orientation and shape of the wing pads (divergent or parallel to the body), shape of the head, body profile and the length of the tails. Biologists use more precise keys like mouth structure and the veining of the adult wings, but these are not readily discernible at the streamside. Color is important when choosing an imitation, but the familiar yellow and black zebra patterning is common to creepers of several families. Not all members of the family known as the Yellow Stoneflies are yellow. Size is also a good indicator, with the earliest winter and spring emergers occupying the small end of the scale and the late spring and early summer Goldens and Giants occupying the top spot.

Just before hatching, the fully grown larvae crawl along the bottom toward rocks or other hard objects projecting above the water line. Then they climb out and split their shucks razor straight along the back of the head and thorax to emerge, leaving clusters of empty casings that are a familiar sight on most streams. Some time elapses before their bodies harden and their wings dry sufficiently for flight. While mayflies rise gracefully from the water, and caddis dart about erratically, the flight of adult stoneflies seems labored, and their wings exaggerate their size. They look like bi-planes taking off.

Adults have two pairs of wings, of essentially equal length, shiny, conspicuously veined and held back flat or slightly curved over the abdomen. They also have two tails, which can be quite long or nearly imperceptible, and working mouths, even though their diet is usually restricted to liquids in the form of water or plant nectars. The life span of the typical adult stonefly is ten days to two weeks, but some may live as long as a month. Adult males are only about sixty percent as large as the females. Stoneflies mate in the streamside vegetation or on the ground. Some males attract females by beating their abdomens against a hard surface to make a drumming sound, which you can hear on quiet

nights. Only virgin females respond, sometimes with a beat of their own. After mating, the females fly over or walk upon the water's surface until their egg masses are either washed or knocked away or dissolve.

The stoneflies described in the following pages include those of greatest importance to New England fly-fishers. Larval imitations are tied

in a wide range of sizes owing to the fact that they are available to fish long before they reach maturity. Body measurements of the mature creepers are taken from the head to the tip of the abdomen, exclusive of tails or antennae. Adult measurements are from the head to the tip of the wing at rest.

Early Dark Stoneflies—Creepers

Family: Taeniopterygidae   Size: 7-15 mm
Nickname: Little Sepia Stonefly
Active: First week of March to last week of April

Each year, in mid-February, early signs of spring appear on my studio window. They are tiny, often wingless winter stoneflies, the Capniidae, hatching from the Mascoma River outside. Soon they are joined by members of other early stonefly families, which continue to hatch even as the first mayflies appear. The larvae of all of these small, dark early season flies subsist on detritus, preferring to burrow among plant debris, and are rarely found in riffles or open current. They come in all shades of brown, from sepia to amber to chocolate. There are two families of small, slender stoneflies, the Capniidae and the Leuctridae. The so-called Broadbacks of the family Nemouridae are also small but more robust. Equally stout are the largest and most common of the early stoneflies, the family Taeniopterygidae. These are of greatest importance to New England fly-fishers and occur in large as well as small rivers. There are over 30 species with unpronounceable names, but the most valued are those that hatch between mid March and late April when stream ice is melting and trout are just becoming active. Most are dark brown to tan with lighter yellowish undersides, subtle dorsal markings and divergent wing pads.

Left to Right: Turkey Tail Nymph, Brown Swannundaze Stonefly, American Pheasant Tail
Hook Sizes 12-18

One of the niceties of the Stoneflies is that their larvae are all structured more or less the same, varying principally in color, size and proportion, and they follow the same pattern of emergence. While this may complicate matters for the biologist trying to identify each species, it is a blessing for the angler who is thereby free from having to carry a huge assortment of imitations. This is particularly true of the early, winter-hatching stoneflies and also of the spring-hatching Chloroperlidae, who not only share size and general appearance but occupy many of the same habitats. Minutiae like shape of the wing case and relative length of the tail become less important in small sizes. For the most part, all of these little larvae are too small to be of much value except when a hatch is imminent or in progress and large numbers are exposed to feeding trout. In New England, it is a time of year when most trout are hunkered down near the bottom avoiding ice and extreme cold. If you see adult flies in the air or on streamside rocks, look for signs of fish feeding in the shallows. Work these areas with one or more nymph imitations in a dead drift while maintaining a low profile. Crawl the nymphs back along the bottom with a hand-over-hand retrieve. Only after thoroughly working the shallow water should you drift the nymphs through pockets and deeper pools.

Early Dark Stoneflies—Adults

Family: Taeniopterygidae   **Size: 8-16 mm**
Nicknames: Little Red Stonefly, Little Sepia Stonefly
Active: First week of March to last week of April

Adult winter stoneflies are remarkably hardy. During the day I'll often see them on streamside rocks or wandering on snow banks many yards from the nearest stream. Although most prevalent in the early afternoons, they have a fairly long adult life and are apt to be active whenever conditions are warm enough. They will perish if exposed to sub-freezing temperatures, but manage to survive by tunneling into the snow. The slender Capniidae and the broad Nemouridae are generally too small to bring early season trout to the surface. Leuctridae adults, which resemble a pine needle, are occasionally important in the fall on cold, fast rivers. Adult Taeniopterygidae grow as large as 16mm and provide the greatest opportunity of all early stoneflies for surface fishing. Some species are apt to emerge at any time of year, but the peak hatch is usually in April. During the cool months of spring they hatch from mid morning to late afternoon, or whenever the sun is strongest, and mate a week later during the middle of the day. Those that hatch during the steamier months of summer emerge and lay eggs after dark. Egg-laying females bear a cluster of tiny, pale golden globes on their abdomens.

(L to R): Early Brown Stonefly, Dancing Stonefly, Sepia Spentwing Stonefly
Hook Sizes 12-18

All stoneflies hatch after crawling out onto stones, but some do end up in the water. Cover both stages by adding a nymph pattern on the point of your dry fly and dead drifting the pair through the shallows. Fish are more likely to rise to early stoneflies when adult females are ovipositing and when there are other insects, like midges or early mayflies, to draw them to the surface. If stoneflies predominate, fish take them selectively, both at and below the surface. They also take the spent insects that accumulate after egg laying. Art Flick fished his version of the Early Brown Stonefly as a wet fly, but fish also took it on top. I first tied the Dancing Stonefly (a shameless appropriation of the LaFontaine Dancing Caddis) after watching sepia females flutter continuously across the surface, always facing upstream, to jettison their eggs. Others skittered across the current into the shallows. A few days later I seduced a 16-inch rainbow with my new pattern. The method of imitation depends on where fish are feeding. If they are in the current, use the sudden inch or cast directly downstream and alternately twitch and drift against the current. In shallows and eddies, cast downstream at an angle to the fish's feeding direction to skate the fly directly in front of it. As with any active presentation, takes occasionally come when you least expect them. Wait until the fish has disappeared below the surface before gently setting the hook.

Little Green Stoneflies—Adults

Family: Chloroperlidae   **Size: 7-14 mm**

Active: First week of May to last week of June

The group of stoneflies nicknamed the Little Greens, whose amber-colored, short-tailed nymphs are 5-12 mm at maturity, is woefully underrated. The creepers have rounded, unpatterned wing pads running parallel to the body and no visible gills. I find these leaf eaters in the crevices of stones on the bottom of swift, gravelly waters, especially the colder upland streams where such detritus is most prevalent. Small to medium-sized streams are their favored habitat. Prior to emergence they migrate downstream by releasing themselves into the drift. Like most smallish stoneflies they are relatively cylindrical and poorly designed for swimming. True to their order, they crawl out of the water to emerge. Not all adults are green bodied—some are yellow or olive—but for angling the most useful are those with bright, nearly chartreuse bodies and a green tint to the wings. During relatively cool spring weather they begin their sporadic emergence in the afternoon and continue until after dark. They lay their eggs by touching down on the water and then flying off to repeat the process in a new spot. These flights can occur whenever heat and sunshine are subdued, usually in the early evening.

(L to R): Little Green Stonefly, Yellow Sally
Hook Sizes 14-18

In terms of creating feather and fur patterns, larvae of the Little Greens are similar to those of winter stoneflies but make their homes in faster water. If you encounter a hatch you can add one as a point fly to a dry adult pattern, which then doubles as an indicator. The hatch, however, is usually too spread out to generate much feeding activity. Ovipositing, by contrast, is a more consolidated affair, with plenty of bright green adults bouncing upon the surface. Since my introduction to this modest little insect, there have been numerous occasions when I've been thankful to have an imitation in my fly box. During the lulls between major spring hatches they are as likely as any other stonefly or caddis to be the predominant insect on the water. I've never known fish to feed on them selectively, but their bright color renders them most attractive to opportunistic feeders at a time when trout are rising to other light hatches without keying on any of them. They are also small enough to use in tandem with another dry fly. Egg-laying females land softly on the surface, and a drag-free dry-fly drift is usually sufficient to lure a fish. But if rises are irregular or fish appear to be cruising, an alternate twitch and drift or a skated fly may be required to entice them from a greater distance.

Giant Stonefly—Creepers

Family: Pteronarcyidae   Size: 25-50 mm
Genera: *Allonarcys* and *Pteronarcys*
Nickname: Salmonfly
Active: First week of May to third week of September

Out west there's a large *Pteronarcys* stonefly called a Salmonfly that hatches in such astounding numbers as to draw even the largest trout to the surface and the most prudent easterners to the next westbound plane. Here in New England we have two *Pteronarcys* species, including *dorsata*, the largest of all stoneflies, and a second genus, *Allonarcys*, which is distinctive in the lateral hooks along the abdomen. The Goliaths of this family take up to three years to mature and grow as large as 50 mm. They are a dark, almost black olive brown and wear sharply cornered, nearly rectangular, shield-like plates over the prothorax ahead of their outward pointing wing pads. They have an oval cross section and luxuriant gill pairs on the thorax and on each of the two front abdominal segments. Although fierce looking, they are primarily vegetarians, and curl into a characteristic defensive posture when threatened. Pteronarcyidae favor cool running mountain streams with good stretches of riffles and plenty of submerged leaves, especially just below stream rapids. Emergence is triggered not by the length of the day but by the river reaching a fixed number of days of warm temperatures. It moves upstream several miles each day.

**(L to R): Crawling Allonarcys, Kaufmann's Black Stone
Hook Sizes 2-8**

Wherever you find Giant Stoneflies they will at least be sufficiently populous that fish will recognize them as food and greedily take a nymph imitation. Because it takes years for them to mature, there are large nymphs throughout the season in the streams they inhabit. Fishing a large dark stonefly nymph can be productive at almost any time, but late spring, when many of them are hatching and fish are on the lookout for them, can be especially good. Unfortunately, we don't get the blizzard hatches of the West. Our spring *Pteronarcys* hatches coincide with those of smaller insects like *Ephemerella dorothea*, and are usually so sparse that fish ignore the adult stoneflies in favor of daintier, more numerous fare. But a nymph once saved the day for me when nothing was rising except the temperature, and the landlocked salmon on the West Branch were down deep. I cast a heavily weighted black stonefly upstream and let it sink rapidly as it drifted past me. When I saw my floating line suddenly dive to the bottom I set the hook into the jaw of my best fish of the week. These gentle stonefly giants are slow moving but determined creatures, and anything but a dead drift followed by a slow, steady retrieve along the bottom is sure to be met with disinterest. At the same time, many of the waters they inhabit are so swift that fish are compelled to seize the fly without a moment's hesitation.

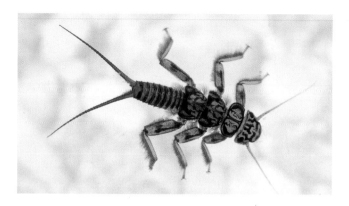

Golden Stoneflies—Creepers

Family: Perlidae   **Size: 18-35 mm**
Subfamilies: Acroneurinae and Perlinae
Nicknames: Great Stonefly, Common Stonefly
Active: All year long

The upper reaches of the Connecticut River are stonefly Heaven. The river is still small, tree-lined and rich enough to support a healthy caddis population, which in turn feeds some very big Golden Stonefly creepers. These larger species require two to three years to mature, so they are always present in the stream. They have branched gills, but on the thorax only. On some species the dorsal surfaces of their heads and thoraxes are decorated with elaborate designs, something like a brown and yellow Rorschach ink blot test, and their abdomens are ringed with stripes. Others are plainer, a more uniform brown. Their undersides are more evenly colored, usually the warm shade of yellow on which many imitations are based. Their wing pads are rounded and rather short, and their heads are wide. In fact their entire bodies are broad but very flat, supported by sturdy, hairy legs. Turn over the rocks in a cool flowing trout stream and you'll soon find the larvae along with the remains of their latest meal. Developing nymphs feed on both dead and living plant matter, but more mature larvae are ferocious predators whose diet includes not only most aquatic insects (including their own species) but fish eggs and small minnows.

(L to R): Glass Bead Golden Stone, Connecticut River Curler, Kaufmann's Golden Stone
Hook Sizes 6-10

Predatory stoneflies are territorial and therefor migratory, distributing their populations well throughout the stream. Their habitat is the most widespread of the order and includes stony riffles and slower, sandy runs and pools. Creepers are most active in the spring, just prior to hatching, and again in the fall, but because there is always a maturing brood, nymph patterns are effective all year long. Owing to their size, their wide distribution and the opportunistic feeding patterns of New England fish, Golden Stonefly nymphs rank high among the most productive patterns during non-hatch periods. Just before or during a hatch, fish the nymph near protruding rocks, especially those near stream edges, where emergers are likely to crawl toward the surface and trout will be lying in anticipation of easy feeding. These nymphs are crawling away from mid stream, so it is important to cast from a position on the bank where you can retrieve your fly toward the banks. Keep your fly on the bottom and use a hand-twist retrieve to move it slowly. Fish the deeper areas in mid stream during non-hatch times using the same technique. When fishing downstream, takes are apt to be solid and sudden as the trout expects the nymphs to resist being plucked from the rocks. For upstream presentations, cast upstream of the likely feeding position and dead drift your nymph towards your target. A buoyant dry fly added as an indicator is often helpful in detecting strikes.

Golden Stoneflies—Adults

Family: Perlidae   **Size: 22-42 mm**
Subfamilies: Acroneurinae and Perlinae
Nicknames: Great Stonefly, Common Stonefly
Active: Last week in May to first week in July, then sporadically into September

From its gentle beginnings in Lake Placid, New York, the Ausable River rolls and tumbles through the Adirondacks on its way to Lake Champlain. At twilight in early June the Coffin Flies vie with the egg-laying flights of big Golden Stoneflies for the attention of the river's hungry brown trout, who rise to naturals and to well-tied imitations with a splash that rivals the river's churning rapids. Like the larvae, adult Golden Stoneflies come in a wide array of sizes and colors, but nearly all have bellies the color of a ripe squash and tawny wings, like scalded coffee with a splash of milk in it. They are flat and wide, just like the creepers, but their overhanging wings make them seem huge even at rest. They emerge above the waterline on streamside rocks where fish can't get them, usually at night to avoid dehydration from the intense summer sun. In the cool of the evening they return en masse to lay eggs on the water's surface, their dark egg sacs visible above their upturned abdomens. Their impact upon the water is a dinner gong to fish, who react without the least hesitation.

(L to R): Clipped Deer Hair Stonefly, Orange Stimulator, Downwing Hornberg
Hook Sizes 4-10

Golden Stonefly hatches are usually sparse on northeastern freestone streams and altogether absent from large, placid rivers, but on whitewaters like the Ausable or the Rapid, heavy hatches are more common. Adult stonefly designs from the west, where dense daytime hatches are legendary, now overshadow eastern patterns, but such high-floating dries are well suited to evening egg-laying flights on eastern rivers and as attractors for both brook trout and landlocked salmon in the fall. Females briefly but repeatedly slap the surface to dislodge their eggs. Fish seem to focus less on the water's surface than on the space above it. They may take no notice of a dead-drifted imitation, but as soon as one sees a fly in its window it crashes up through the surface to nail it. The current obscures their vision, enabling the angler, equipped with a long rod to reach the fly into position, to approach and deliver the fly with short casts and very short drifts. New Englanders have developed their own unique style of imitating adult Goldens where they are less populous. Many become trapped in the surface film to be carried by the currents into the feeding lanes of opportunistic fish. Their struggles in the water have given rise to several New England wet-fly patterns, including John Blunt's downwing version of the Hornberg Special for the Kennebago River in Maine. Fished with quick and constant action through the pockets and around the rocks, it is more temptation than the river's brookies and landlocks can withstand.

Little Yellow Stoneflies—Creepers

Family: Perlodidae   **Size: 8-16 mm**
Nickname: Yellow Sally
**Active: Second week of April to last week of June, then
sporadically through August**

When compared to the large, flat forms of the Big Golden creepers, the
Yellow Stoneflies are smaller and more cylindrical. These plain to
patterned forms are very similar to the Golden Stonefly nymphs in their
yellow and brown markings, but they lack the branched thoracic gills
and general hairiness of their larger cousins. Their habitat is more widespread, and they are plentiful in most rivers and streams that are suitable for trout. They come in many sizes, but there are two subfamilies,
Perlodinae and the smaller Isoperlinae, and it is the latter that occurs in
greatest abundance in eastern trout waters. There are over 50 species of
the genus *Isoperla* alone, making it one of the largest stonefly genera.
Their normal life cycle is one year, with most of their growth occurring
during the spring. Algae and other living plant matter make up much of
the early larval diet, but as they mature they become more predatory.
Because they produce only one annual brood these smaller creepers are
more seasonal as a food source. But different species hatch in different
seasons, with many emerging during the spring and a few appearing in
late summer after the larger golden stoneflies have tapered off.

(L to R): Bird's Nest, Yellow Swannundaze Stonefly, Albino Stonefly
Hook Sizes 8-14

During a hatch of Little Yellow Stoneflies the procedure for fishing the nymphs is the same as for any stonefly hatch. Cast toward the middle of the stream and slowly work your nymph along the bottom and in toward the shallows where the adults are hatching. Because of the diversity in size and appearance, it is essential to provide yourself with a sample of the natural in order to arrive at the proper choice of imitation. Hatch times are always the most productive for fishing any stonefly nymph, but it is certainly possible to induce fish to take them at other times. Cast well upstream and let the fly sink as it drifts toward your spotted target or a suspected feeding lie. Then alternately raise and lower the rod tip to inscribe a graceful waveform in the air until the fly is directly below the fish. The up-and-down motion of the fly beneath the surface suggests a creeper struggling against the current and triggers all but the wisest fish to strike. In slower reaches and pocket waters, where the current allows you to sweep a wet fly while keeping it close the bottom, you can couple the swing with a hand-over-hand retrieve to imitate the stonefly struggling to move across the stream. To minimize snags, use an unweighted fly with a split shot on a four-inch extension of fine monofilament tied to your fly. At worst you'll have to break off the weight.

Little Yellow Stoneflies—Adults

Family: Perlodidae   Size: 10-19 mm
Nickname: Yellow Sally
Active: First week of May to last week of June, then sporadically through August

As with the creepers, adult stoneflies of the family Perlodidae are easily distinguished from the larger Perlidae by their more cylindrical cross sections, their smaller size and their tail of more or less the same length as their abdomens. In spite of their collective nickname, they come in a wide range of colors including brown, sepia, yellow and orange. This means, of course, that you really need a specimen in hand if you wish to match the color of the predominant species. Most of us are familiar with the Yellow Stoneflies that are ever present and occasionally abundant during the late summer, but members of this family start hatching in the early spring and continue to emerge throughout the season. They emerge at twilight or after dark and until sunrise. Egg laying also begins at twilight and continues throughout the night, but you will also see them laying eggs in the daytime, particularly in the early hours of the morning. Females protect their fully ripened, nearly black egg clusters by tucking their abdomens up under their wings. At egg-laying time they settle on or skitter across the surface of the stream to dissolve and remove these clusters.

(L to R): Yellow Egglaying Stonefly, Yellow Sally, Yellow Stimulator
Hook Sizes 10-14

One evening, long before I began my studies of bugs, I was enjoying my usual lack of success when suddenly the twilight sky above the White River filled with fairy-like forms of floating insects, quietly touching down and rising from the water. Blissfully believing that I was witnessing a Little Yellow Stonefly hatch, I tied on a creamy Deer Hair Caddis. In retrospect I learned that this was the flight of egg-laying females, but I was too happily hooking trout to be concerned with this apparent divergence between good science and good sport. The experience taught me that during heavy egg-laying flights a simple dead drift of a palmered, high-floating pattern gets the job done. But I've never encountered such a swarm in the years since. Now, when there is light fish or bug activity I use a skated fly to stir some action. With either presentation the rises are splashy, as fish are anticipating an insect about to fly away. Summer hatches of Little Yellows usually begin after dark, but they linger into the early daylight hours when you'll see them come off the water and fly to the protection of the trees. If fish are working the surface, cast your fly into the shallows where stoneflies are emerging or into the current seams and eddies where the cripples collect. Add the occasional light twitch to your dead drift. If there is no surface activity, tie a nymph below your dry pattern and fish them in the shallows.

CHAPTER 7

Otheroptera

In addition to the three orders described in the preceding chapters, many other insect orders are represented in the diets of New England's freshwater game fish. The true flies of the order *Diptera*, for instance, at approximately 3500 species, vastly outnumber even the caddisflies. Most are too small (or too annoying) to be of importance to the angler but a few, like the craneflies, are not only sizable but very much a menu item for fish and other stream dwellers. Black flies are relished by the brookies in Maine, as are mosquitoes there and elsewhere, but neither is a hatch that I, for one, care to be out in. Midges, the Chironomids, so much a part of western fly fishing, are extremely important on our ponds and lakes but of somewhat less consequence on the less-fertile rivers and streams east of the Hudson.

The order *Odonata* incorporates two related but distinct suborders, the Dragonflies (*Anisoptera*) and Damselflies (*Zygoptera*). Together, these include only about 450 species in North America but are globally much more widespread. Like the *Ephemeroptera*, the *Odonata* are primitive insects, unable to fold their wings down over their abdomens.

Although the larval forms are rather drab, the adults come in a dazzling array of patterns and colors that would not be out of place in a Mardi Gras parade. Dragonflies and Damselflies usually emerge above the water level on streamside rocks or vegetation. A very few lay their eggs directly on the bottoms of shallow streams, but most of the business of their adult life is accomplished out of the reach of fish.

Beyond the true aquatic insects that spend at least part of their lives beneath the water's surface there is an endless parade of terrestrials that haplessly fall upon it. These include ants, beetles, leafhoppers, grasshoppers, caterpillars, wasps, spiders and a vast array of delicacies that fish seize at every opportunity. They arrive mainly by mistake, during mating or migrational flights, by falling out of trees or in failing to properly calculate the distance of a leap. Their occurrences are seasonal but generally unpredictable, and I never head for the stream without my box of terrestrial patterns secured in its assigned pocket of my vest.

Insects of the *Megaloptera* spend only their larval stages under water but, as their ordinal name indicates, they are all relatively large and therefor an important part of the subaquatic food chain. These include the true alderflies and the large, ferocious hellgrammites and fishflies. Other aquatic orders include *Hemiptera,* the water bugs; *Neuroptera*, or spongillaflies; *Coleoptera*, also known as water beetles; and *Lepidoptera*, the aquatic caterpillars and moths. All play a part in the diets of freshwater fish. Few are of such significance that they warrant special patterns to imitate them, but that has been no obstacle to those wishing to establish new if questionable frontiers in the art of fly fishing. Fortunately, space limitations compel us to confine our examinations to a mere fragment of the possibilities provided by the bounty of the stream.

Dragonflies—Larvae

Order: Odonata   **Size: 25-55 mm**
Suborder: Anisoptera
Active: First week of April to second week of September

We tend to think of dragonflies as stillwater insects, which is partly true, but I seldom dig up the substrate in my search for nymphs without netting several of their distinctive larvae. They are unmistakable in their roundness, like a six-legged spider, with large eyes mounted on opposite sides of their wide heads, substantial mandibles and two short antennae. Their abdomens are very wide, but in profile the insects are fairly flat. They are equipped with a double set of wing pads. The larvae come in many colors, from bright orange to olive green to a bluish brown, governed in part by diet and habitat. The grayish cream of a freshly molted instar may darken to a chocolate brown within a few hours. Their hairy bodies collect stream debris more quickly than Velcro, providing a convenient camouflage. I find them well out of the main current in shallow, silty water along the stream banks or in quiet pools and backwaters. Their gills are positioned at the rectum, and they use this feature to scoot around by jet propulsion. Dragonflies are skillful predators. They are exclusively carnivorous, sometimes cannibalistic, and most attracted to moving prey, which they stalk or ambush like a cat.

Left to Right: Olive Woolly Bugger, Kennebago Muddler, Kaufmann's Dragon
Hook Sizes 6-10

Dragonflies achieve maturity in one to four years, depending upon species and climate. Emergence takes place all season long, from the first warm months of spring into early autumn. They hatch directly from larval to adult form after crawling out of the water onto reeds, logs or other streamside objects. Some larvae are little more than an inch long at maturity, but this is deceptive. On emergence, the compressed, club-like tail unfolds to the long familiar club shape, and the usually drab coloring of the nymphs gives way to vivid patterns. In contrast to the more delicate damselflies, who repose with their wings held rearward, dragonfly adults hold their wings to the side, outstretched, when at rest. You'll see them everywhere in the spring, from slow ponds to the most rollicking rivers. In matching the natural larvae, which often display the ability to camouflage themselves, the general coloration of the stream or its vegetation is a good starting point. This is a situation in which digging around for a live model could mean the difference between success and frustration. Predictably, most patterns are olive colored. Fish these patterns actively on the shallow edges of streams, and especially around grasses and other vegetation, both on the bottom and through the midwater. Short, quick strips or rod movements of an inch or so will mimic their unusual means of locomotion. Alternatively, where fish are cruising and currents allow, creep an unweighted imitation along the bottom with a hand-over-hand retrieve.

Damselflies—Larvae

Order: Odonata   **Size: 20-50 mm**
Suborder: Zygoptera
Active: First week of April to last week of August

Like their dragonfly cousins, damselflies also inhabit flowing as well as stillwater habitats, and I have found them in river systems throughout New England. The larvae share the wide head and large eyes of their order, but beyond these the similarities are less evident. Damselfly larvae are much more slender, resembling the larger swimming mayfly nymphs more that the robust dragonflies. The key indicator, however, is the almost cylindrical abdomen terminating in a triplet of gills that could easily be mistaken for the tails of a mayfly nymph except for their distinctive paddle shape. These appendages serve not only as the damselflies' breathing apparatus but as a propulsion device as effective as any set of flippers. Like the dragonfly larvae, their size is deceptive. I've witnessed graceful adults of two inches or more emerging from mature nymphs as little as an inch long. It is an astonishing transformation. Shortly before hatching, the damselfly nymphs crawl out into the open on subsurface rocks or vegetation, still obscured by their habitat-matching coloration, to await the appointed time. Then, they crawl above the water level and cling, usually to an upright object, to hatch. From there, they are beyond the reach of any trout.

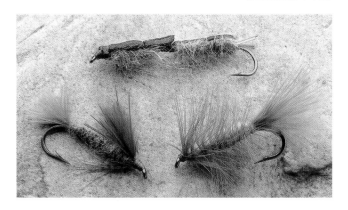

(L to R): Green Damsel Nymph, Damsel Wiggle Nymph, Olive Woolly Bugger
Hook sizes 8-12

River-dwelling Zygoptera larvae are often found crawling on underwater leaf litter and vegetation, including submerged roots. Their coloration is less varied than the dragonflies, limited to various olive hues and a few with a dark, purplish cast. Their common name is misleading, for these damsels, like their more aggressively named cousins, are vicious predators, lying in wait and then seizing their prey with a sudden flash of their labia. Consequently, you'll find the best populations in tailwaters and other nutrient-rich rivers where they have plenty of midge larvae and swimming nymphs to devour and vegetation in which to hide. You'll rarely find them in open water or idling in the drift. Damsel imitations, especially hinged patterns like the Wiggle Nymph, always work best when fished actively. Cast them where the current is slack and where there is plenty of underwater vegetation, including the roots of streamside shrubs and trees. Allow the weighted fly to sink, then retrieve it with very short strips, or by quickly moving the rod in a series of lateral strokes and then stripping in the slack. In the early morning, when damsels are hatching, they rise to the surface in the process of swimming to shore, and fish are likely to follow, but very cautiously. Resist the temptation to enter the water, cast an unweighted pattern towards the center of the stream, and use the same stripping or stroking retrieve to swim it back to the shore.

True Flies—Larvae

Order: Diptera **Size: 3-60 mm**

Active: All year long

The four major orders of fly fishing insects are Mayflies, Caddisflies, Stoneflies and True Flies. This last order, scientifically known as the Diptera or two-winged insects, exceeds the other three combined in the number of species, but the amount of space they occupy in angling literature is woefully small. Diptera include midges, mosquitoes, craneflies, black flies and gnats. Larvae range from 1 to 100 mm and are recognized by their lack of legs or wingpads and by the absence of any clear delineation between head, thorax and abdomen. Many, like the cranefly larvae, have conspicuous anal prolegs or other fleshy protuberances. Basically, they look like watery worms, expanding or contracting telescopically. Often the outer skin is so transparent as to reveal the functioning of their innards, which really grosses out my kids. They breed just about anywhere, from salty estuaries to backyard puddles, from the arctic to the tropics. Some are free swimming. As a result, they are an incredibly important food source for game fish, both in the drift and on the bottom. Depending on size and habitat, development can be anywhere from a week to a year or more. At maturity, they enter pupation in a variety of ways. As adults, their appearances are diverse.

**(L to R): Brassie, Vernille Larva, Gross Cranefly Larva
Hook Sizes 6-26**

Colors run from creams, tans and the earthy grayish browns of the crane-fly larvae to the bright reds of some midge (Chironomid) larvae known as bloodworms. Presentation of larval imitations is dependent upon both size and habitat. Many larger forms, especially cranefly larvae, remain on the bottom, where I usually find them on smaller rivers in the spring before the major mayfly hatches get under way. I've often suspected them as the reason that worm fishermen do so well by getting their bait down deep in mid April. Black fly larvae are seasonal and cover the surfaces of rocks in fast-flowing streams before hatching in the spring. But the most valuable to imitate all season long, particularly in winter when little else is available, are the midge larvae, especially the Chironomidae, which engage in well-coordinated waves of behavioral drift at any time of the day or night. Sample the drift with a seine net to determine the size and color of the prevailing species. You can fish larger imitations singly using a dead-drift nymph presentation, but the tiny, unweighted midge imitations should be added as a dropper or tied to the bend of a larger, weighted nymph that will not only keep both flies near the bottom, but serve as an additional attractor. When the streams warm up and fish are on the move, you can drift midge larvae closer to the surface by using a dry fly as an indicator.

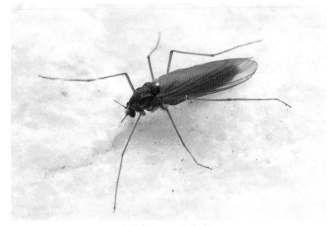

Midges—Adults

Order: Diptera   **Size: 2-7 mm**
Families: Dixae, Chironomidae, others
Active: First week of March to last week of November

Over the years the term "midge" has been generally applied to just about any small stream insect, including mayflies, microcaddis and tiny terrestrials like ants. More recently, as anglers have become increasingly aware of the importance of matching insect behavior, the definition has been properly limited to a few families of two-winged insects of the order Diptera, the "true flies." There are more species of midges alone than of any of the other three major orders. Midges come in a wide array of sizes and colors, even shapes, but they are all characterized by their long, almost spidery legs, slender abdomens, large, often hunched thoraxes and large eyes, and by the absence of tails. Their single pair of wings is held back over the body, either flat or tent style. Almost all adult midges are non feeding and short-lived. They hatch in the early part of the day and lay their eggs during the afternoon and evening, often gathering in clusters, which are the preferred targets of efficiency-minded fish. Their pupae are aquatic, sometimes free-living, and hover just under the surface film in the moments before a hatch, breathing through respiratory thoracic gills or horns.

**(L to R): Griffith's Gnat, Yellow Midge, Grouse and Flash
Hook Sizes 20-28**

I must confess at the outset that although I have caught some of my biggest trout with tiny midge imitations on ponds and on rare trips to western rivers, I'm not greatly inclined toward fishing midges on New England streams. And yet even here the art has its devotees. As a major component of fish diets they are undeniably important, and if fish are feeding and midges are all they are taking, they are certainly valuable to the angler. I rarely encounter that situation, but I keep a few imitations in my box of tiny flies just in case. They are most useful during hot stretches of summer or in the colder extremes of the season when nothing else is hatching. Whatever the season, presentation to surface-feeding trout requires the utmost in stealth and patience. The water is typically smooth, or we would have little chance of seeing either the dimpling rises or the subtle takes, and any movement which disturbs the surface immediately telegraphs our presence. Likewise, an outsized leader or the merest hint of drag is likely to put down the fish. Approach cautiously to within casting range, then allow the surface to settle and the fish to resume feeding. Determine whether they are rising to adults or to emerging pupae. Place your fly only a foot or two ahead of a rising fish or a cruiser. To aid in the detection of strikes and to keep pupal patterns near the surface, tie your imitation in tandem with a larger dry fly.

Hellgrammites and Fishflies—Larvae

Order: Megaloptera   Size: 25-90 mm
Family: Corydalidae
Active: All year long

It's no secret to bait fishermen that one of the best ways to catch a lunker is to put your hook through the thoracic plate of a big ol' hellgrammite and drift it deep. And it is a rare New England river that doesn't have at least a modest population of these large, fierce insects. In fact, our rivers and streams contain two easily confused subfamilies of these larvae. The true hellgrammite is the larval form of the Dobsonfly, and its nearly identical cousin is the larval fishfly. Fully grown, they can be almost frightening to behold. They are dark, olive brown or sepia to almost black, with vicious-looking mandibles that they will use when provoked. They resemble a colossal caddis, with two hooked anal prolegs that they use to drag themselves backwards. When threatened, they curl up tight, just like a large stonefly. Their powerful bodies are somewhat flat, supported at the thorax by six legs, and eight of the abdominal sections are flanked by a pair of lateral filaments, giving them the appearance of a centipede. A shield over the prothorax matches the head in pattern and color. They are carnivorous, with a decided preference for caseless caddis larvae.

(L to R): Whitlock's Hellgrammite, Kaufmann's Brown Stonefly, Brown Woolly Bugger
Hook Sizes 6-8

The distinguishing feature of the hellgrammite is its conspicuously branched gills at the base of its abdominal filaments. Fishfly larvae not only lack this endowment but exhibit far less fringing on the filaments themselves. Both dwell hidden in the riffles of clean, moderate to fast-flowing streams for up to three years before leaving the water to pupate under wet logs or leaf debris, where they cease to be of any real value to fly fishermen. This long growth period keeps them available to trout throughout the year in many sizes up to at least three inches, making it by far our largest stream insect. Known to many as bass bait, these larvae prefer relatively warm environments and are absent from cold tailwaters or spring-fed streams. Their effectiveness as live bait is due in large part to their conspicuous motion on the hook. The trick is to find a pattern that will behave like a hellgrammite that has been jarred loose from its safe haven under the rocks. A free-drifting hellgrammite adopts a defensive posture, curled up to a fraction of its size, except when it is thrashing about in an attempt to regain control. Most patterns designed as hellgrammites look nothing like the naturals, but a few familiar standards give the illusion of motion. Fish weighted flies deep in the riffles, at the heads of pools and even in the rapids. The heavy Megaloptera larvae rarely rise more than a few inches from the bottom.

Ants and Diving Wasps—Adults

Order: Hymenoptera
Active: All season long
Size: 4-8 mm

One of fly fishing's best-known phrases is "Ant the hatch." Ants have the sole honor of being so relished by trout as to divert their attention during selective feeding. In fact, the editor of a major fishing magazine once confided that he ties on a foam ant at the beginning of dry-fly season and leaves it there until closing day. During most of the year ants are wingless. They either fall from trees or are blown onto the water, where fish seize them opportunistically. At swarming time they sprout wings and land on the water in sufficient numbers to trigger steady and selective surface feeding. Individual swarming females are often escorted by a smaller male, and fish can display a definite preference for one over the other. Similar in appearance to the ants are the small diving wasps, who engage in the gruesome practice of laying eggs in the larvae and eggs of subaquatic creatures, who must then play host to the developing wasps even as they are devoured from within. Ants and wasps belong to the same order, and are easily identified by their membranous wings (whence the name of the order) and the narrow attachment between the thorax and abdomen.

(L to R): Flying Cinnamon Ant, Black Foam Ant, Wet Black Ant Hook sizes 18-22

Surface fishing with ant patterns is mainly confined to a dead-drift presentation. Ants can do little beyond squirming on the water, but any attempt to twitch the fly causes a correspondingly large commotion with the leader. Pattern considerations include size and color, which range considerably through the spectrum of browns, reds and blacks, to winged or wingless imitations, and to upright, downwing or spent-wing positions, all of which must be determined by observing a specimen. Wingless ants are initially concentrated near the shoreline and under overhanging trees and bushes where it can be pretty challenging to place a fly with sufficient slack to maintain a drag-free drift (and extremely satisfying when you succeed). Winged ants and diving wasps are more scattered, but currents can disperse the wingless just as easily as they can collect the winged. I spent a blissful hour on the Ellis River in early June as brookies took wingless ants all over the pool. Initially they ride high on the surface, but sooner or later, as if in quicksand, ants trap themselves with each movement, ever deeper into the meniscus, until they drown. Fish sinking wet patterns by casting just ahead of rising fish. You can also cast your fly upstream and let it drift just under the surface, on a greased leader, like a drowned insect. For a dry fly, begin by floating it on the surface and allow it to drag under at the end of the drift.

Grasshoppers—Adults

Order: Orthoptera   **Size: 25-50 mm**
Active: First week of July to second week of October

From the dog days of summer to the first killing frosts of fall, grasshoppers abound in New England meadows in an almost constant migration for fresh forage. Their powerful legs and wings enable them to bound over great distances, but no so great as they think. Many of them end up in the stream, where they struggle mightily in an effort to liberate themselves. They are a gift of the wind and their own folly. Fish have difficulty sucking down so large an insect, so it is necessary for them to raise their heads out of the water to engulf their struggling victims. Smaller fish tend to fail in the effort, merely dousing your fly. A rise to a grasshopper is loud, often startling. But not all hoppers are taken on the surface, and, lacking any buoyancy, many sink quickly after landing upon it, as my few experiments have demonstrated. Most appear to be an overall tannish gray, but when they open their wings to fly or struggle in the water they reveal a palette of bright hues including reds, yellows and greens, sometimes in combination. They first appear in the spring but don't become major players until mid summer when they reach maturity.

(L to R): Letort Hopper, Kennebago Muddler, Parachute Hopper
Hook Sizes 10-12

If enough hoppers are landing on the water you'll find fish holding near the banks where most of the insects are coming from. It doesn't take many of these large morsels to trigger feeding, and trout will travel outside their normal feeding lanes to nab one. The explosive rises are enough to clue you in to what's happening. Most of the time a dead drift will suffice, but a well-timed twitch over a skeptical trout may be needed to simulate a struggling insect and provoke a strike. Rocks lining the stream provide the means to bounce your fly off the bank to further the deception. Delicacy of presentation is hardly an issue, in fact a fly that lands a bit hard can provoke a response. Just don't overdo it. And even the most indiscriminate trout is likely to refuse a dragged imitation. It is important that your fly lie flush within the surface, or even an inch or two below it to imitate a drowned insect. There are a lot of clever hopper patterns on the market, and most of them work just fine. Famous names like Schenk, Marinaro and Schwiebert all designed patterns to solve problems with finicky trout. In a pinch, you probably keep a Muddler Minnow in your fly box. It not only bears a passing resemblance to a hopper, it sits just right in the surface film, and it allows us to fish a favored attractor while professing to be matching the hatch.

Fly Patterns

Where two or more names appear in parenthesis, the name(s) of the originator appear(s) first, then a "/", followed by the name of the tier. All patterns not otherwise attributed are designed and/or tied by the author, who has taken the liberty of modifying the designs of others, with proper attribution, to suit the local fauna. Those who prefer to purchase their flies from the originators will find a list of the professional tiers, with contact information, at the conclusion of this chapter.

Mayflies

Tiny Fork-Gilled Nymph

Paraleptophlebia Nymph
(The Dettes/Mary Dette Clark)
Hook: Mustad 94840
Thread: White waxed 6/0
Tail: Light blue dun hackle fibers
Ribbing: White thread, counter-wound, then lacquered
Abdomen: Stripped peacock quill
Wingcase: Mallard wing quill section
Thorax: Mixed muskrat and rabbit dubbing
Legs: Light blue dun hackle fibers

Sawyer Pheasant Tail
(Frank Sawyer/Hunter's Angling Supply)
Hook: Nymph, 2XL
Thread: Copper wire
Tail: Four or five ring-necked pheasant tail barbs
Rib: Copper wire
Abdomen: Ring-necked pheasant tail barbs, twisted
Thorax: Ring-necked pheasant tail barbs, twisted
Wingcase: Ring-necked pheasant tail barbs

Slate Winged Mahogany Dun

Blue Quill
(Tied by George Schlotter)
Hook: Standard dry fly
Thread: Gray
Tail: Medium blue dun hackle barbs
Body: Stripped peacock quill
Wing: Mallard flank, divided
Hackle: Medium blue dun

Blue Wing Mahogany
(Designed and tied by Jack Pangburn)
Hook: Standard dry fly
Thread: Olive/brown 6/0
Tail: Brown microfibbets
Body: Tying thread, built up
Wing: Gray and blue mixed poly yarn
Hackle: Chocolate dun
Head: Burnt orange thread

Clipped Mahogany Dun
(The Dettes/Mary Dette Clark)
Hook: Mustad 94840
Thread: White waxed 6/0
Tail: Medium blue dun hackle fibers
Body: Clipped brown hackle quill
Wing: Woodduck breast feather, dyed dun, clumped and divided.
Legs: Medium blue dun

Two-Tailed Clinger, Nymph

Hare's Ear Wet
(Tied by Hunter's Angling Supply)
Hook: Standard wet fly

Thread: Brown 6/0
Tail: Ginger hackle barbs
Ribbing: Flat gold tinsel
Body: Dubbed hare's mask fur
with guard hairs
Wing: Mallard wing quill section

Gold Ribbed Hare's Ear

(Tied by Hunter's Angling Supply)
Hook: Standard nymph hook
Thread: Brown or tan 6/0
Tail: Hare's mask guard hairs
Ribbing: Flat gold tinsel
Abdomen/Thorax: Dubbed hare's
mask fur with guard hairs
Wingcase: Mallard wing quill
section
Legs: Thorax dubbing picked out

Ginger Quill Wet

(Tied by Mary Dette Clark)
Hook: Mustad 3906B
Thread: White waxed 6/0
Tail: Golden ginger hackle fibers
Body: Stripped peacock quill
(ribbed with white 6/0
thread and lacquered)
Hackle: Golden ginger
Wing: Gray mallard wing quill

Quill Gordon, Dun

Quill Gordon

(Tied by Del Mazza, his
variation)
Hook: Standard dry fly
Thread: Gray
Tail: Grizzly hackle barbs, dyed
blue dun

Body: Stripped peacock quill,
coated with lacquer
Wing: Woodduck flank
Hackle: Grizzly, dyed blue dun

Hare's Ear Dry

Hook: Standard dry fly
Thread: Brown 6/0
Tail: Ginger hackle barbs
Body: Dubbed hare's mask fur
with guard hairs
Ribbing: Flat gold tinsel
Wing: Mallard wing quill section
Hackle: Light or barred ginger

Light Hendrickson

(Art Flick, adapted from the Roy
Steenrod original/Hunter's
Angling Supply)
Hook: Standard dry fly
Thread: Yellow
Tail: Rusty dun hackle barbs
Body: Fawn-colored fur from
belly of a red fox
Wings: Male woodduck flank
feather
Hackle: Rusty dun

Quill Gordon, Spinner

Red Sparklewing Spinner

Hook: Standard dry fly
Thread: Rust 6/0
Tail: Light gray microfibbetts
Abdomen/Thorax: Blended
brown, claret and rusty fur
dubbing
Wings: White Antron or craft
yarn

Quill Gordon Spinner
Hook: Standard dry fly
Thread: Brown 6/0
Tail: Cree hackle fibers
Body: Stripped peacock eye quill
Wings: Hackle tips from a hen neck
Legs: Cree hackle, clipped top and bottom
Thorax: Brown fur dubbing

Clipped Hackle Hacklewing Spinner
Hook: Standard dry fly
Thread: Rust 6/0
Tail: Light dun hackle barbs, split
Abdomen: Clipped brown hackle quill
Wings: Light dun spade hackle, clipped top and bottom
Thorax: Rusty fur dubbing

Gray Winged Yellow Quill, Dun

Little Marryatt
(Note: This is a modernized version.)
Hook: Standard dry fly
Thread: Primrose yellow
Tails: Light ginger hackle fibers
Body: Yellow fur dubbing
Wing: Light dun hen hackle tips
Hackle: Light ginger

SASH
Hook: Standard nymph hook
Thread: Rust or orange
Tails: Grouse or partridge
Body: Spectrumized amber and olive acrylic yarn
Ribbing: Silver oval tinsel
Hackle: Grouse or partridge

Rusty Usual
(Designed and tied by Fran Betters)
Hook: Dry fly no. 12-16
Tail: Snowshoe rabbit foot hair
Wing: Same as the tail
Body: Rust fur dubbing
Head: Hot orange thread

Salmon Spinner

Ginger Ginger Quill Spinner
Hook: Standard dry fly
Thread: Orange
Tails: Barred ginger hackle, divided
Abdomen: Stripped ginger quill
Thorax: Salmony fur dubbing
Wings: Amber Antron fibers over white CDC puffs, tied spent

Clipped Hackle Sparklewing Spinner
Hook: Standard dry fly
Thread: Orange
Tails: Barred ginger hackle fibers
Abdomen: Ginger hackle, clipped close to quill
Wings: White Antron yarn, combed
Thorax: Salmon fur dubbing

Salmon Parachute Spinner
Hook: Standard dry fly
Thread: Orange 6/0
Tail: Barred ginger hackle barbs

Body: Salmony fur dubbing
Rib: Brown tying thread
Wingpost: White Antron yarn
Hackle: Barred ginger or Cree

Crawlers, Nymphs

Hendrickson Nymph
Hook: Standard nymph hook
Thread: Rust, 6/0
Tail: Dark woodduck flank barbs
Ribbing: Rust thread, 6/0
Abdomen: Blended rust/olive
     fur dubbing
Wingcase: Dark woodduck flank
     feather, stroked with
     flexible cement
Thorax: Same as abdomen
Legs: Dark woodduck flank barbs

Gold Ribbed Hare's Ear
(Tied by Hunter's Angling Supply)
Hook: Standard nymph hook
Thread: Brown or tan 6/0
Tail: Hare's mask guard hairs
Ribbing: Flat gold tinsel
Body: Dubbed hare's mask fur
     with guard hairs
Wingcase: Mallard wing quill
     section
Legs: Thorax dubbing picked out

Gilled Ephemerella Nymph
Hook: Nymph hook 2XL
Thread: Olive brown 6/0
Tail: Four dun ostrich herl tips
Gills: Herl from tail, divided in
     two section and brought
     forward on sides of abdomen

Rib: Fine copper wire
Body: Blended olive, brown and
     rust fur dubbing
Wingcase: Shiny segment from a
     wild turkey flat
Legs: Thorax dubbing picked out

Hendrickson/Red Quill, Dun

Light Hendrickson
(Art Flick, adapted from the Roy
Steenrod original/Hunter's
Angling Supply)
Hook: Standard dry fly
Thread: Yellow
Tail: Rusty dun hackle barbs
Body: Fawn colored fur from
     belly of a red fox
Wings: Male woodduck flank
     feather
Hackle: Rusty dun

Red Quill
(Art Flick/George Schlotter)
Hook: Standard dry fly
Thread: Black or gray
Tail: Dun hackle barbs
Body: Stripped Rhode Island Red
     (brown) quill
Wing: Woodduck drake flank,
     divided
Hackle: Natural blue dun

Parachute Vertical Emerger
(Designed and tied by Harold
McMillan)
Hook: Tiemco TMC 400T
Thread: Burgundy 8/0

Tail (Shuck): Brown or rust Z-lon
Nymph Body: Brown nymph
  dubbing
Ribbing: Fine gold wire
Adult Body: Pink rabbit dubbing
Wingpost: White Z-lon or calf
  body hair
Hackle: Light honey dun

Hendrickson Thorax
(Tied by David Goulet)
Hook: Standard dry fly
Thread: Black or gray
Tail: Dark dun hackle barbs
Body: Light pink fur dubbing
Wing: Light gray Hi-Vis
Hackle: Dark dun, clipped from
  bottom

Red Quill/Hendrickson, Spinner

Rusty CDC/Antron Spinner
Hook: Standard dry fly
Thread: Rust 6/0
Tail: Medium gray microfibbets
Body: Rust-colored fur dubbing
Wings: White Antron fibers over
  white CDC puffs, tied spent

Red Quill Parachute Spinner
Hook: Standard dry fly
Thread: Rust 6/0
Tail: Honey dun hackle barbs
Body: Stripped red hackle quill
Thorax: Blended rust, brown and
  claret fur
Wingpost: White Antron yarn
Hackle: Honey dun

Semi-spent Henwing Egglayer
(Based on a pattern by Vincent
Marinaro)
Hook: Standard dry fly
Thread: Rust 8/0
Tail: Watery dun hackle fibers
Egg Sac: Chartreuse acrylic yarn
Body: Rusty fur dubbing
Wing: Pale dun hen feathers
Hackle: Watery dun

Pale Evening Dun

Parachute Sulphur
(George Schlotter)
Hook: Standard dry fly
Thread: Yellow
Tail: Medium dun hackle barbs
Body: Yellow fur or synthetic
  dubbing
Wingpost: Pale gray poly yarn
Hackle: Medium dun

Parachute Vertical Emerger
(Designed and tied by Harold
McMillan)
Hook: Tiemco TMC 400T
Thread: White 8/0
Tail (Shuck): Brown or rust Z-lon
Nymph Body: Light brown
  nymph dubbing
Ribbing: Fine gold wire
Adult Body: Pale yellow fur dubbing
Wingpost: Pale gray Darlon or
  calf body hair
Hackle: Light ginger

Tufted Wing Sulphur
(The Dettes/Mary Dette Clark)

Hook: Mustad 94840
Thread: White waxed 6/0
Tail: Light ginger hackle fiber
Body: Pale creamy yellow
    dubbing
Wing. Woodduck breast feather,
    dyed dun, clumped and
    divided
Hackle: Light ginger

Pale Evening Spinner

Parachute Invaria
(Designed and tied by Bill Thompson)
Hook: Standard dry fly
Thread: Dark brown
Tail: Dun hackle fibers
Body: Red/brown goose biot
Post: Light gray turkey wing
Hackle: Blue dun

Rusty CDC/Antron Spinner
Hook: Standard dry fly
Thread: Rust 6/0
Tail: Medium gray microfibbets
Body: Rust-colored fur dubbing
Wings: White Antron fibers
over white CDC puffs,
    tied spent

**Clipped Hackle Hacklewing
Spinner**
Hook: Standard dry fly
Thread: Rust 6/0
Tails: Light dun hackle fibers
Abdomen: Brown hackle,
    clipped close to quill
Wings: Light dun spade hackle
Thorax: Rusty fur dubbing

Sulphur, Dun

Sulphur Dun
(George Harvey/Hunter's
Angling Supply)
Hook: Standard dry fly
Thread: Primrose yellow
Tail: Cream hackle barbs
Body: Cream fur dubbing
Wings: Cream hackle points
Hackle: 2 Cream and 1 dyed
    orange, mixed

Parachute Sulphur
(Tied by George Schlotter)
Hook: Standard dry fly
Thread: Yellow
Tail: Medium dun hackle barbs
Body: Yellow fur or synthetic
    dubbing
Wingpost: Pale gray poly yarn
Hackle: Medium dun mixed

Loopwing Vertical Emerger
(Designed and tied by Harold
McMillan)
Hook: Tiemco TMC 400T
Thread: White 8/0
Tail: Ginger Z-lon
Nymph Body: Light brown fur
    dubbing
Ribbing: Fine gold wire
Adult Body: Yellow fur dubbing
Wing: White CDC

Sulphur, Spinner

Polywing Sulphur Spinner
(Tied by George Schlotter)
Hook: Standard dry fly

Thread: Yellow 8/0
Tail: Watery dun hackle fibers
Body: Sulphur yellow acrylic yarn
Wing: White poly yarn

P.E.D. Parachute Spinner
(Designed and tied by Jack Pangburn)
Hook: Standard dry fly
Thread: Yellow/amber 6/0
Tail: Pale microfibbets
Body: Tying thread, built up
Wingpost: Clear Antron
Hackle: Light ginger

Wingless Sulphur Spinner
Hook: Standard dry fly
Thread: Yellow 8/0
Tail: Watery dun hackle fibers
Body: Sulphur yellow fur dubbing
Ribbing: Tying thread
Hackle: Watery dun

Common Clingers
March Brown Nymph
(Art Flick/Hunter's Angling Supply)
Hook: Nymph hook
Thread: Brown
Tail: Three long pheasant tail fibers, divided
Body: Amber seal fur (substitute) and fawn colored fox belly fur, mixed
Wingcase: Pheasant tail fibers, dull side up
Hackle: Partridge

American Pheasant Tail
(Tied by the Orvis Company)
Hook: Standard nymph
Thread: Rust 6/0
Tail: Ring-necked pheasant tail barbs
Body: Ring-necked pheasant tail barbs, twisted and wrapped with thread
Rib: Fine copper wire
Wingcase: Ring-necked pheasant tail section
Thorax: Peacock herl
Legs: Wingcase fibers tied back

March Brown Floating Nymph
(Larry Solomon/Mary Dette Clark)
Hook: Mustad 9671
Thread: White waxed or brown 6/0
Wing bulge: Dyed brown deer hair extending to center of shank
Tail: Ring-necked pheasant tail barbs
Body: Beige-brown fox fur dubbing
Legs: Brown partridge
Head: Brown thread or white thread coated in brown lacquer

American March Brown, Dun
American March Brown
(Art Flick/Hunter's Angling Supply adapted from the Preston Jennings Original)
Hook: Standard dry fly

Thread: Orange
Tail: Ginger hackle barbs
Body: Light fawn colored fox fur
Wing: Woodduck flank, well
    marked
Hackle. Dark grizzly and dark
    ginger grizzly

Gray Fox ComparaDun
Hook: Standard dry fly
Thread: Rust or tan 6/0
Tail: Ginger hackle barbs, divided
Body: Mixed tan, yellow and
    brown fur dubbing
Wing: Variegated deer body hair

March Brown Henwing Emerger
(Designed and tied by George
Schlotter)
Hook: Standard dry fly
Thread: Rust/orange
Tail: 3 pheasant tail barbs
Body: Blended Australian opossum
Legs/Wing: Speckled hen
    feather, wrapped twice as a
    collar, then folded back to
    form the wing

Great Red Spinner
Clipped Henwing Spinner
(March Brown)
Hook: Standard dry fly
Thread: Orange
Tails: Dark dun grizzly hackle
    fibers
Abdomen: Brown hackle, clipped
    close to quill

Wings: Light dun hen hackle
    points
Thorax: Rusty fur dubbing

Great Red Sparkle/CDC Spinner
Hook: Standard dry fly
Thread: Rust, 6/0
Tails: Dark dun microfibbets
Abdomen: Blended mahogany
    fur dubbing
Wings: Gold Antron fibers over
    light dun CDC
Thorax: Brown fur dubbing

Red Parachute Spinner
Hook: Standard dry fly
Thread: Brown
Tails: Dark dun grizzly hackle
    fibers
Body: Rusty red fur dubbing
Ribbing: Tying thread
Wingpost: Light dun Hi Vis
Thorax: Dark dun grizzly

Cream Cahill, Dun
Cream Cahill Parachute
Hook: Standard dry fly
Thread: Tan 6/0
Tail: Barred ginger hackle fibers
Body: Cream fur dubbing
Wingpost: Mottled white turkey
    flat
Hackle: Barred ginger

Usual
(Designed and tied by Fran Betters)
Hook: Dry fly no. 12-16

Tail: Snowshoe rabbit foot hair
Wing: Same as the tail
Body: Cream or light gray fur
Head: Hot orange thread

Cream Wulff
(Designed and tied by Jack
Pangburn)
Hook: Standard dry fly
Thread: Red
Tail: Squirrel, badger or lynx,
tied full
Body: Cream poly yarn
Wing: White poly yarn, tied full
Hackle: Barred ginger or Cree

Cream Cahill, Spinner
Light Cahill Parachute Spinner
(Tied by Jack Pangburn)
Hook: Standard dry fly
Thread: Yellow/tan 6/0
Tail: Ginger microfibbets
Body: Tying thread, built up
Wingpost: Clear Antron
Hackle: Barred ginger

Polywing Jenny Spinner
Hook: Standard dry fly
Thread: Rust 6/0
Tail: White microfibbets
Tip/Thorax: Rust acrylic yarn,
dubbed
Abdomen: White acrylic yarn,
dubbed
Wing: Clear Antron fibers

Cream Egglayer
Hook: Standard dry fly

Thread: Yellow
Egg Ball: Rusty orange fur dubbing
Tail: Cream hackle barbs, divided
Body: Cream fur dubbing
Wings: Antron yarn, divided
Hackle: Cream

Light Cahill, Dun
Light Cahill
(William Chandler/Hunter's
Angling Supply)
Hook: Standard dry fly
Thread: Primrose yellow
Tails: Ginger hackle fibers
Body: Light red fox belly fur
Ribbing: Tying thread
Wings: Lemon woodduck flank
Hackle: Ginger

Yellow Ginger ComparaDun
Hook: Standard dry fly
Thread: Orange 6/0
Tail: Barred ginger or Cree
hackle fibers, divided
Body: Amber spectrumized
fur dubbing
Wings: Deer hair, well
variegated

Rusty Usual
(Designed and tied by Fran
Betters)
Hook: Dry fly no. 12-16
Tail: Snowshoe rabbit foot
hair
Wing: Same as the tail
Body: Rust fur dubbing
Head: Hot orange thread

Isonychia Nymph

Lead Wing Coachman Wet
(Tied by Mary Dette Clark)
Hook: Mustad 3906B
Thread: White waxed 6/0
Tag: Fine flat gold tinsel
Body: Peacock herl
Hackle: Brown (cock or hen)
Wing: Gray mallard wing quill

Isonychia **Nymph**
(The Dettes/Mary Dette Clark)
Hook: Mustad 9672
Thread: White waxed 6/0
Underbody: Lead wire
Tail: Ring-necked pheasant tail barbs
Ribbing: Brown thread, counter-wound
Abdomen: Natural gray ostrich herl over a dubbed blend of two-thirds muskrat and one-third red wool
Wingcase: Light mallard wing quill section
Thorax: Muskrat fur
Legs: Brown partridge
Head: Brown lacquer over tying thread

Zug Bug
Hook: Nymph, 2XL
Thread: Brown or rust 6/0
Tail: Peacock swords
Body: Peacock herl
Wingcase: Woodduck flank feather, lacquered and trimmed to shape
Hackle: Brown

Leadwing Coachman, Dun

Dark Hendrickson
(Tied by George Schlotter)
Hook: Standard dry fly
Thread: Black or gray
Tail: Dark blue dun hackle barbs
Body: Muskrat fur
Wing: Woodduck drake flank, divided
Hackle: Dark blue dun

Adams
(Tied by the Orvis Company)
Hook: Standard dry fly
Thread: Gray or black
Tail: Mixed brown and grizzly hackle fibers
Body: Muskrat fur dubbing
Wing: Grizzly hackle points
Hackle: Mixed brown and grizzly

Dun Variant
(Art Flick/Hunter's Angling Supply)
Hook: Dry fly, short shank
Thread: Olive
Tail: Dark dun spade or saddle
Body: Stripped Rhode Island Red (brown) quill
Wing: None
Hackle: Dark dun spade or saddle, stiff

White Gloved Howdy, Spinner

Bent Body Spinner
(Designed and tied by Bill Thompson)

Hook: Swimming nymph
Thread: Dark Brown
Tail: Dun microfibbets
Body: Rusty brown rabbit fur
Wing: Wing Zing cut or burned to shape
Hackle: Blue Dun

Great Red Sparkle/CDC Spinner

Hook: Standard dry fly
Thread: Rust, 6/0
Tails: Dark dun microfibbets
Abdomen: Blended mahogany fur dubbing
Wings: Gold Antron fibers over light dun CDC
Thorax: Brown fur dubbing

Red Parachute Spinner

Hook: Standard dry fly
Thread: Brown
Tails: Dark dun grizzly hackle fibers
Body: Rusty red fur dubbing
Ribbing: Tying thread
Wingpost: Light dun Hi Vis
Hackle: Dark dun grizzly

Gray Drake Spinner

Mirus Spinner

(Designed and tied by Dick Stewart. This pattern has evolved since its introduction in *Flies for Trout*)
Hook: Dry fly, long shank
Thread: Dark brown
Tail: Yellow microfibbets

Body: Yellow dubbing
Hind Wing: Brown Z-lon, looped and skirted on top behind thorax
Hackle: Bleached grizzly or barred ginger, trimmed flat on the bottom.

Siphlonurus Spinner

(Designed and tied by Dick Stewart)
Hook: Dry fly, long shank
Thread: Rusty brown
Tail: Dun microfibbets or hackle fibers
Body: Stripped red quill
Wing: Dun hackle points, angled back
Hackle: Dun

Bent Body Spinner

(Designed and tied by Bill Thompson)
Hook: Swimming Nymph
Thread: Dark brown
Tail: Dun microfibbets
Body: Rusty brown rabbit fur
Wing: Wing Zing cut or burned to shape
Hackle: Blue dun

Common Burrower, Nymphs

Wiggle Nymph

(John Blunt/Don Sicard)
Rear Hook: Mustad 9672
Thread: Yellow
Tail: Pheasant tail tips

Abdomen: Light yellow dubbing with tail fibers pulled forward on top
Rib: Yellow thread
Joint: 20-pound white braided line
Front Hook: Mustad 3399, cut at bend
Gills: Light gray filoplume, to cover hook joint
Thorax: Light yellow dubbing
Wingcase: Pheasant tail barbs
Legs: Tips from wingcase pulled down and back
Head: Black tying thread

Kennebago Emerger
(Tied by Don Sicard)
Hook: Mustad 3665A
Thread: Black
Tail: Mallard flank
Abdomen: Medium dun dubbing
Wings: Bleached elk
Thorax: Medium light tan dubbing with guard hairs
Head: Rust dubbing

Burk's Hexagenia
(Andy Burk/Kaufmann's Streamborn)
Hook: Tiemco 200R
Underbody: Lead wire or substitute, wrapped and flattened
Thread: Primrose or pale yellow
Tail: Gray marabou
Back: Dark turkey tail
Gills: Gray filoplume from pheasant

Rib: Copper wire
Abdomen: Pale yellow rabbit
Wingcase: Turkey tail
Thorax: Same as abdomen
Legs: Mottled hen saddle

Green Drake, Dun

Gray Fox Variant
(Art Flick/Hunter's Angling Supply)
Hook: Dry fly, short shank
Thread: Primrose yellow
Tail: Ginger
Body: Stripped light ginger or cream hackle quill
Wing: None
Hackle: 1 light ginger, 1 dark ginger and 1 grizzly, tied oversize

Green Drake
(The Dettes/Mary Dette Clark)
Hook: Mustad 79580
Thread: White waxed 6/0
Wing: Mallard flank dyed pale green
Tail: Three peccary fibers, divided
Body: Creamy yellow dubbing fur
Hackle: Golden badger

Parachute Vertical Emerger
(Designed and tied by Harold McMillan)
Hook: Swimming nymph hook
Thread: Tan or brown 6/0
Tail: Brown Z-lon

Nymph Body: Brown fur or
   synthetic dubbing
Ribbing: Fine copper wire
Adult Body: Olive fur or synthetic
   dubbing
Wingpost: Bright green Z-lon
Hackle: Grizzly dyed bright green

Coffin Fly, Spinner

Hairwing Spent Spinner
Hook: Dry fly, 3XL
Thread: Cream 6/0
Tail: 3 Moose or peccary hairs
Body: White fur dubbing
Ribbing: Cream tying thread
Wing: White Antron over dark
   deer hair, tied spent
Thorax: Brown fur dubbing

Coffin Fly
(The Dettes/Mary Dette Clark)
Hook: Mustad 79580
Thread: White waxed 6/0
Wing: Two teal flank feathers,
   divided
Tail: Three peccary fibers, divided
Ribbing: White thread 3/0
Underbody: White poly yarn
Body: White saddle hackle,
   trimmed before winding
Hackle: Golden badger

AuSable Coffin Fly
(Vic Betters, Ray Bergman and
Red Wilbur/Fran Betters)
Hook: Dry fly no. 10
Tail: Ivory cream elk or badger
   hair

Hackle: Badger hackle, tied
   heavy
Body: Ivory cream dubbing
Head: Hot orange thread

Brown Drake, Spinner

Brown Loopwing Hatchmatcher
(Tied by Don Sicard)
Hook: Mustad 3399D
Thread: Brown
Tail/Abdomen: Mallard flank
   feather dyed to desired
   color, tied in at the
   butt loopwing style,
   trimmed at the tip
   to form the tails
Loop Wing: Dyed mallard flank
   feather
Thorax: Brown fur dubbing
Hackle: Grizzly

Brown Antron/Poly Spinner
Hook: Dry fly, 2XL
Thread: Brown 6/0
Tail: 6 microfibbets, divided into
   three pairs
Body: Blended brown and cream
   fur dubbing
Wing: Sparse gold Antron fibers
   over white poly yarn

Sparkle Paradrake
Hook: Standard dry fly
Thread: Brown 6/0
Tail: Moose mane, tied in with
   body
Abdomen: Natural dark elk
   hair

Wingpost: White Antron or poly yarn
Thorax: Brown fur dubbing
Hackle: Ginger

Yellow Drake, Spinner

Cream Variant

(Art Flick/Hunter's Angling Supply)
Hook: Dry fly, short shank
Thread: Yellow
Tail: Cream hackle barbs
Body: Stripped cream hackle quill
Wing: None
Hackle: Cream spade or saddle, stiff

Cream Haystack

(Designed and tied by Fran Betters)
Hook: Dry fly no. 10
Tail: Cream elk or deer hair
Wing: Same as the tail
Body: Cream Australian opossum dubbing
Head: Hot orange or chartreuse thread

Hackle Wing Spinner

Hook: Standard dry fly
Thread: Cream 6/0
Tail: Barred ginger hackle fibers
Body: Blended cream and yellow fur dubbing
Wings: Stiff barred ginger spade hackle with a "V" cut from top and bottom
Thorax: Blended tan and yellow fur dubbing

Great Leadwinged Drake, Dun

Deer Hair Spent Hex

Hook: Standard dry fly
Thread: Tan 6/0
Tail: Moose mane, tied in with body
Abdomen: Bleached deer hair
Wing: Bleached deer hair
Thorax: Blended yellow and brown fur
Wingcase: Wild turkey shoulder feather

Hexagenia Hatchmatcher

(Tied by Don Sicard)
Hook: Mustad 3399D
Thread: Yellow
Tail/Abdomen: Mallard flank feather dyed to desired color, tied in at the butt loopwing style, trimmed at the tip to form the tails
Wing: Dyed mallard flank feather
Thorax: Blended yellow and brown fur
Hackle: Grizzly

Yellow Haystack

(Designed and tied by Fran Betters)
Hook: Dry fly no. 10
Tail: Hot orange elk or deer hair
Wing: Same as the tail
Body: Australian opossum dubbing
Head: Hot orange or chartreuse thread

Fringe Gilled Nymph

Light Cahill Nymph
Hook: Standard nymph hook
Thread: Primrose yellow 6/0
Tail: Lemon woodduck flank fibers
Abdomen/Thorax: Cream fox belly fur
Wingcase: Lemon woodduck flank feather, stroked with flexible cement
Legs: Lemon woodduck flank fibers or guard hair from the fox fur

Speckled Hen Nymph
Hook: Nymph hook 2XL
Thread: Tan
Tails: Fibers near base of speckled hen feather
Body: Rabbit fur dubbing
Wings/Legs: Speckled hen feather, turned twice, coated with flexible cement, folded back and notched with a "V"

Hare's Ear Soft Hackle
Hook: Standard or 2X wet fly
Thread: Brown or tan 6/0
Tail: Hare's mask guard hairs
Ribbing: Fine oval gold tinsel
Body: Dubbed hare's mask fur with guard hairs
Hackle: English grouse body feather

Golden Drake, Dun

Cream Variant
(Art Flick/Hunter's Angling Supply)
Hook: Dry fly, short shank
Thread: Yellow
Tail: Cream hackle barbs
Body: Stripped cream hackle quill
Wing: None
Hackle: Cream spade or saddle, stiff

Anthopotamus Emerger
(Designed and tied by David Goulet)
Hook: Standard dry fly
Thread: Yellow 6/0
Tail: Brown ostrich herl
Abdomen: Brown synthetic dubbing
Wing: Yellow CDC
Head/Thorax: Yellow fur or synthetic dubbing

Anthopotamus ComparaDun
(Al Caucci and Bob Nastase/Tied by David Goulet)
Hook: Standard dry fly
Thread: Yellow 6/0
Tail: Cream hackle dyed yellow
Abdomen: Blended yellow fur dubbing
Wing: Bleached deer hair

Drunella Nymph

Black Gnat Wet
(Modified from the traditional and Leisenring patterns)

Hook: Partridge L2A
Thread: Black
Tail: Crow body feather fibers
Body: Crow wing fibers wound
    with tying thread
Hackle: Starling shoulder feather

American Pheasant Tail
(Tied by the Orvis Company)
Hook: Standard nymph
Thread: Rust 6/0
Tail: Ring-necked pheasant tail
    barbs
Body: Ring-necked pheasant tail
    barbs, twisted and wrapped
    with thread
Rib: Fine copper wire
Wingcase: Ring-necked pheasant
    tail section
Thorax: Peacock herl
Legs: Wingcase fibers tied back

Dark Crawler Nymph
Hook: Nymph, 2XL
Thread: Dark brown
Tail: Soft-hackle fibers from a
    crow
Body: Blended black and brown
    fur dubbing
Wingcase: Iridescent turkey
    shoulder feather
Legs: Tips of a turkey tail feather

Blue-Winged Olive Dun
Blue-Winged Olive
(Tied by Hunter's Angling Supply)
Hook: Standard dry fly
Thread: Olive

Tail: Dun hackle barbs
Body: Olive fur, dubbed
Wing: Dun hen hackle points
Hackle: Dun

Attenuata CDC Emerger
(Designed and tied by David
Goulet)
Hook: Dry fly, 2XL
Thread: Olive 8/0 or 12/0
Tail: Single strand of olive thread
Body: Silk fur dubbing
Ribbing: Tying thread
Wing: Single clump of
    dun CDC

Blue-Winged Olive Parachute
(Tied by David Goulet)
Hook: Standard dry fly
Thread: Olive 8/0
Tail: Dun hackle barbs
Body: Olive silk dubbing
Wingpost: White poly yarn
Hackle: Dun

Dark Olive Spinner
Blue-Winged Olive Parachute
(Same as pattern for BWO Dun,
above)

Olive CDC Spinner
Hook: Standard dry fly
Thread: Olive 8/0
Tail: Three light dun
    microfibbets, divided
Body: Blended olive and black
    fur dubbing
Wings: Natural dun CDC

Olive Sparklewing Spinner
Hook: Standard dry fly
Thread: Olive 8/0
Tail: Light dun microfibbets
Abdomen: Olive tying thread
Wings: Light gray Antron fibers
Thorax: Olive fur dubbing
　　with guard hairs

Dark Clinging Nymphs
Dark Clinger Nymph
Hook: Nymph, 2XL
Thread: Black
Tail: Soft hackle fibers from a crow
Underbody: Lead wire or
　　substitute, lashed to sides
　　of hook
Gills: Black ostrich herl, palmered
　　over the abdomen and
　　trimmed top and bottom
Body: Black fur dubbing
Wingcase: Guinea fowl body
　　feather, stroked with
　　flexible head cement
Legs: Guinea fowl fibers

Sumner's Secret
(Sumner "Stowie" Stowe/The
Fly Rod Shop)
Hook: Nymph, 2X
Thread: Black 6/0
Rib: Fine silver oval tinsel
Body: Black tying thread or floss
Wing: Guinea fowl

Black Gnat Wet
(Modified from the traditional
and Leisenring patterns)

Hook: Partridge L2A
Thread: Black
Tail: Crow body feather fibers
Body: Crow wing fibers wound
　　with tying thread
Hackle: Starling shoulder feather

Little Yellow Spinner
Wingless Sulphur Spinner
Hook: Standard dry fly
Thread: Yellow 8/0
Tail: Watery dun hackle fibers
Body: Sulphur yellow fur dubbing
Ribbing: Tying thread
Wing: None
Hackle: Watery dun

Parachute Sulphur
(Tied by George Schlotter)
Hook: Standard dry fly
Thread: Yellow
Tail: Medium dun hackle barbs
Body: Yellow fur or synthetic
　　dubbing
Wingpost: Pale gray poly yarn
Hackle: Medium dun mixed

Polywing Sulphur Spinner
(Tied by George Schlotter)
Hook: Standard dry fly
Thread: Yellow 8/0
Tail: Watery dun hackle fibers
Body: Sulphur acrylic yarn
Wing: White poly yarn

Ephoron Nymph
White Fly Nymph
Hook: Nymph hook, 2XL

Thread: Primrose 6/0
Tail: Tan fibers from the base
of a speckled hen feather
Body: Cream fur dubbing
Gills: Filoplume
Wingcase: Amber feather from
a mallard drake, stroked
with flexible cement
Legs: Same as tail

Light Cahill Nymph
Hook: Standard nymph hook
Thread: Primrose yellow 6/0
Tail: Lemon woodduck flank
Abdomen/Thorax: Cream
fox belly fur
Wingcase: Lemon woodduck
flank feather, stroked
with flexible cement
Legs: Lemon woodduck flank
fibers or guard hair from
the fox fur

White Fly, Dun/Spinner
Harold's White Fly
(Catskill style, tied by Harold
McMillan)
Hook: Standard dry fly
Thread: White 6/0 or 8/0
Tail: White hackle fibers
Body: Creamy white fur dubbing
Wing: White hen hackle tips
Hackle: White

White Wulff
(Designed by Lee Wulff)
Hook: Dry fly, 2XL
Thread: Black

Tail: White calf tail or bucktail
Body: Cream-colored fur
Wing: White calf tail or bucktail
Hackle: Light badger

Usual
(Designed and tied by Fran Betters)
Hook: Dry fly
Tail: Snowshoe rabbit foot hair
Wing: Same as the tail
Body: Cream or light gray fur
Head: Hot orange thread

Spentwing Whitefly Spinner
Hook: Standard dry fly
Thread: Yellow 8/0
Tail: White microfibbets
Abdomen: White fur dubbing
Thorax: Natural rabbit dubbing
Wing: White craft yarn

Tiny Swimming Nymphs
Sawyer Pheasant Tail
(Frank Sawyer/Hunter's Angling
Supply)
Hook: Nymph, 2XL
Thread: Fine copper wire
Tail: Four or five ring-necked
pheasant tail barbs
Abdomen: Ring-necked pheasant
tail barbs, twisted
Thorax: Ring-necked pheasant
tail barbs, twisted
Wingcase: Ring-necked pheasant
tail barbs

Floating Baetis Nymph
Hook: Curved dry fly hook, 3XL

Thread: Brown or tan 8/0
Tail: Brown Z-lon
Body: Natural rabbit fur dubbing
Rib: Fine copper wire
Wing Bud: Black closed-cell foam
Legs: Cross section of a hen feather

Flashback Hare's Ear
Hook: Nymph hook, 2XL
Thread: Brown or tan 8/0
Tail: Hare's mask guard hairs
Body: Dubbed hare's mask fur with guard hairs
Wingcase: Several pieces of narrow Flashabou
Legs: Thorax dubbing picked out

Tiny Blue-Winged Sulphurs, Rusts and Olives, Duns

(Note: Patterns are given here for olive dressings, but any body color can be substituted)

Blue-Winged Olive CDC Emerger
(Designed and tied by David Goulet)
Hook: Dry fly, 2XL
Thread: Olive 8/0 or 12/0
Tail: Single strand of olive thread
Body: Silk fur dubbing
Ribbing: Tying thread
Wing: Single clump of dun CDC

Blue-Winged Olive
(Tied by Hunter's Angling Supply)

Hook: Standard dry fly
Thread: Olive
Tail: Dun hackle barbs
Body: Olive fur, dubbed
Wing: Dun hen hackle points
Hackle: Dun

Double U
(Designed and tied by David Goulet)
Hook: Standard dry fly
Thread: Olive tying thread
Tail: Single piece of olive thread
Body: Built up olive tying thread
Wing: White closed-cell foam cylinder, tied semi-spent

Tiny Blue-Winged Sulphurs, Rusts and Olives, Spinners

(Note: Patterns are given here for olive dressings, but any body color can be substituted)

BWO Sparklewing Spinner
Hook: Standard dry fly
Thread: Olive 8/0
Tail: Light dun microfibbets
Body: Olive tying thread
Wings: Light gray Antron fibers
Thorax: Olive fur dubbing with guard hairs

BWO Parachute
(Tied by David Goulet)
Hook: Standard dry fly
Thread: Olive 8/0
Tail: Dun hackle barbs

Body: Olive silk dubbing
Wingpost: White poly yarn
Hackle: Dun

Sparkle Blue Dun Wet
Hook: Standard wet/nymph
Thread: Olive 6/0
Tail: Medium dun hackle barbs
Body: Olive tying thread
Wing: Gray Antron fibers
Hackle: Medium dun hackle
barbs

Trico, Duns

Trico CDC Emerger
Hook: Standard dry fly
Thread: Black 8/0
Tail: Brown Z-lon fibers
Abdomen: Olive fur dubbing
Wings: Light dun CDC
Head/Thorax: Black fur
dubbing

Trico Hairwing
(ComparaDun style, tied by
Umpqua Feather Merchants)
Hook: Standard dry fly
Thread: Black 8/0
Tail: Black hackle barbs or
microfibbets
Body: Black silk dubbing or 6/0
thread
Wing: White bleached deer or
elk hair

Wingless Trico
Hook: Standard dry fly
Thread: Black 8/0

Tail: Light dun hackle barbs
Abdomen: Olive fur dubbing
Head/Thorax: Black silk
dubbing
Hackle: Medium dun over
the thorax

Trico, Spinners

Head to Head Trico Spinner
Hook: Dry fly, size 16-18, 2XL
Thread: Black
Tails: White microfibbets, 3 at
the bend, 2 at the eye
Body: Black silk dubbing
Wings: White poly yarn
Hackle: None

Spent Trico Female
(Designed and tied by George
Schlotter)
Hook: Dry fly, straight eye 2XL
Thread: White 8/0
Tail: Light dun hackle fibers
Abdomen: White tying
thread
Thorax: Black fur dubbing
Wing: White poly yarn

Foam Trio Spinner
Hook: Standard dry fly
Thread: Black 8/0
Tail: 3 white microfibbets
Body: Black silk dubbing
Ribbing: White thread 3/0
Thorax: Black closed-cell foam
tied under dubbing and
brought forward
Wing: Gray Antron fibers

Caddisflies

American Grannom, Larva

Herl Cased Caddis
Hook: Nymph, 3XL
Thread: Olive
Underbody: Bright green acrylic yarn
Case: Palmered strand of peacock herl
Worm: Bright green acrylic yarn
Legs: Grouse

Dark Cased Caddis
(Designed by Gary LaFontaine)
Hook: Nymph, 2XL
Thread: Olive
Underbody: Lead wire or substitute, well covered in tying thread
Case: Grouse body feather(s), wrapped forward and trimmed to shape
Worm: Green fur or synthetic dubbing
Legs: Grouse

Fur Peeping Caddis
(Carl Richards and Bob Braendle. Owen Edwards has published a similar pattern.)
Hook: Nymph hook, 2 or 3XL
Thread: Olive 8/0
Worm: Green synthetic yarn, singed
Legs: Partridge fibers

Underbody: Lead wire or substitute wound around front half of hook
Case: Natural rabbit's fur, dubbed in a loop and trimmed to shape

American Grannom, Pupa

Deep Sparkle Pupa
(From the design by Gary LaFontaine)
Hook: Standard wet/nymph
Thread: Olive
Shuck: Olive Antron yarn, tied in at bend and brought forward to envelop the body
Body: Bright green Antron fibers and olive yarn, blended and dubbed
Legs: Grouse feathers
Head: Brown fur or ostrich herl

Emergent Sparkle Pupa
(From the design by Gary LaFontaine)
Hook: Standard dry fly
Thread: Olive
Shuck: Olive Antron yarn, tied in at bend and brought forward to envelop the body with a few strands trailing back
Body: Bright green Antron fibers and olive yarn, blended and dubbed
Wings: Dark brown deer hair
Head: Brown thread or ostrich herl

Grouse and Flash
(Designed and tied by Nick Yardley)
Hook: Mustad 79580
Thread: Black 8/0 or 12/0
Underbody: Thread to match natural
Overbody: Pearl Krystal Flash
Thorax: Hare's ear dubbing
Hackle: Grouse

American Grannom, Adult

Henryville Special
(Tied by Del Mazza)
Hook: Standard dry fly
Thread: Olive
Body: Olive fur dubbing
Ribbing: Grizzly hackle, palmered
Wing: Mallard or goose quill sections tied tent style over sparse woodduck flank fibers
Hackle: Dark ginger or grizzly dyed brown

Quad Wing Spent Caddis
(Carl Richards/Bob Braendle)
Hook: Tiemco 100
Thread: Black
Body: Spun fur or synthetic dubbing
Wings: Tips of partridge body feathers
Body: Green spun fur or synthetic dubbing
Legs: Rooster hackle

Dette Caddis
(The Dettes/Mary Dette Clark)
Hook: Mustad 94840 or equivalent
Thread: White waxed silk or UNI-Thread, 6/0
Egg Sac: Medium olive chenille
Body: Muskrat dubbing
Wing: Brown partridge
Hackle: Dun and brown mixed

Saddle Case Maker, Larva

Pink Caddis
Hook: Curved caddis nymph hook
Thread: Brown 8/0
Body: Pink acrylic yarn
Rib: Rust thread, 6/0
Thorax: Brown ostrich herl
Head: Brown tying thread

USD Cream Caddis
Hook: Curved caddis nymph hook
Thread: Tan 8/0
Head: Brown fur dubbing
Legs: Furnace hen hackle fibers
Body: Blended tan/cream fur dubbing
Head: Brown tying thread

Brassie
Hook: Nymph, 2XL
Thread: Black or brown 6/0
Abdomen: Copper or brass wire
Head: Peacock or ostrich herl

Glossosoma, Pupa

Foam Caddis Emerger
(Designed by members of the
FRAA and tied by
David Goulet)
Hook: Nymph hook, curved or
straight
Thread: Black or brown 8/0
Body: Brown cylindrical foam,
lashed to hook and
brought forward
Hackle: Black

Ginger Partridge SLF
(Dan Noyes/The Fly Rod Shop)
Hook: Curved nymph hook
Thread: Brown 6/0
Abdomen: Ginger SLF Dubbing
Head: Partridge

Tan Caddis Emerger
(Designed and tied by
George Schlotter)
Hook: Curved caddis hook
Thread: Brown 6/0
Abdomen: Tan fur dubbing
Rib: Brown tying thread
Wing: Grouse fibers
Head: Rust fur dubbing

Glossosoma, Adult
Black Caddis
(Designed and tied by
Jack Pangburn)
Hook: Standard dry fly
Thread: Dark gray or black
Body: Fur dubbing to match
species

Wing: Dark gray catbird, starling
or pigeon feather, folded
and cut to shape
Hackle: Dun, clipped flat on
bottom

Diving Caddis
(Based on the design by Gary
LaFontaine)
Hook: Standard Wet Fly
Thread: Brown
Body: Blended tan, brown
and yellow Antron yarns
Wings: Gold Antron over dark
dun grizzly hackle fibers
Hackle: Dark ginger

Deer Hair Caddis
(Al Troth style)
Hook: Standard dry fly
Thread: Brown
Body: Blended brown and
yellow rabbit fur
dubbing
Rib: Dark ginger hackle,
palmered
Wing: Light-tipped brown deer
hair
Hackle: Brown

Net Spinner, Larva
Simple Caddis Larva
(Carl Richards and Bob
Braendle/Bob Braendle)
Hook: Tiemco TMC 2487
Thread: Black
Underbody: Lead wire or
substitute, wrapped

Body: Spun fur or synthetic
   dubbing
Legs: Cream soft hackle
Rib: Copper wire
Tail: Cream soft hackle

Netspinner Larva
Hook: Curved caddis nymph
   hook
Thread: Olive brown 6/0
Tail: Ostrich herl tips
Back: Turkey tail section
Rib: Copper wire
Body: Olive acrylic yarn, dubbed
Legs: Grouse or hen partridge
   feather
Head: Brown fur dubbing

Glass Bead Caddis Larva
(Designed and tied by Harold
McMillan)
Hook: Daiichi 1150
Thread: Olive 6/0
Tail: Blended olive synthetic
   dubbing and chartreuse
   rabbit fur
Abdomen: 3 green bi-colored
   beads
Thorax: Same as tail
Head: 1/8" tungsten bead

Spotted/Cinnamon Caddis, Pupa

Teardrop Emergent Pupa
(Designed and tied by Bob
Braendle)
Hook: Tiemco TMC 2487
Thread: Black

Abdomen: Spun fur or synthetic
   dubbing
Shuck: Ginger Z-lon, seared and
   glued
Wingcase: Snowshoe rabbit,
   folded forward
Thorax: Same as abdomen
Legs: Rooster hackle

Grouse and Flash
(Designed and tied by Nick
   Yardley)
Hook: Mustad 79580
Thread: Black 8/0 or 12/0
Underbody: Thread to match
   natural
Overbody: Pearl Krystal Flash
Thorax: Hare's ear dubbing
Hackle: Grouse

Yellow Caddis Emerger
(Designed and tied by
George Schlotter)
Hook: Curved caddis hook
Thread: Brown 6/0
Abdomen: Yellow fur dubbing
Rib: Brown tying thread
Wing: Grouse fibers
Head: Rust fur dubbing

Spotted/Cinnamon Caddis, Adult

Cinnamon Caddis
(Designed and tied by Jack
Pangburn)
Hook: Mustad 94840 (Standard
   dry fly)
Thread: Brown 6/0

Ribbing: Cinnamon hackle, palmered and clipped on top
Body: Cinnamon dubbing
Wing: Cinnamon Swiss straw, cut and tied in tent style
Antennae: Microfibbets, longer than body

Hare's Ear Caddis (a. k. a. Vermont Caddis)

(Designed by committee and first tied by George Schlotter)
Hook: Standard dry fly
Thread: Tan
Body: Hare's ear, roughly dubbed
Hackle: Mixed grizzly and brown

AuSable Caddis

(Designed and tied by Fran Betters)
Hook: Dry fly no. 12-16
Tail: None
Body: Rusty orange Australian opossum
Down Wing: White calf tail
Hackle: Grizzly and brown mixed
Head: Hot orange thread

Little Sister Sedge

Spent Polywing Caddis

(Carl Richards and Bob Braendle/Bob Braendle)
Hook: Tiemco 100
Thread: Black
Body: Spun fur or synthetic dubbing
Wings: White Antron

Solomon Caddis B

(Larry Solomon/Mary Dette Clark)
Hook: Mustad 94840
Thread: White waxed 6/0 or 8/0
Body: Medium olive fur dubbing
Wing: Natural brown deer hair
Hackle: Bronze dun

Olive Hare's Ear Caddis (a. k. a. Vermont Caddis)

(Designed by committee and first tied by George Schlotter)
Hook: Standard dry fly
Thread: Olive
Body: Hare's ear dyed olive, roughly dubbed
Hackle: Mixed grizzly and brown

Dark Blue Sedge, Larva

Sparkle Yarn Caddis

Hook: Wet fly, 3 or 4XL
Thread: Black 6/0
Underbody: Lead wire or substitute wrapped around front half of hook shank
Body: Bright green yarn, wrapped over underbody
Case: Blended black and tan acrylic yarn and light gray Antron fibers
Legs: Grouse body feather fibers
Head: Mixed brown and black fur dubbing

Fur Peeping Caddis

(Carl Richards and Bob Braendle.

Owen Edwards has published a
similar pattern.)
Hook: Nymph hook, 2 or 3XL
Thread: Olive 8/0
Worm: Green synthetic yarn,
singed
Legs: Partridge fibers
Underbody: Lead wire or
    substitute wound around
    front half of hook
Case: Natural rabbit's fur,
    dubbed in a loop and
    trimmed to shape

Herl Cased Caddis
Hook: Nymph, 3XL
Thread: Olive
Underbody: Bright green acrylic
    yarn
Case: Palmered strand of
    peacock herl
Worm: Bright green acrylic yarn
Legs: Grouse

Dark Blue Sedge, Pupa
Deep Sparkle Pupa
(From the design by Gary
LaFontaine)
Hook: Standard wet/nymph
Thread: Black
Shuck: Gray Antron yarn, tied in
    at bend and brought for-
    ward to envelop the body
Body: Bright green Antron fibers
    and olive yarn, blended and
    dubbed
Legs: Crow shoulder feathers
Head: Black fur or ostrich herl

Emergent Sparkle Pupa
(From the design by Gary
LaFontaine)
Hook: Standard dry fly
Thread: Olive
Shuck: Gray Antron yarn, tied in a
    bend and brought forward to
    envelop the body with a few
    strands trailing back
Body: Bright green Antron fibers
    and olive yarn, blended and
    dubbed
Wings: Dark brown deer hair
Head: Black thread or ostrich herl

Crow's Nest Soft Hackle
Hook: Curved nymph hook, 2XL
Thread: Black 6/0
Body: Blended olive and natural
    rabbit
Ribbing: Oval silver tinsel
Hackle: Crow shoulder feather

Dark Blue Sedge, Adult
Black Deer Hair Caddis
(Al Troth Style)
Hook: Standard dry fly
Thread: Black
Body: Blended muskrat and olive
    fur
Rib: Dark blue dun hackle,
    palmered
Wing: Deer hair dyed black

Solomon Caddis D
(Larry Solomon/Mary Dette Clark)
Hook: Standard dry fly
Thread: Black

Body: Dark gray fur dubbing
Wing: Deer hair dyed dark dun
Hackle: Dark blue dun

Dancing Caddis
(From the design by Gary LaFontaine)
Hook: Swedish dry fly, upside down
Thread: Black
Body: Blended olive and muskrat synthetic dubbing
Wing: Black dyed deer hair
Hackle: Dark dun

Green Caddis, Larva
Glass Bead Caddis Larva
(Designed and tied by Harold McMillan)
Hook: Daiichi 1150
Thread: Olive 6/0
Tail: Blended olive synthetic dubbing and chartreuse rabbit fur
Abdomen: 3 green bi-colored beads
Thorax: Same as tail
Head: 1/8" tungsten bead

Simple Caddis Larva
(Carl Richards and Bob Braendle/Bob Braendle)
Hook: Tiemco TMC 2487
Thread: Black
Underbody: Lead wire or substitute, wrapped
Body: Spun fur or synthetic dubbing

Legs: Cream soft hackle
Rib: Copper wire
Tail: Cream Soft hakle

Rhyacophila Larva
Hook: Yorkshire sedge hook
Thread: Dark green 6/0
Tail: 6 pheasant tail fibers
Underbody: Bright green Antron dubbing
Dorsal Underlay: Feathers for tail brought forward
Overbody: Chartreuse (fluorescent) Swannundaze
Thorax: Rabbit fur dubbing, brown
Legs: Grouse

Green Caddis, Adult
Quad Wing Spent Caddis
(Carl Richards/Bob Braendle)
Hook: Tiemco 100
Thread: Black
Body: Fur or synthetic dubbing
Wings: Tips of partridge body feathers
Body: Green spun fur or synthetic dubbing
Legs: Rooster hackle

Diving Caddis
(Based on the design by Gary LaFontaine)
Hook: Standard wet fly
Thread: Bright olive
Body: Dubbed green craft yarn

Wings: Light blue/gray Antron over dark dun grizzly hackle fibers
Hackle: Dark dun grizzly

Henryville Special
(Tied by Del Mazza)
Hook: Standard dry fly
Thread: Olive
Body: Olive fur dubbing
Ribbing: Grizzly hackle, palmered
Wing: Mallard or goose quill sections tied tent style over woodduck flank fibers
Hackle: Dark ginger or grizzly dyed brown

"Alder Fly," Larva

Glass Bead Caddis Larva
(Designed and tied by Harold McMillan)
Hook: Daiichi 1150
Thread: Olive 6/0
Tail: Blended olive synthetic dubbing and chartreuse rabbit fur
Abdomen: 3 green bi-colored beads
Thorax: Same as tail
Head: 1/8" tungsten bead

Simple Caddis Larva
(Carl Richards and Bob Braendle/Bob Braendle)
Hook: Tiemco TMC 2487
Thread: Black

Underbody: Lead wire or substitute, wrapped
Body: Green fur or synthetic dubbing
Legs: Cream soft hackle
Rib: Copper wire
Tail: Cream soft hackle

Green Caddis Larva
Hook: Curved Yorkshire sedge
Thread: Olive 6/0
Abdomen: Blended green and olive craft yarn
Legs/Thorax: Hare's mask fur, with guard hairs
Head: Olive tying thread

"Alder Fly," Pupa

Olive Partridge SLF
(Dan Noyes/The Fly Rod Shop)
Hook: Curved nymph hook
Thread: Brown 6/0
Abdomen: Ginger SLF Dubbing
Head: Partridge

Golden Maple
(Dan Noyes/The Fly Rod Shop)
Hook: Curved nymph, 6XL
Thread: Olive 6/0
Tail: Golden pheasant crest
Body: Olive floss
Thorax: Brass bead held by a tuft of rabbit dubbing
Hackle: Grizzly

"Alder Fly" Pupa
Hook: Standard dry fly
Thread: Brown

Body: Blended black, green
and yellow acrylic
yarn, dubbed

Wing Buds: Turkey tail segments,
trimmed to shape

Antennae: Long fibers from base
of a brown hen hackle feather

Legs: Shorter brown hen fibers
tied over antennae

"Alder Fly," Adult

Diving Caddis

(Based on the design by
Gary LaFontaine)

Hook: Standard wet fly

Thread: Bright Olive

Body: Blended black and green
craft yard, dubbed

Wings: White Antron over brown
hackle fibers

Hackle: Ginger

Pheasant Zebra Caddis

(Designed and tied by Bill
Thompson)

Hook: Standard dry fly

Thread: Dark brown

Body: Gray rabbit fur

Hackle: Blue dun palmered
through the body

Wing: Pheasant body feather,
cut to shape and coated
with flexible cement

Antennae: Stripped hackle quill

Deer Hair Alder Fly

Hook: Standard dry fly

Thread: Brown

Body: Blended black and olive
dubbing

Rib: Brown hackle, palmered

Wing: Dark natural deer hair

Hackle: Brown

Northern Casemaker, Larva

Sparkle Yarn Caddis

Hook: Wet fly, 3 or 4XL

Thread: Brown 6/0

Underbody: Lead wire or
substitute wrapped around
front half of hook shank

Body: Pale yellow yarn

Case: Chopped, mixed and
dubbed black and tan
acrylic yarn and light gray
Antron fibers

Legs: Grouse body feather fibers

Head: Mixed brown and claret
fur dubbing

Chopped Deerhair Caddis Larva

Hook: Partridge D4A

Thread: Brown

Weight: Lead wire or substitute,
wrapped near hook bend

Head: Ball of brown yarn, dubbed

Legs: Partridge or grouse fibers

Body: Light yellow acrylic yarn

Case: Chopped deer hair and rabbit fur, blended and dubbed
in a loop

Fur Peeping Caddis

(Carl Richards and Bob
Braendle/Bob Braendle)

Hook: Nymph hook, 2 or 3XL
Thread: Olive 8/0
Worm: Yellow Antron yarn, singed
Legs: Partridge fibers
Underbody: Lead wire or substitute wound around front half of hook
Case: Natural rabbit's fur, dubbed in a loop and trimmed to shape

Northern Casemaker, Pupa

Pumpkin Pupa
Hook: Partridge D4A
Thread: Orange 6/0
Ribbing: Tying thread
Body: Blended amber Antron fibers and orange-yellow yarn, dubbed
Wing Buds: Turkey tail segments
Legs: Grouse feathers
Head: Rusty fur dubbing

Ginger Partridge SLF
(Dan Noyes/The Fly Rod Shop)
Hook: Curved nymph hook, long shank
Thread: Brown
Body: Ginger SLF dubbing
Hackle: Partridge body feather

Ginger SLF Bird's Nest
(This is Dan Noyes variation on the Cal Bird pattern)
Hook: Nymph or wet fly, 3XL
Thread: Orange

Tail: Teal flank, dark natural
Abdomen: Ginger SLF dubbing, #40
Rib: Copper wire
Legs: Same material as tail, tied in at top and sides in three sparse sections
Thorax: Same as abdomen

Great Brown Autumn Sedge, Adult

Ginger Deer Hair Caddis
Hook: Standard dry fly
Thread: Orange, 6/0
Body: Blended orange, yellow and brown fur dubbing
Rib: Ginger hackle, palmered
Wing: Bleached deer or elk hair, dyed ginger
Hackle: Ginger

Ginger Diving Caddis
(From the design by Gary LaFontaine)
Hook: Wet fly, 3XL
Thread: Yellow
Body: Yellow Antron fibers, orange and brown craft yarn, blended and dubbed
Wing: Mixed ginger and brown hackle fibers
Overwing: White or gold Antron fibers
Hackle: Ginger

Golden Demon Hairwing
Hook: Wet fly, 3XL
Thread: Black 6/0

Tail: Golden pheasant crest
Body: Flat gold tinsel
Wing: Red squirrel tail
Throat: Dyed red saddle hackle
Head: Black lacquer over
    tying thread

Stoneflies

Early Dark Stoneflies,
Larvae

Brown Swannundaze Stonefly
Hook: Nymph hook, 3XL
Thread: Rust 8/0
Tail: 4 brown hen hackle fibers
Abdomen: Brown Swannundaze
Wingcase: Turkey tail section,
    coated with flexible cement
Thorax: Rabbit fur dubbing, rust
Legs: Thorax dubbing picked out

American Pheasant Tail
(Tied by the Orvis Company)
Hook: Standard nymph
Thread: Rust 6/0
Tail: Ring-necked pheasant tail
    barbs
Body: Ring-necked pheasant tail
    barbs, twisted and
    wrapped with thread
Rib: Fine copper wire
Wingcase: Ring-necked
    pheasant tail section
Thorax: Peacock herl
Legs: Wing case fibers tied back

Turkey Tail Nymph
Hook: Nymph hook, 3XL

Thread: Brown 8/0
Tail: 6 turkey tail tips
Ribbing: Rust thread, 6/0
Abdomen: Turkey fibers from
    tail twisted and wrapped around
    shank
Wingcase: Turkey tail section
Thorax: Mahogany fur dubbing
Legs: Thorax dubbing picked
    out

Early Dark Stoneflies,
Adults

Dancing Stonefly
(Adapted from Gary LaFontaine's
Dancing Caddis)
Hook: Curved dry fly, 6XL,
    straight eye, upside down
Thread: Yellow
Tails: None
Body: Mixed brown and claret
    fur dubbing
Wings: Natural deer hair, light
Hackle: Light ginger

Early Brown Stonefly
(The Dettes/Mary Dette Clark)
Hook: Mustad 3906B
Thread: White waxed 6/0
Tail: Medium blue dun
    hackle fibers
Body: Dark, red-brown
    stripped quill
Wing: Dark gray mallard wing
    quill
Hackle: Dun and brown mixed
Head: White thread lacquered
    brown

Early Brown Spentwing

Hook: Dry fly 2XL
Thread: Rust, 6/0 or 8/0
Tail: Medium blue dun hackle
 fibers
Body: Mixed brown and rust fur
 dubbing
Wing: Tan poly yarn in two
 sections, one swept
 backward and the other
 forward

Little Green Stonefly, Adult

Little Green Stonefly

Hook: Dry fly, 2XL
Thread: Primrose yellow
Body: Pale green dubbing
Ribbing: Cream hackle, palmered
Wing: Bleached deer body hair
Hackle: Cream

Yellow Sally

(Tied by Hunter's Angling
Supply)
Hook: Dry Fly, 3 or 4XL
Thread: Primrose yellow
Tail: Pale chartreuse deer body
 hair
Body: Pale yellow dubbing
Ribbing: Cream hackle, palmered
 and trimmed on top
Wing: Pale gray duck quill
 section, coated with
 cement, trimmed to
 shape and tied rolled
 over the body
Hackle: Cream

Giant Stoneflies, Larvae

Kaufmann's Black Stone

(Randall Kaufmann/Kaufmann's
Streamborn)
Hook: Tiemco 300 or 5263 (6XL),
Thread: Black
Underbody: Wrapped lead wire
 or substitute, flattened
Tails: Black turkey biots, in a "V"
Abdomen: 60% mixture of
 blended black, claret,
 amber, purple, red, fiery
 brown, blue and hot
 orange Angora goat hair
 and 40% Hare-Tron, to
 match color of natural
Rib: Transparent black
 Swannundaze
Wingcases: Three turkey tail
 sections, coated with flexi-
 ble cement and "V"shaped
Thorax: Same as abdomen
Antennae: Black turkey biots,
 tied in a "V"
Head: Same as body

Crawling Allonarcys

Hook: Salmon hook, upside
 down
Thread: Brown or black 6/0
Tails: Black goose biots
Underbody: Three lengths of
 heavy wire, lashed to
 bottom of hook shank
Abdomen: Blended black and
 brown fur or synthetic
 dubbing, sides picked out
Rib: Brown monofilament

Wingcases: Turkey tail segment, folded in three sections
Legs: Furnace hen hackle, brought forward with wingcases
Thorax: Same as abdomen
Antennae: Peccary hairs
Head: Body dubbing

Golden Stonefly, Larvae

Glass Bead Golden Stone
(Designed and tied by Harold McMillan)
Hook: Curved stonefly hook, 4XL
Thread: Yellow 6/0
Tail: Yellow goose biots
Tag: Golden yellow Wapsi Super Bright dubbing
Abdomen: Gold Killer Caddis glass beads
Thorax: Golden yellow Wapsi Super Bright dubbing (add two 3/16" brass beads for a faster-sinking fly)
Wingcases: Turkey wing section
Legs: Brown goose biots
Antennae: Yellow goose biots

Kaufmann's Golden Stone
(Randall Kaufmann/Kaufmann's Streamborn)
Hook: Tiemco 300 or 5263 (6XL)
Thread: Brown
Underbody: Wrapped lead wire or substitute, flattened
Tails: Golden brown turkey biots, tied in a "V"

Abdomen: 60% mixture of blended gold, amber, rust, blue and orange Angora goat hair and 40% Hare-Tron, to match color of natural
Rib: Amber Swannundaze
Wingcases: Three turkey tail sections, coated with flexible cement and "V"shaped
Thorax: Same as abdomen
Antennae: Golden brown turkey biots, tied in a "V"
Head: Same as body

Connecticut River Curler
(Based on the Catskill Curler of Matt Vinciguerra)
Hook: Wet fly, 3XL
Thread: Yellow
Tails: Amber goose biots
Weight: 2 heavy wire strips lashed to hook sides
Abdomen: Pale yellow acrylic yarn, dubbed
Ribbing: Fine copper wire
Back/Wingcases: Turkey tail segment, coated with flexible cement
Thorax: 3 light gray ostrich herls over yellow acrylic yarn
Legs: Light brown hen feather tied behind thorax and brought forward with cases
Antennae: Excess of wingcase clipped to shape

Golden Stonefly, Adult

Orange Stimulator
(Randall Kaufmann/Kaufmann's
Streamborn)
Hook: Curved dry fly, 3XL
Thread: Orange
Tail: Natural elk or deer body
    hair
Abdomen: Orange dubbing
Rib: Brown hackle, palmered
Wings: Same as tail
Thorax: Red or amber
    dubbing
Hackle: Grizzly, over
    thorax

Downwing Hornberg
(John Blunt's adaptation of the
traditional wet fly)
Hook: Wet fly 3XL
Thread: Black
Body: Flat silver tinsel
Underwing: Yellow saddle
    hackle fibers
Wing: Woodduck flank
    feather, tied downwing
Cheeks: Jungle cock eyes
Hackle: Grizzly

Clipped Deerhair Stonefly
Hook: Dry fly, 3XL
Thread: Orange
Body: Golden yellow synthetic
    dubbing
Rib: Brown hackle, palmered
Wings: Natural deer body
    hair
Head: Deer hair, clipped

Little Yellow Stonefly, Larva

Albino Stonefly Nymph
Hook: Tiemco TMC 200R
Thread: Primrose yellow 6/0
Tail: White goose biots
Abdomen: Palest cream
    dubbing
Rib: Clear Swannundaze
Wingcases: Mallard flank feather,
    stroked with cement
Thorax: Same as abdomen
Legs: Picked out thorax
    dubbing

Yellow Swannundaze Stonefly
Hook: Tiemco TMC 200R
Thread: Yellow 6/0
Tail: Amber goose biots
Underbody: Amber acrylic yarn
Body: Yellow Swannundaze
Ribbing: Black thread 3/0
Wingcase: Hen or pheasant body
    feather, stroked with
    flexible cement
Thorax: Same as underbody
Legs: Ginger hackle fibers

Bird's Nest
(Cal Bird/Umpqua Feather
Merchants)
Hook: Nymph, 2XL or 3XL
Thread: Tan or brown
Tail: Mallard or teal flank, dyed
    brown
Abdomen: Blended tan and olive
    natural and synthetic fur
Rib: Copper wire

Legs: Same material as tail, tied in at top and sides in three sparse sections
Thorax: Same as abdomen

Little Yellow Stonefly, Adult

Yellow Sally
(Tied by Hunter's Angling Supply)
Hook: Dry fly, 3 or 4XL
Thread: Primrose yellow
Tail: Pale chartreuse deer body hair
Body: Pale yellow dubbing
Ribbing: Cream hackle, palmered and trimmed on top
Wing: Pale gray duck quill section, coated with cement, trimmed to shape and tied rolled over the body
Hackle: Cream

Egglaying Stonefly
Hook: Dry fly, 2XL
Thread: Yellow
Egg Sac: Black closed-cell foam
Body: Pale yellow fur
Wing: Bleached deer hair
Hackle: Light ginger

Yellow Stimulator
(Randall Kaufmann/Kaufmann's Streamborn)
Hook: Curved dry fly, 3XL
Thread: Orange
Tail: Natural elk or deer body hair

Abdomen: Yellow dubbing
Rib: Brown hackle, palmered
Wings: Same as tail
Thorax: Red or amber dubbing
Hackle: Grizzly over thorax

Otheroptera
Dragonfly

Olive Kennebago Muddler
(Designed and tied by Mike Arsenault)
Hook: Mustad 9672
Thread: Black or brown 6/0
Tail: Woodduck flank fibers
Body: Flat gold tinsel
Underwing: Gray squirrel tail
Overwing: Woodduck flank feathers
Head: Olive dyed deer hair, tied Muddler style

Kaufmann's Lake Dragon
(Randall Kaufmann/Kaufmann's Streamborn)
Hook: Tiemco 5263
Underbody: Wrapped lead wire or substitute, flattened
Eyes: Burned monofilament
Tails: Green marabou
Rib: Copper wire
Abdomen: Olive or brown Hare-Tron and blended goat hair
Legs: Pheasant body feathers
Wingcase: Turkey tail segments, cut to shape and colored with Pantone pen
Head: Same as abdomen

Olive Woolly Bugger
Hook: Partridge D4A
Thread: Olive 6/0
Tails: Olive marabou
Underbody: Wrapped lead wire
or substitute
Body: Olive chenille or acrylic
yarn
Hackle: Olive saddle hackle

Damselflies
Damsel Wiggle Nymph
(Designed and tied by Jack
Pangburn)
Hooks: Wet fly, 2, linked with
nylon loop, and with front
point removed
Thread: Brown or olive
Tail: Brown Swannundaze or biots
Body, rear: Olive brown dubbing
Ribbing: Fine copper wire
Body, front: Olive brown dubbing
Legs: Picked out dubbing
Back/Wingcase: Brown Nymph
Skin coated with cement
Eyes: Bead-chain balls, painted

Green Damsel
(Designed by E. H. "Polly"
Rosborough)
Hook: Wet fly, 3XL
Thread: Light olive
Tails: Golden olive marabou
Body: Blended olive yarn
Wing: Darker green
marabou
Legs: Mallard or teal flank,
dyed olive

Olive Woolly Bugger
(Same pattern as for Dragon Fly,
column to left)

True Flies, Larvae
Brassie
Hook: Nymph, 2XL
Thread: Black or brown 6/0
Abdomen: Copper or brass wire
Head: Peacock or ostrich herl

Vernille Larva
Hook: Curved Caddis, up-eye
Thread: 6/0, to match body
Body: Vernille, singed on ends,
tied in at two points

Gross Cranefly Larva
Hook: Nymph, 2XL
Thread: Brown 6/0
Tail: Natural ostrich herl
Underbody: Blended acrylic
yarn
Body: Light brown transparent
Swannundaze
Head: Natural rabbit dubbing

Midges, Adult
Griffith's Gnat
(George Griffith/The Orvis Co.)
Hook: Mustad 79580
Thread: Black 8/0 or 12/0
Body: Peacock herl
Hackle: Grizzly, palmered

Grouse and Flash
(Designed and tied by Nick
Yardley)

Hook: Mustad 79580
Thread: Black 8/0 or 12/0
Underbody: Thread to match natural
Overbody: Pearl Krystal Flash
Thorax: Hare's ear dubbing
Hackle: Grouse

Yellow Midge
(This pattern can be tied in any color to suit the naturals)
Hook: Standard dry fly
Thread: Primrose 8/0 or 12/0
Tail: Cream hackle barbs
Body: Yellow fine silk dubbing
Wing: Clear Antron fibers
Hackle: Cream, tied splayed

Hellgrammites and Fishflies

Whitlock's Hellgrammite
(Dave Whitlock/Umpqua Feather Merchants)
Hook: Streamer, straight eye, 6XL, upside down and bent upwards
Thread: Black
Tail: Brown goose biots
Abdomen: Dark gray fur
Back: Dark gray raffia (Swiss straw)
Rib: Copper wire
Thorax: Same as abdomen
Legs: Dark speckled hen feather
Wingcases: Same as back
Mandibles: Brown goose biots

Kaufmann's Brown Stone
(Randall Kaufmann/Kaufmann's Streamborn)
Hook: Tiemco 300 or 5263
Thread: Brown
Underbody: Wrapped lead wire or substitute, flattened
Tails: Brown turkey biots, tied in a "V"
Abdomen: 60% mixture of blended Angora goat hair and 40% Hare-Tron, to match color of natural
Rib: Transparent brown Swannundaze
Wingcases: Three turkey tail sections, coated with flexible cement and "V"shaped
Thorax: Same as abdomen
Antennae: Brown turkey biots, tied in a "V"
Head: Same as body

Brown Woolly Bugger
Hook: Partridge D4A
Thread: Brown 6/0
Tails: Brown marabou
Underbody: Wrapped lead wire
Body: Brown chenille or acrylic yarn
Hackle: Brown or furnace saddle hackle, palmered

Ants and Wasps

Foam Ant
Hook: Standard dry fly
Thread: Black

Body: Closed-cell foam cylinder
Legs: Dark dun hackle

Flying Cinnamon Ant
(This pattern can be tied in any color to suit the naturals)
Hook: Standard dry fly
Thread: Rust
Abdomen: Fine gray silk dubbing
Wing: Poly yarn
Legs: Dark ginger hackle
Head/Thorax: Bare tying thread

Black Wet Ant
(Designed by Ed Koch)
Hook: Standard dry fly
Thread: Black 6/0 or 8/0
Body: Built up thread, coated with black lacquer
Legs: Black hen hackle

Grasshoppers

Letort Hopper
(Ed Schenk/Hunter's Angling Supply)
Hook: Dry fly, 2XL
Thread: Yellow 6/0
Body: Yellow fur dubbing
Wing: Mottled brown turkey quill
Overwing: Deer body hair

Head: Butts of the wing hair (and some of the tips) clipped to shape

Kennebago Muddler
(Designed and tied by Mike Arsenault)
Hook: Mustad 9672
Thread: Black or brown 6/0
Tail: Woodduck flank fibers
Body: Flat gold tinsel
Underwing: Gray squirrel tail
Overwing: Woodduck flank feathers
Head: Natural deer hair, Muddler style

Parachute Hopper
(Tied by Hunter's Angling Supply)
Hook: Dry fly, 3XL
Thread: Tan 6/0
Body: Yellow fur dubbing
Wing: Mottled brown turkey quill, coated with flexible cement
Legs: Ring-necked pheasant tail barbs
Wingpost: White calf tail or body hair
Hackle: Grizzly

Resources

Many of the patterns listed in this index are available from the following commercial tiers or retailers, as attributed:

Fran Betters
AuSable Wulff Products
adirondackflyfishing.com
(518) 647-8414

John Blunt
Grants Kennebago Camps
(800) 633-4815
(207) 864-3608

Bob Braendle
Great Lakes Fly Fishing Co.
Rockford, MI
(800) 303-0567

Mary Dette Clark
Dette Trout Flies
Roscoe, New York
(607) 498-4991

David Goulet
Classic and Custom Fly Shop
New Hartford, CT
(860) 738-3597

Hunter's Angling Supplies
New Boston, NH
(800) 331-8558

Kaufmann's Streamborn
Portland, Oregon
(800) 442-4359

Harold McMillan Jr.
Housatonic River Outfitters
West Cornwall, Connecticut
(860) 672-1010

Dan Noyes and Sumner Stowe
The Fly Rod Shop
Stowe, VT
(800) 535-9763

Jack Pangburn
17 Mist Lane
Westbury, NY 11590

Don Sicard
Casco Bay Fly Tying Studio
(207) 353-9433

George Schlotter
The Angler's Nook
Route 313,
Arlington-Cambridge Road
Shushan, NY 12873

Illustrations
For information on the watercolors you may contact the artist directly:
David B. Tibbetts
22 Burpee Lane
New London, NH 03257

Bibliography

Burian, Steven K. and Gibbs, K. Elizabeth; *Mayflies of Maine: An Annotated Faunal List*. University of Maine, Orono, ME, 1991

Flick, Arthur B.; *The New Streamside Guide to Naturals and their Imitations*. Nick Lyons Books, New York, NY, 1991

Gordon, Sid W.; *How to Fish From Top to Bottom*. The Stackpole Company, Harrisburg, PA, 1955

Jennings, Preston J.; *A Book of Trout Flies*. Crown Publishers Inc., New York, NY, 1935, 1970

Kaufmann, Randall; *Tying Nymphs*. Western Fisherman's Press, Portland, OR, 1994

Knopp, Malcolm and Cormier, Robert; *Mayflies: An Angler's Study of Trout Water Ephemeroptera*. Greycliff Publishing Company, Helena, MT, 1997

LaFontaine, Gary; *Caddisflies*. Lyons & Burford, New York, NY, 1981

Leisenring, James E. and Hidy, Vernon S.; *The Art of Tying the Wet Fly* and *Fishing the Flymph*. Crown Publishers Inc., New York, NY, 1971

Leiser, Eric and Boyle, Robert H.; *Stoneflies for the Angler*. Stackpole Books, Harrisburg, PA, 1982

Marinaro, Vincent; *A Modern Dry Fly Code*. Crown Publishers Inc., New York, NY, 1950, 1970

McCafferty, Dr. W. Patrick; "Nymphing With Mayflies: A New Look at Matching the Drift". *American Angler*, Nov./Dec. 1998, Abenaki Publishing, Bennington, VT

McCafferty, Dr. W. Patrick; *Aquatic Entomology: The Fishermen's and Ecologists' Guide to Insects and Their Relatives*. Jones and Bartlett, Sudbury, MA, 1983

Pobst, Dick and Richards, Carl; *The Caddisfly Handbook: An Orvis Streamside Guide*. The Lyons Press, New York, NY, 1998

Richards, Carl and Braendle, Bob; *Caddis Super Hatches: Hatch Guide for the United States*. Frank Amato Publications, Portland, OR, 1997

Rosenbauer, Tom; *Prospecting for Trout*. Dell Publishing, New York, NY, 1993

Swisher, Doug and Richards, Carl; *Emergers*. Lyons & Burford, New York, NY, 1991

Sawyer, Frank; *Nymphs and the Trout*. Crown Publishers Inc., New York, NY, 1958, 1970

Skues, G. E. M.; *The Way of a Trout With a Fly and Some Further Studies in Minor Tactics*. A. and C. Black Ltd, London, England, 1949

Solomon, Larry and Leiser, Eric; *The Caddis and the Angler*. Stackpole Books, Harrisburg, PA, 1977

Schwiebert, Ernest G., Jr.; *Matching the Hatch*. The MacMillan Company, Toronto, Ontario, Canada, 1955

Schwiebert, Ernest G., Jr.; *Nymphs*. Winchester Press, New York, NY, 1973

Stewart, Kenneth W. and Stark, Bill P.; *Nymphs of North American Stonefly Genera (Plecoptera)*. The Entomological Society of America, Lanham, MD, 1988

Stewart, Dick and Allen, Farrow; *Flies for Trout*. Mountain Pond Publishing, North Conway, NH, 1993

Wright, Leonard; *Fishing the Dry Fly as a Living Insect: An Unorthodox Method*. E. P. Dutton and Co., Inc., New York, NY, 1972

List of Watercolor Illustrations

Index

Index of Fly Patterns